ALWAYS ON CALL

ALWAYS ON CALL

A unique account of a cop's remarkable life of law enforcement in outback Queensland.

Peter Andrew Cahill

Disclaimer

This autobiography is a work of creative non-fiction. All events are accurate to the best of the author's memory. Some names and identifying features have been changed to protect the innocent and the not so innocent. This book deals with sexual assault, physical assault, domestic violence, community violence and suicide. While the author has taken great lengths to ensure the subject matter is dealt with in a compassionate and respectful manner, it may be troubling for some readers. Therefore reader discretion is advised. Aboriginal and Torres Strait Islander people are advised that this material may contain the name or image of Indigenous Australians who have died. The author in no way represents any company, corporation, or brand mentioned herein. The views expressed in this autobiography are solely those of the author.

Always on Call
Copyright © Peter Cahill, 2021
ISBN: 978-0-6451916-9-1 Paperback
ISBN: 978-0-6452837-0-9 E-Book
First published 2021

All rights reserved. Without limiting the rights under copyright reserved above, no part of this publication may be reproduced, stored in, or introduced into a database and retrieval system or transmitted in any form or by any means (electronic, mechanical, photocopying, recording or otherwise) without the prior written permission of both the owner of copyright and the above publishers.

Original Map illustration by Ivan Vanbli Photographs Cahill

ABOUT THE AUTHOR

Peter Cahill, who once was described by a senior cop as "The man is a legend in his own time", invites the reader into his life as a police officer and experience the ups and downs of working in various Queensland police stations. He tells his stories with remarkable candour of times where life-threatening danger was often not far away. Peter now lives in far North Queensland, where he likes spending time with his wife Pimmie, their loyal German shepherd dog Tonto, the always mischievous sausage dog mix, Simba, and an elderly rainbow lorikeet named Jacko.

ENDORSEMENTS

Peter's book is an honest reflection of working as a police officer in remote and regional communities in an era where resources and support were often in short supply and where creative problem solving was the norm. Peter's book reminds us that for police officers, regardless of when or where, confronting violent, dangerous or difficult situations is an ever-present possibility and that it takes courage and conviction to bring about a solution. The book also explores the human element of policing and the toll the work can have on its officers. It is a book that many serving and former police officers, their families and friends will relate to.
   -**Graham Lohmann**, *Queensland Police Service 1975-2019*

In *'Always on Call,'* Peter Cahill uses his firsthand experiences to explain in detail exactly what dangers a police officer was confronted with on a daily basis throughout his career. Its splash of Aussie humour only adds to the tale. Every event in the book actually happened and is part of this nation's history. It's said, "Every person has a story,' and this man's story is worth retelling, for its men like Peter, who help build this nation. So, to sum up my appreciation of his dedication and service, allow me to quote from C.J. Dennis. *"To you sir, I dips me lid!"*
   -**Dennis L. Wells**, author of *'Forgiven Sins'*

DEDICATION

First and foremost, I like to dedicate this book to my lovely wife, Pimmie, whose knowledge and enthusiastic perseverance turned my long term wish of writing a book about my years in the police force into a reality.

Secondly, I dedicate this book to the scores of Indigenous Community Policemen and Police Trackers, who singularly and collectively provided me with an insight into a dimension I could never have experienced had I not been a policeman in Outback Queensland. You have my respect.

*"People sleep peaceably in their beds at night
only because rough men stand ready
to do violence on their behalf."*

- George Orwell

Mama, take this badge off of me
I can't use it anymore
It's getting dark, too dark to see
I feel I'm knocking on heaven's door
Knock knock knocking on
heaven's door

Mama, put my guns in the ground
I can't shoot them anymore
That long Black cloud is comin' down
I feel I'm knockin' on heaven's door
Knock knock knocking on
heaven's door.

- Bob Dylan

CONTENTS

About The Author v
Foreword xvii
Map Encompassing My Career In The Police Force xix
Introduction xxi

Petrie Terrace
Beginning 1
Post-Mortem Training 6
Sworn In 6

Fortitude Valley
On The Beat 9

Stafford
The Station 13
V12 Daimler Crash 14
Vietnam War Demonstrations 16
Springbok Tour 1971 17
The Mental Health Act 22
Delirium Tremens 25

St George
The Ranking System 29
Grocery Run Fatality 32
Crop Duster Crash 33
Explosives Experts 34
Bravery Award 36
The Youth Club 40

Mount Isa
The Town, The Station 45
Dead Horses 46
The Elephant And The Orangutan 48
The Paedophile's Death 50

Death Of A Shunter 52
We Found A Dead Body 53
The Driving Test 53
Motorcycle Death 55
The Prank 55
Mornington Island 57
Paying Rates 58
Moonlighting 59
Dajarra Welcome 61
Settling Scores 63
Time's Up 63
Sam 64
Aircraft Crash 65
Perilous Ute Drive 67
The Motorcycle Gang 68
Sea Search 69

Camooweal
Cave Rescue 71
Camooweal Duties 73
The Shovel Man 75
Boots The Dog 76
Slim Dusty 77
Stockmen On Leave 78
From Camooweal To Bedourie 78
The Snake 80
The Flood Boat 81
Missing Horses 82
Back To The Isa 84
The Garbos 85
Search At Massacre Inlet 86

Caloundra
Transfer From Mount Isa 92
Dealing With A Drunk 94
The Dead Body 97
The Drowning 98
False Identity 100
Staring Evil In The Eye 102

The Burly Garbos 103

Landsborough
Motorcycle Licence 105
Uninvited Guest At The Table 106
The Squatter 108
Outlaw Motorcycle Gangs 111
The Overturned Truck 114
Ute Burnouts 115
Animal Cruelty 117
Accidents 117
Section Fifteen Of The Traffic Regulations 118
The Humorous Side Of Things 119
Dead Body On The Sunlander 121
Head On Triple Fatality 122
Maleny Rescue 124
Landsborough To Thursday Island 125

Thursday Island
Thursday Island, Getting There 127
Distemper 129
Caught In A Storm 130
Baked Beans 132
Coral Poisoning 134
Family Lost At Sea 135
Prisoner Escape 137
Murder At Close Range 139
The Paddy Wagon Snake 142
Scotty's Revenge 143
The Escaped Leper 144
The Floating Body 145
Wayward Bullets In The Night 147
The Badu Island Rape 149
The Bar Fight 152
The Nurse And The Islander 154

Cairns
Transfer Perils 158
The First Shift 160

U.S. Navy Shore Patrol And The Showies 163
The Runaway Tractor 165
We Nicknamed Him Pom 168
Death In Custody 168
Port Douglas 170
Yarrabah 173
Furniture Court Rifleman 179
Back In Cairns 182

Coen
Getting There 184
The Race Meeting 188
Coen Town Power 191
Roller Skates 192
Illegal Immigrants 193
Suspect Drug Producer 196
The Man-Eater 199
Off Duty Perils 200
Nikko Thongs 204
Overseer Lockhart River 205
Not Feeling Good 207
Checking The Fences 209
The Driving Test 210
Drug Raid 212
Barry Port 214
Drinking At The Canteen 214
Transfer To The Sunshine Coast 217

Tewantin
Sunshine Coast Posting 218
Aircraft Crash 219
It's All Part Of The Job 219
School Bus Rollover. 220
The Visiting Detectives 221
Sledgehammer 223

Tannum Sands
The Station 225
Carl The German Shepherd 226

From Tannum Sands To Burketown 227

Burketown
The New Year's Eve Trap...229
Hashtag's Day In Court..232
Morning Glory 236
Helicopters Gulf Country 237
Entertainment Comes To Burketown..............................239
The Cop Who Outran A Charging Buffalo.....................240
Shiloh Goes To School 241
The Stabbing 242
The Heli-Muster Pilot 245
Pilot Payback...246
Sarge, The Pigs Are Out 247
The Unforgettable Plane Ride 250
Conference Perks..253
Black Soil Bog Down..254
Car Rollover 256
A Compromised Battle 257
Staring Into The Barrel 259
Tropical Cyclone Alert 266
Cardio-Pulmonary Resuscitation.....................................268
Pointed With The Bone..269
The Video Camera 273
Crash-Landing In The Dark..275
Tv Comes To Burketown..277
The Wild Pig Hunt...277
Christmas Mornings 279
Cahill's Law States 279
Outback Characters 280
Burketown Farewell..282

Tully
The Phone Call..283
Cyclone Winifred 284
Lifesaving Arrest 285

Sandgate
Sergeant First Class 286
Removalists Meet With My Attack Dog 287

Palm Island
The Island 289
Commissioner Lewis 292
Break-In At The Bakery 293
Suicide Carnage 294
Winning And Losing 296
RAAF FA18 Hornet Crash 301
Always On Call 304
Karma 309
Perilous Leave 311
Ground Zero 317
When The Going Gets Tough 322
Leprosy 323
Palm Island Police Truck 324
Almost A Deep Six 325
Violence, Disillusions And New Beginnings 330

Glossary

FOREWORD

I first met the author when we joined the Qld Police Force as cadets when teenage boys at the Police Barracks, Petrie Terrace. After our three year stint there, our paths took different directions, and we didn't cross professional paths again until Mt. Isa and then later in Cairns and Cape York, although we'd catch up once in a blue moon when he was in the Big Smoke.

Peter, or "Killer" as he was colloquially and affectionately known, was a legend as a country cop and was particularly widely known in the Far North and Cape York. He operated in the days when respect was not granted because of the police uniform or badge but had to be earned, and political correctness PC didn't exist. He volunteered for most of his remote and country postings, spending years in inhospitable areas that most police wouldn't cope with for long periods. There was nil to little back-up due to the vast distances involved, with communications to Police HQ only sparsely available. A vast amount of the time, he operated by himself, and as a remote country police officer, he was on call 24/7.

It takes a policeman with a unique, strong character to earn respect and be able to police Aboriginal communities, which Pete achieved over many years at various locations. He was highly regarded by both Aboriginal and Islander Tribal Elders. He practised Community Policing long before it became a mainstream method of policing.

To survive and successfully police a lot of the remote, vast Police Divisions, a cop had to have good wits, excellent people skills, street smarts and large gonads. He also had to be able to physically handle himself as this was standard frontier policing. Practical policing then was not a black and white affair but, through necessity, sometimes operated in the "grey" zone.

A number of highly risky actions that Peter took over the years, especially in disarming offenders, usually when outnumbered and out gunned, would have resulted in Bravery Awards had there been official witnesses.

I thought of comparing him to the fantasy figure of Crocodile Dundee, but Peter was the real deal.

I highly recommend ALWAYS ON CALL to the prospective reader who is interested in remote, country policing, where the Marquis of Queensbury rules didn't always apply, as practised by the few who were up to it. It is an exciting, unique page-turner that will appeal to the adventurous at heart.

Stoll Watt
ex Inspr. B.M. V.A.
Brisbane 9/2021.

MAP ENCOMPASSING MY CAREER IN THE POLICE FORCE

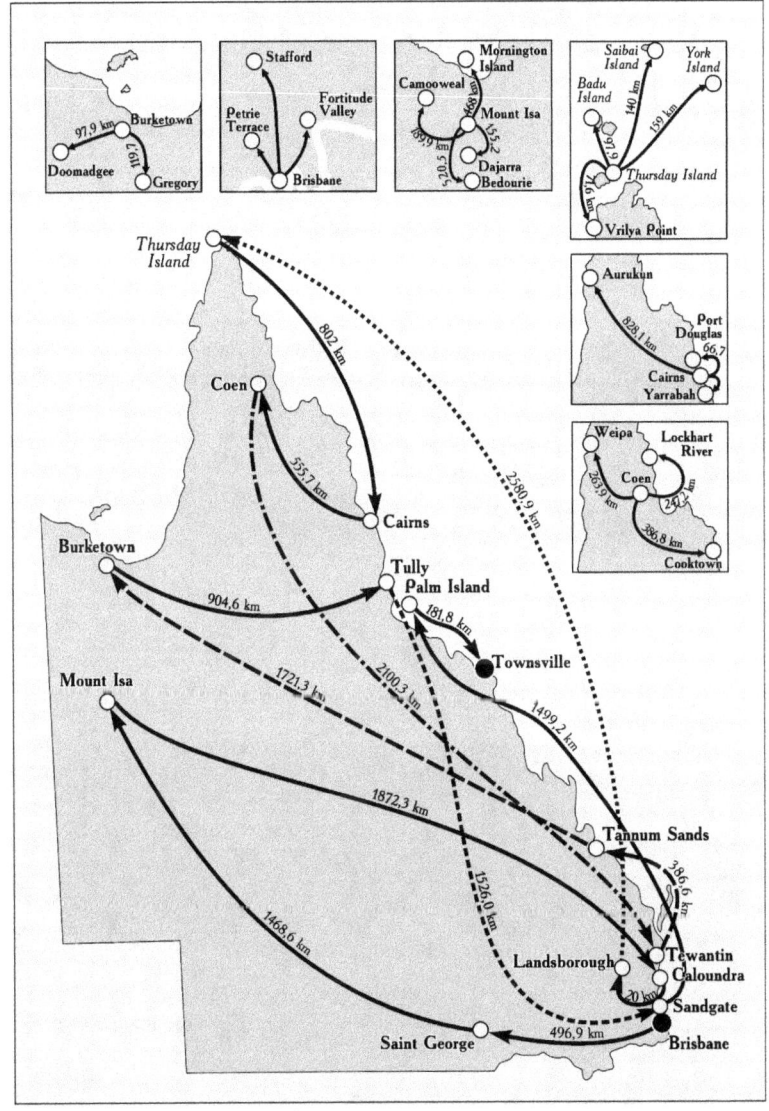

INTRODUCTION

My great-grandfather, Andrew Cahill, was a police officer in the Royal Irish Constabulary responsible for the peace of Ireland. There was the need for a militaristic structure to combat the continuous unrest within the country. Those serving in the Royal Irish Constabulary were regarded as the best-trained police force in the world. During that time, New Zealand and Australian colonies offered money and land grants to attract much-needed immigrants. Andrew's older brother, Malachy, had ventured to the land Down Under two years previously, and it was he who sent word to his brothers that the colonies needed men to join the newly established Queensland Police Force. Andrew was eager to escape his hunger ravaged homeland, and in 1866, he set sail for colonial Queensland, followed a year later by his brother Patrick. Unknowingly at the time, the three brothers set forth a generational family tradition of policing, which, during my time in the force, included one uncle, two cousins and one brother.

Always on Call

PETRIE TERRACE

BEGINNING

At sixteen, I started my training as a Queensland Police Cadet in the old Petrie Terrace Depot in Brisbane. On my first day, I fronted up dressed in a suit and tie, believing that this would be the best way to go, but I didn't know that it was deemed a crime to have the buttons of your coat undone. The drill instructor, Tom Molloy, a second-class sergeant, had been in this training position for most of his service. He stopped in front of me, looked me up and down, and broke into a loud, close to my face lecture informing me of my shortcomings, many of which I was unaware. After he had his say, I was permitted to go inside the depot and was allocated a two bunk, second-floor share room.

Each morning, one hundred and thirty cadets arrived at the Lang Park PCYC for physical training, first aid training, self-defence and whatever else was thought necessary. This location was also where we played a game loosely described as "basketball". With ten cadets per side and not too many rules, it was not dissimilar to the army game known as "murderball". The object was to score a goal in the hoops at each end of the court by whatever means, which meant lots of pushing, shoving, and tripping of opponents. One large cadet seemed to be taking an extra interest in intimidation. After he had several goes at me, I decided that enough was enough, and when I saw him come towards me for another try, I jumped around to face him and delivered a foot sweep that sent him sprawling along the floor. The instructors were watching but did not comment. The game continued with the bully from there on in, losing total interest in me.

For decades, the depot's training of cadets and probationaries had been the domain of the Irish drill instructor Tom Molloy. In WWII, he had been a petty officer in the Royal Navy and had seen extensive active service on British Navy ships. A strict disciplinarian, he ran the place much like a naval training establishment. Yet, though the discipline was strict, with physical training a high priority, it was conducted in an overall sensible manner. Although, I do admit that I might not have felt that way at the time.

It became apparent that Tom was secretly and justifiably proud of his war service and had a propensity for asking cadets and probationaries during the regular morning room inspections if their fathers had seen service in WWII. An answer in the affirmative seemed to produce a more favourable treatment by him. Unlike some, my parents had served in the army during the war; therefore, I didn't have to worry about fabricating an answer. He also asked a cadet, with an apparent German surname, if his father had served during the war, to which the cadet proudly replied,

'Yes, Sergeant, he did'.

'What branch of the service was he in?'

'In the Navy, Sergeant'.

The Sergeant is ecstatic at this point, having some connection with what he thought to be a fellow traveller and went on to ask,

'And what ship was he on?'

The answer was,

'The Bismarck!'

Well, you should have seen old Tom's facial expression! Even though he might not have encountered the famous German battleship during his years in the Navy, he nevertheless was left speechless for once.

Like all police cadets, I kept fit, and at six feet tall, I well and truly met the stated required height to join the police. However, the problem remained that I wasn't "big" enough to meet the weight and body measurement requirements. Quite simply, I was skinny as a rake. A senior cop described my physique as being akin to that of a "greyhound gone bad". As my probationary training approached, it became evident that I would never make the weight and measurement requirements needed to qualify before my nineteenth birthday. Fortunately, the physical training instructor, Arthur Millwood, at the Police Youth Club at Paddington, took it upon himself to put me on a weightlifting regime over the next twelve months. He was a police sergeant who, even though in his fifties at that stage, still had a couple of weightlifting records to his credit, making him just the bloke I needed at that time. I got on well with him, and he started using me as his crash dummy in his regular unarmed combat classes for cadets and probationaries. The course was successful, and I bulked up considerably, with the result that I passed my probationary entrance physical requirements with ease.

The improved build felt good and added that little bit of extra confidence needed when placed in a situation where physical strength becomes a distinct tactical advantage, and I was to have plenty of those situations in the coming years. Over time I became more robust, and the imposed regime gave me a lifetime's interest in lifting weights. I have always been grateful for the Sergeant's interest and knowledge, including the techniques in unarmed combat he taught me.

Following the mornings at the PCYC, we proceeded to various police stations, where most blokes did the filing duties. I was lucky enough to be placed in a large Criminal Investigation Branch office at the Valley with a staff of thirty-two plainclothes men, a uniform, senior constable, and a typist. My duties varied enormously, covering filing, typing, running errands, organising Christmas parties, send-offs and more. I also knew verbatim the phone numbers of all the hotels frequented by detectives. It was handy that I knew where the two-man-teams were so that at any given time, I could jump on the phone and call them if the bosses were looking for them. During my cadet training, I learned how to type and gained an intermediate star qualification in freshwater lifesaving. It didn't hurt that my uncle, who was also in the police, was a well-respected and well-known cop, and as a result, some detectives occasionally took me with them on their Saturday night "graveyard" shift.

One day, they were short of men, so I was asked to watch a couple of suspects for property offences. I was surprised on entering the interview room to see two former classmates who'd been bits of rogues back at school. Most of my former schoolmates entered various careers as clergymen, military, police, and as was apparent here, a few crooks as well. These experiences with detectives stood me in good stead. During one of my duties, I identified a crook, which led to a commendation from the commissioner for recognising and reporting a wanted man.

During the years as a police cadet at the old Petrie Terrace Depot, I generally had a second job somewhere, either in the evenings or weekends. I also had a couple of old lawnmowers in my Holden ute and mowed a few lawns in my spare time. I was always on the lookout for jobs that would bring in a bit of money, so someone asked, would I wash a few windows?

'No worries,' I said, 'I'll do that.'

When I arrived on the job, I looked up skywards onto the twenty-six levels newly built, high-rise building. All I had to do, they said, was wash all the windows - from the outside! Then I was required to climb out from the inside of the rooms, out through the open window and onto a narrow ledge. All this while carrying a bucket, a spray bottle containing Metho, and rubbing newspaper. The trick was to keep my balance, which was more manageable if one didn't look down. There were no such things as safety requirements in those days, and a harness and scaffolding were non-existent. I told my Mum that I had scored a job with a cleaner, but I didn't tell her that it involved venturing out on narrow ledges of high-rise buildings. I figured it was best that way.

One Saturday afternoon, my mate Jim and I were heading back to the depot from our window washing job when we noticed a huge man running along the footpath dressed in pyjamas. As it was near the Brisbane General Hospital, I figured he might have absconded from the psychiatric ward. I pulled over to the kerb, and as soon as the man ran past the vehicle, I yelled,

'Where are you headed?'

'Botany Bay.' was the reply.

I said, 'Well, so are we. Jump in.'

Jim opened the car door, and the man settled in next to him on the front seat. I drove around the back of the Fortitude Valley Police Station, where the constables on duty collected the patient. The escapee didn't object and was all smiles when he was lead inside the station.

POST-MORTEM TRAINING

During the four months spent in training as a probationary, the Force endeavoured to include as many scenarios as possible a young constable might encounter once sworn in.

During one occasion, we were transported down to the Brisbane City Morgue to attend a post-mortem examination. The body ready for dissection was that of a twenty-four-year-old male killed in a vehicle collision the previous day. It was pretty confronting to see the forensic pathologist using the electric saw to remove the top of the skull and a large tin snip type tool to open the chest cavity.

Some years earlier, my late father had been an undertaker and, living at the rear of the funeral home, it wasn't unusual to see the occasional dead body. However, the dissection was a first for me. With mixed feelings, I sat through the whole process, after which we returned to the depot. At the time, I did not know that in the not-too-distant future, I would have a much greater involvement with a post-mortem, one where the visual and smell impacted me in such a way that it remained ingrained in my mind for a very long time.

SWORN IN

It was during my probationary training that the British royals paid a visit to Brisbane. As there was a marked shortage in police numbers at the time, and with the need for police presence along the route taken by the visiting royals, they made use of probationaries, thus taking us out on the street a week or so before being sworn in. On Monday the 27th of April 1970, I graduated, and after taking The Oath of Service, I was sworn in as constable 8013.

> *"I, Peter Andrew Cahill swear by almighty God that I will well and truly serve our Sovereign Lady Queen Elizabeth the Second and Her Heirs and Successors according to law in the office of constable or in such other capacity as I may be hereafter appointed, promoted, or reduced, without favour or affection, malice or ill-will, from this date and until I am legally discharged; that I will see and cause Her Majesty's peace to be kept and preserved; and that I will prevent to the best of my power all offences against the same; and that while I shall continue to be a member of the Police Force of Queensland I will to the best of my skill and knowledge discharge all the duties legally imposed upon me faithfully and according to law. So help me God."*

Little did I know that morning how soon that section of the Oath, concerning the preservation of life, would personally affect me for the remainder of my service.

At a young age, I was aware that, at times, police officers were killed in the line of duty. As a kid, I lived a street up from a residence where a young cop was shot while responding to a domestic dispute. Another was shot during my cadet service, walking up to the front door of a house. The murderer had fired a powerful .303 Lee Enfield rifle, with the projectile passing through the front door, before mortally wounding the policeman. I was constantly reminded of this incident as I passed by that residence, where the bullet hole remained as a stark reminder.

Despite these and other police shootings around the state, I doubted that it would happen to me. However, I was wrong, and during my career, I experienced some compromised situations that could have ended badly for me. It made me aware that I wasn't ten feet tall and bulletproof after all.

Following the swearing-in ceremony on the grassed quarter-deck at the depot, we received our best wishes and transferred over to our allocated training stations. Thus, my career started as a beat and traffic cop at the uniformed section at Fortitude Valley, which kicked off with a very unsettling trip to the morgue.

FORTITUDE VALLEY

ON THE BEAT

The senior sergeant briefed me on my duties as a beat policeman, which involved eight-hour rotational shifts, starting and ending at the Valley's main intersection. At the time, a police officer on patrol was contacted via a wooden police telephone box which, in my case, was situated on the footpath of the Valley's main intersection. If the senior sergeant in charge of the shift wanted to speak to you, he would activate the red light on top of the police phone box, and the police officer nearest the phone box was to answer the call. On my first evening on the beat, I saw the red light come on, so I grabbed the supplied phone box key, opened the door, and squeezed into the relatively small space. Lifting the receiver, I said,

'Constable Cahill speaking.'

The senior sergeant's voice boomed through the receiver.

'You are required to accompany an ambulance to the morgue. It will be there shortly.'

I'd barely replaced the receiver when the ambulance pulled up, and a young ambo, about the same age as me, greeted me.

'G'day, I'm Mark', he said, 'hop in.'

We drove the ten minutes to the morgue with Mark telling me that the deceased old lady we had on board had died earlier in hospital. Nearing the banks of the Brisbane River, he swung the ambulance towards the premises enshrined in complete eerie darkness. In this place, I learned that a torch was an essential item. If you didn't have one, you had to feel your way around the cold walls to find the light switch, and inside the cold room, it seemed even darker. Police often engaged in pranks like turning off the lights while some poor bastard was inside, who then had to feel his way to a wall and walk himself round to the door. It was eerie to see how many bodies on the gurneys had one hand draped over the side of the tray. It was just the thing you wanted to feel brushing against your leg in the dark when trying to find the wall.

The body we had for the morgue was quite heavy, and I learned there's truth to the term "dead weight". Over in the loading zone, there was a device with lifting straps to give us a hand, so I grabbed a morgue trolley and lined it up next to the wheeled gurney of the ambulance holding the deceased. When we were satisfied that the straps underneath the arms and legs were in place, we pulled the chain to start the lift of the body upwards.

The compression caused by the lift resulted in a rush of air escaping from the dead woman's mouth. Neither of us had ever done this lift before, and already slightly ill at ease, the dreadful groaning sound coming forth from the dead body gave us a dreadful fright. In unison, we let go of the lifting straps. The body dropped down, back onto the gurney, and we ran like possessed, making for a fast exit. Our fear propelled sprint lasted only metres when we realised that it was just a noise. And as you do in situations like that, we burst out laughing and sheepishly returned to the dock and got on with the job at hand.

I spent my days walking the beat at the prescribed pace of four kilometres per hour. Apart from a meal break back at the station, I virtually walked the entire eight-hour shift. Occasionally a sergeant and his driver in a patrol vehicle pulled up to check on things, which was the only police contact the beat cop had during the shift. The requirement to perform traffic duty at several points around the Valley area was a job I didn't like at all. I would never be like some of the brilliant traffic point blokes who had a celebrity-like following. One of the most well-known traffic policemen was "Dancing Dickie Daniels", who made a complete production out of directing traffic. People came from far and wide to see him in action, dancing, twirling, and leaping through the air while flawlessly directing the traffic. Other duties assigned to me were taking reports at the scene of traffic collisions and various other complaints, such as lost property, shoplifting, barking dogs, fence disputes and the like.

Back in the sixties and seventies, several derelicts and homeless people resided in parks and abandoned buildings. The overwhelming majority being older males addicted to alcohol, with WWII veterans forming the bulk. They frequented establishments, termed "Wine Bars". These were low-grade booze outlets whose existence depended entirely on derelicts and those of low socioeconomic status. As eventually the last of these old blokes died, so did the wine bars with their compromised and dwindling source of income. Many of these men died during the cold winter months due to poor health and lack of shelter to escape the cold and rain.

Eventually, more than pleased to have completed my training, I wasted no time packing up and moving on to my new posting, a small suburban station at Stafford. Had I remained in my current capacity, I probably would've had second thoughts about continuing police work. However, it was nothing like I had expected and nothing like the police work I'd been on the periphery of whilst a cadet at the large Criminal Investigation Branch. It was also nothing like the challenging outback police work I encountered spanning a twenty-three-year career in the police force.

STAFFORD

THE STATION

I packed my bags and headed for Stafford, a suburb in the northern part of Brisbane, where I started work as a general duties' constable. The job turned out to be interesting enough because it covered everything I had so far learned and studied. Cases of simple shoplifting, conducting general inquiries, including taking statements from people involved in collisions, serving summons, and satisfying warrants. I enjoyed the interaction with the local members of the community, who knew their local police by name.

We sometimes had a bit of fun during interactions, like when a colleague and I executed a warrant for non-payment of an old fine on a bloke with a criminal history. He and his brother were not all that well disposed towards police, and after trying to dispute the fine, they finally paid and reluctantly handed over the cash. My colleague said, making sure they'd hear,

'We get to keep half of whatever we collect.'

Upon hearing that, the two brothers went ballistic, and for a moment, I thought it would almost certainly escalate. Seeing them blow a fuse was so funny that we couldn't contain ourselves and burst out laughing. That's when they realised it was a joke and slammed the door shut on us.

I will never forget Stafford because of the pong coming from the local tannery works that greeted me when I opened the office on the morning shift. The suburb also had shopping and banking facilities, as well as schools and an industrial area. Most of the residents lived in housing commission areas, blocks of flats, and middle-class homes, with new developments underway delivering an estate of upmarket homes.

The two main thoroughfares, Webster and Stafford Road, intersected, with the old Stafford police station situated on its corner. Regardless of the traffic lights on the intersection, collisions occurred daily. In cases like that, it was either the slowest or most junior cop who had to go and take the report. Several serious crashes occurred while I was there, but none so spectacular as the one involving a V12 Daimler sports car.

V12 DAIMLER CRASH

Up until that fateful night of the crash, there were only three V12 Daimlers to be found in Australia. I wasn't on duty that night, which was a good thing as I knew Frank, the driver of the Daimler, personally. He and I had become acquainted at the local bowls club, where we met up from time to time to have a few beers. Frank liked to play the ladies and enjoyed his booze maybe a bit too much. His white sports car had the longest bonnet I had ever seen on a vehicle. It housed a V12 engine, which made the driving compartment and boot sections seem small in comparison. All in all, it was an extremely fast motor car.

The collision happened a fair way to the north of the main intersection at a juncture where Stafford Road intersected with one of the smaller side streets. By the time my shift started the next day, the vehicles had been removed from the scene and taken to the police holding yard. The Daimler's damage was extreme, with the entire front section destroyed. The other vehicle, an FC Holden sedan, lay ripped into three sections: the engine area, the seating, and the boot section. The local towing company had to make four trips, loading and delivering the various pieces to the police holding yard. The wrecks attracted a lot of public attention. There were people continually wandering into the ungated holding yard, and with often only one cop rostered on the late shift, getting rid of the gawkers as well as performing regular police duties became quite a challenge.

During one late shift, I had been out serving summonses and doing general inquiries, leaving the station temporarily unattended. Disgusted, I saw upon my return that one ghoul had found a wig on the floor of the Daimler. It had been worn by the female passenger of the sports car at the time of her violent death. He was parading around wearing the wig, thinking it to be hilarious.

I learned that Frank had been driving the Daimler, and both he and his female passenger had died on impact. The young man driving the Holden was transferred to hospital with severe injuries, and after he'd recovered enough, I was able to interview him. I lined up all the evidence, and it soon became clear how the collision had occurred. The Holden sedan had entered from a side street onto Stafford Road intending to turn right and was therefore required to give right of way. With the road clear and two headlights barely visible in the far distance, it provided enough time for the Holden to veer out onto the road and make the right-hand turn. At that moment, the Daimler suddenly had appeared and collided side on with the Holden. The impact separated the seating part from the rear and front sections, resulting in the instant deaths of its two occupants.

Later the Holden driver told me during the interview, 'I stopped at the intersection to make sure no cars were coming. I could see the lights of a vehicle a long way off, leaving me plenty of time to make the turn. I drove out onto Stafford Road, and the next thing I knew was this car hitting me side-on.'

Previously, I'd interviewed another witness, a retired racing car driver, who was having a beer on his front porch that evening. He saw the Daimler go past travelling at high speed, estimated to be around two hundred and ten kilometres per hour in a sixty zone. The witness wasn't far out in his estimate as the investigation found that the speedometer of the Daimler was jammed on that exact speed. Considering this speed, and from the perspective of the driver of the Holden, the vehicle he saw approaching was indeed a long way off, but travelling at this incredible speed, it wouldn't have taken much time to cover the distance. Fortunately, the construction of the Holden was a deciding factor in the survival of the young bloke driving it, who eventually made a full recovery.

VIETNAM WAR DEMONSTRATIONS

While I was at Stafford, the Viet Nam war was in full swing with Australian troops engaged in the thick of the hostilities. The National Service, or "Nashos", had been called up at the roll of a dice. Your date of birth dictated whether you saw military service or otherwise. After completing three years as a Navy cadet, I served twelve months in the Royal Australian Navy and was happy to have missed out, but I felt for the blokes who did get called up.

On at least two occasions, with anti-war demonstrations in the inner-city areas of Brisbane, I was rostered on along with cops who came in from all over Queensland. They assisted in keeping order, ensuring the protesters remained on the route, for which they had a permit. During my shift, work involved linking hands and forming a human police chain, thus containing the protesters on their route. It was pretty much nonviolent at that stage, and I was often just a few inches away from their faces. They would try to start conversations with you, but it didn't matter what your view was. You were required to uphold the law and carry out instructions regardless. For one of the demonstrations, I was positioned with another young cop in a narrow lane, having been given instructions not to allow the protesters access. At the time, I thought, if enough of them wanted to, there wouldn't be much we could do to impede them, but nothing eventuated.

SPRINGBOK TOUR 1971

During my time at Stafford, the South African rugby union team known as the "Springboks" came to Australia for a six-week rugby union tour. The springbok, a gazelle, was the emblem used by White South African teams during the apartheid, with Black South Africans excluded from national teams. The apartheid ideology was introduced in South Africa, calling for individual advancement of the different racial groups. A state of emergency was declared in Queensland during the anti-apartheid demonstrations of the Springbok Tour of 1971, where protestors were prepared to resort to extreme violence. These demonstrations were an altogether different situation from the

Vietnam demos. The protestors vengeance was even unleashed onto animals such as a big white police horse in Melbourne, where marbles were thrown onto the bitumen, causing the horse to lose its footing and fall. Once he was on the ground, they slashed him with sharp objects, mainly metal toy thumb clickers, a kids' toy in the shape of a frog or cricket. How anyone can justify barbaric cruelty like that in a protest against the apartheid policy in South Africa, is beyond me.

But whether I had an opinion or otherwise on the South Africa policy, I was simply required to carry out my duty in helping to keep the peace. The Springbok Rugby team toured Eastern Australia in 1971, and wherever they went, they went accompanied by large numbers of police. The force, drawn from all over Queensland, were sent to Brisbane as reinforcements. The country police still wore the drab olive uniforms, in contrast to the new blue ones worn by coastal police. It had the public confused as to the identity of the country police, thinking they were soldiers.

Before the arrival of the Springboks, I was placed with a huge group of police at the Enoggera army barracks in Brisbane. Here we received instructions for what was to come, and quite frankly, I was surprised by some of the revelations, and the extent to which protesters had gone, to injure police. One example was when an attractive young woman had given a uniformed police officer a wrapped sandwich. The young cop, for some reason, had felt uneasy about it, which was just as well. However, forensic examination of the food revealed that the bread contained ground-up glass. As well as that, explosives were found on the grounds and had to be removed by the bomb squad. A video of those bombs detonated inside a forty-four-gallon drum gave us an idea of what would've happened had they not been found in time. In addition, they showed us photos of agitators who were in all the protest marches. They were always up near the front but a few ranks back, urging the mob onwards. I wondered at the time if they were ideologues or if some organisation paid them to do it.

The Springboks, whilst in Brisbane, were staying at the Tower Mill Motel up in Wickham Terrace. Rostered on the night shift, we were positioned directly in front of the motel. Those nights were cold, wet, and windy and facing us from across the road, large numbers of protesters spent their time screaming abuse at the police. The insults came thick and fast, accompanied by a bombardment of food and water hurled at us. It went on relentlessly for a couple of nights, and we were all getting sick of it. Finally, the new commissioner who was present could see that something had to be done, as the protesters were going just too far.

Early in the second night, two Springbok players left the motel and walked across the road to the park. The big, tall blond fellows, proudly wearing their Springbok blazers, walked straight into the large mob of protesters. Even though they were readily recognisable, they wandered leisurely around, unharmed, and then simply returned to the motel. The incident made me wonder whether the mob were at all interested in the apartheid policy. It threw substantial doubt on their perception and knowledge of that, which they were protesting. It started to feel very much like they were simply there for the action, for whatever thrill it gave them, trying to harm police officers.

By late that second night, the protesters redoubled their efforts throwing abuse, food, and water at the four lines of police outside the motel. The commissioner decided to act with the instruction to draw our batons and walk towards the screaming mob, thinking that would discourage them. As we were moving in lines towards them, an older, obviously fed up with the situation cop yelled,

'Charge!'

It was a relief to hear that order as the bulk of us young blokes had had enough of the bullshit. Encouraged, we all took off at a gallop with our batons at the ready, towards the mob of protesters. Well, you should have seen them go, knocking each other over in their haste to escape, even though they heavily outnumbered the police. None of us heard the call attributed to the commissioner which came over the loudspeaker.

'Come back, the police, come back!'

We pressed onwards and quickly caught up with the scattering horde as we combined with the mob racing down through the park. The platform, holding floodlights and cameras, was knocked over in the fray, engulfing the park in complete darkness. I galloped along, pushing people out of the way, and telling them to get going. My main concern was not to get whacked on the head from behind, either by protesters or police, as it was hard to distinguish who was who in the pitch dark.

I saw two big old cops lumber past, holding a screaming protester by an ankle each, disappear into the gloom, swinging their batons decisively with their free hand. The melee was all over in minutes, with the road and park now almost devoid of the screaming mob. A few blokes in white coats with the words "Legal Observer" on the back remained. They called out repeatedly,

'Anyone injured? Anyone injured?'

There was a plaintive cry,

'Over here. Over here.'

It came from the large patch of shrubbery at the bottom end of the park. The white coats rushed into the greenery, only to be set upon by two larrikins who sent them straight out again, kicking their backsides. Then, before anyone could establish their identity, the unknown assailants disappeared, laughing into the dark.

A bloke wearing a WWII British army steel helmet approached us, and at the top of his voice, he announced,

'I have been trained to kill with my hands by Her Majesty's Government!'

He followed this up by adopting a fighting stance I'd not seen before, right in front of a senior constable. The cop responded swiftly by bringing his baton down, striking the flat edge of the would-be assassin's steel helmet and asked,

'Does that ring?'

We couldn't help but laugh as we watched him take off down the road, desperately trying to remove his helmet. That pretty much wrapped things up outside the motel, with none of the protesters having the courage to return. It was the last baton charge carried out by any police force in Australia.

Next, I accompanied the Springboks to Toowoomba, where one protester wearing a long coat walked up and down the sidelines dispersing hydrogen sulphide, also known as rotten egg gas. The smell was putrid, and without further ado, the protester was swiftly removed. I then followed the rugby team to the Gold Coast, which fortunately was an uneventful trip.

The last game the Springboks played was at the Brisbane Exhibition Grounds, where half of us police constables watched the crowd, while the other half watched the game, then we swapped directions at halftime. The game ended smoothly with no further demonstrations. Upon returning to our respective stations, we heard that the Premier had granted all police-involved an extra week leave. The thing is that no matter what opinion the public may or may not have had of the then

Premier, he did have the back of police out there on duty. In addition, his team of cameramen attended events, making it difficult for the now termed "fake news" to be fabricated.

THE MENTAL HEALTH ACT

The involvement of police within the Mental Health Act provided further challenges. Due to the division's population density, it was inevitable that police encountered a few of these cases. In those days, police had the power to apprehend a person who appeared to have a mental illness if it meant preventing them from inflicting severe harm to themselves or others. One such incident involved a highly successful local businessman named Harold Prior. Often, he was seen on the footpath in front of his business, giving cash to passers-by who couldn't believe their luck. The family finally had enough, and as they could not resolve the issue internally, the sons resorted to having a warrant taken out against their father under the Mental Health Act. The request was for his removal from the premises and an examination in a psychiatric unit.

Armed with a warrant, five police officers, including myself and two of his sons, made our way to the family business premises. As soon as he saw two police cars arrive, Harold walked out onto the footpath. I appraised immediately that this huge man with big muscular arms was strong. I looked into his bulging red eyes, and the conversation that took place, explaining why we were there, wasn't going the way it was supposed to, and the big fellow was getting agitated. This situation was the last thing we wanted as some of these blokes have superhuman strength. As I stood closest to Harold, I could see

him eyeballing me, and I thought,
'This is going to be something else.'
'I like you colt', he said. 'I will go with you.'

Then, with his massive hand, he firmly grabbed me by the old-style police scout belt and lifted me clear off the ground! Left dangling, I steadied things up by grabbing his forearm with both my hands and said,

'I can arrange that, but first, you'll have to put me down.'

He seemed pleased with that reply and, I felt somewhat relieved when he lowered me back onto the ground.

Harrold Prior followed me to the police car, and together, we drove off towards the Royal Brisbane Hospital. The second car with the remaining six blokes followed behind. Harold willingly came in the lift with me up to the psychiatric unit and quietly went inside, where I left him in the care of the staff. My job was done once the doors closed behind him.

On another occasion, I was one of three cops who went to a house in Stafford Road with a mental health warrant to collect a man named Stan. We were to take him to the psychiatric ward as he had become unmanageable for his aging parents. For three days now, Stan had been on top of a wardrobe in one of the bedrooms, and after a brief but very spirited struggle and a few broken louvres, we got him down and escorted him to the car. There were no such things as cargo barriers separating the front from the rear of police sedans back then, and it took a fair bit of strength to keep him under control while in transit. We took Stan to the admittance area of the hospital, where a young doctor was waiting to examine him before admission. We told the doc what had gone on before and that we'd hang about should he require assistance. Quite indignantly, he said,

'You are not required here, and you might as

well leave.'

But knowing what Stan was capable of, we decided to hang around, out of sight. We heard the doc ask Stan about his relationship with his mum, and he answered,

'She's a bitch.'

The doc then asked him what the date was, to which he replied screaming,

'You can't fool me. It's the thirty-third day of December.'

The date was, in fact, the second of January. With that, he lunged at the startled medico, grabbing him by the throat intent on strangling him.

'This is what you get for trying to trick me.' he screamed.

We ran back inside, managed to restrain Stan for a second time, and immediately took him up to the ward. We heard the doc mutter his apologies, adding that he had judged wrong.

A few nights later, my partner and I received a call for assistance during the late shift. Headquarters had received a report of a mentally ill man living in a small flat outside our division, and they needed backup. What I saw inside I'd not witnessed before.

An older bloke with a shaved head was wearing a German beret and a long leather coat but nothing else. He told us quite calmly that he was, in fact, both the Archangel Gabriel and Erwin Rommel, the German general, and that he was impervious to pain. These delusions in themselves weren't a problem until he put his hand into the gas fire. I could smell the flesh burning, but this man did not indicate that he was affected by the pain. Springing into action, we grabbed him and pulled him away from the flames. It didn't take much to get him into the police car and subsequently to the psychiatric ward at the Royal Brisbane Hospital. And as always, my job was done once the ward doors closed behind the patient.

DELIRIUM TREMENS

Rostered on the Thursday morning shift, my colleague and I patrolled the quiet streets. It was a peaceful morning, and half of Stafford still seemed to be asleep, but it wasn't to last. A call came through on the radio that a large man, wearing the bottom half of a tracksuit, was seen running down Stafford Road, screaming incoherently while wildly flinging his arms about. This message caused the inevitable radio banter to start up,

'Must be an off-duty policeman' and 'Sounds like the Sarge on his morning run.'

Someone had spotted the man in our patrolling area, so we headed out to Stafford Road. The definition "large" used in the radio description of the man was a bit light on, as what we found running down the road was a giant. I pulled the police car over and, upon seeing us, he accelerated into a sprint while turning up the volume on his vocals. I immediately gave chase with the intention of a flying tackle to get him on the ground. As I closed in on him, he suddenly stopped, turned around to face me and, with his arms raised above him like King Kong, let out a mighty roar, and with that, he rushed at me.

I saw a road gang, who were doing some pick and shovel work, drop their tools and bolt into the nearest house. Seeing this giant propel towards me, I immediately aborted the idea of a flying tackle. I had to improvise on the spot as there wasn't a formulated plan B. With some experience in grappling, which I'd learned during my years as a cadet and some Greco Roman amateur wrestling, I was about to find out how much of the combined techniques would help me bring this giant down. I simultaneously delivered a palm heel to his chest and a foot sweep behind both legs. It worked and my opponent, now off-balance, fell to the ground, and like most people with severe mental health issues I'd encountered, he seemed to possess immense strength. By now, my partner had caught up, and the idea was to handcuff this bloke and transport him to the psychiatric ward, a twenty-minute drive away. Unfortunately, executing this plan was easier said than done.

Within no time, our uniform shirts were ripped to pieces during the giant's attempts of escape. Unfortunately, backup wasn't forthcoming as no spectator had called the police, including the road gang, who remained safely inside their refuge. All I could see of them were several sets of eyes looking through the louvres that covered the windows. The fight on the ground continued while the blood oozed from our cuts and scratches and mingled with the dirt and soaked into our clothing. Every attempt made to apply the handcuffs failed, and, rather than tiring, the big man's strength seemed to increase.

Our luck changed when the crew of a passing fire truck and ambulance spotted us on their way back from an accident. Recognising that we were in trouble, they immediately pulled over, and the four firies and two ambos ran over to give us a hand. There were now eight of us in the struggle, and the sheer weight of numbers finally started to wear the big man down. He seemed exhausted, and we were finally able to handcuff him and transfer him into the back of the police car. We drove to the Prince Charles Cardiac Hospital, only a few minutes away as it was too far to the General Hospital. It was not our usual practice but getting medical assistance for this bloke was paramount.

The staff at the hospital were great and immediately sedated him with enough Largactil to put a few blokes to sleep for several hours. So far, so good. The big bloke now lay calm and quiet in the back of the ambulance en-route to the General. We put him onto a gurney and into the patient lift, sending it upwards to the psychiatric ward, and that's when he came good. He started to resist again, which was quite a problem in the small space of the lift. It was a desperate struggle to keep him on the gurney until we reached the ward floor. I'll never forget the tremendous feeling of relief when the ward door opened and a couple of orderlies came out to take over the patient.

As it turned out, the big bloke had been celebrating the end of the rugby season, drinking heavily for at least a week straight and had stopped the boozing about three days before we found him. Unfortunately, by that time, he had developed delirium tremens, a severe alcohol withdrawal complication that can occur after a period of heavy drinking. Fortunately, the DTs are temporary, and when I saw this bloke on the train a few weeks later, he didn't recognise me. It was good to know that he was back to normal again and going about his day.

I spent a few more months at Stafford, gaining valuable experience and working as a team with a good group of colleagues. It was a station I could've remained at longer, but I wanted to get out into the West to experience a completely different type of policing to that of metropolitan areas. My send-off was held at the Stafford animal refuge, in a big shed, where we sat around on bales of hay drinking a few beers. My good mate and uncle, Pat, came down for the occasion. He was a good fighter and had held two serious middleweight boxing titles during WWII. He also received two "Favourable Records" from the Police Department following his assistance to police with his considerable pugilistic ability. One of those occasions concerned a young policeman being assaulted by a group of six foreign merchant seamen when Pat jumped out of his cab and levelled the playing field for the young cop. I left Stafford on a good note and drove to St George, over five hundred kilometres west of Brisbane, to commence the next part of my police service.

ST GEORGE

THE RANKING SYSTEM

St George, which at the time had a population of around two thousand, was the farthest west I had ever been. I immediately took a liking to the place. The Balonne River flowed through town right across from the police station. It provided any keen fisherman with plenty of Yellowbelly and Murray Cod. The willow trees that grew along its banks were alive with birds, particularly at sunset. The area was thriving with sheep and wheat industries as well as a few cotton farms providing employment.

Seven police officers staffed the police station, and the barracks, located around the back, became my home for the duration. Besides the occasional relieving cop, I had them primarily to myself. St George had a reputation for violence at the time, with a few recorded murders, such as that of a bloke shooting a woman with a .303 calibre rifle in the main street. The hotel population comprised the usual western Queensland mixture of graziers, business owners, council employees, government workers, roo shooters, stick pickers and the like, and with four pubs in town, fights were a regular occurrence.

There was even a ranking system in place according to fighting ability. A bloke named Fergus held the number one title, closely followed by Pongo, who had a relentless, peculiar, and unpleasant smell about him. Laurie John Gibbo, a roo shooter, came in a close third and was quite proud of himself for requiring three police officers to arrest him. The "ranking event" had happened a month or so before my arrival.

I had been in St George for about three weeks when I decided to have a few beers at one of the hotels. I barely sat down at the bar when a rough-looking bloke approached me. As he stood in front of me, he made this announcement,

'I'm Laurie John Gibbo, I am number three in town, and the law's as weak as piss.'

By his fighting stance, it was clear that this was a direct challenge, and I immediately recognised that this bloke was one of the town's troublemakers looking for a fight and to show me that he was in charge. I didn't waste time discussing the matter, so following my usual modus operandi, in cases such as this, I hit him without hesitation, delivering a right uppercut to his solar plexus. I watched him go down to the floor upon which I immediately declared loudly,

'It looks like you are now number four, Gibbo.'

The watching crowd roared their approval. As I didn't want to give Gibbo the advantage of getting back up to continue his fight, and knowing that I couldn't kick him, as that was against pub fighting protocol, I decided that the best course of action would be to continue the fight at floor level.

Again, it seemed that, by doing this, I was following the correct pub fight etiquette according to the now large crowd of onlookers, who yet again roared their collective approval. Soon other police materialised, and Gibbo, now slightly worse for wear, was promptly taken to the watch house. Following his court appearance, he received a sentence of imprisonment, so I escorted him to Boggo Road Jail. It involved a seventy-kilometre car trip to the Thallon railway station and a nineteen-hour train journey in a coal-powered locomotive. The train was a freighter, with two wooden carriages at the rear, which stopped at every siding. Gibbo was quiet during the entire trip, and I had no further trouble with him.

Upon my return, I learned that now apparently, I was ranked number three in town. Number two, Pongo, had previously served three years imprisonment for stabbing number one, Fergus, who'd survived. Pongo reputedly stated that he should've received a life sentence for not delivering the stab properly and kill Fergus. Not long afterwards, there was a brawl involving Fergus, who faced eleven opponents. He fought mean and hard and emerged victorious, leaving his opponents in various stages of injury, with one suffering permanent brain damage. Together with a few other police, I went down to arrest him. We told Fergus why we were there, and looking at me, he said,

'I will only go to the station with you.'

I believe this was in part because of my number three ranking in the fighting hierarchy. Fergus was subsequently charged and had to face the circuit court down the track. Out on bail during the intervening period, he came knocking at the barracks door and snarled,

'If I'm going to jail over this, I will kill you and the detective.'

It was evident that he'd been on the booze, so I told him to wait right there for a minute so I could get dressed. I went inside and grabbed the .32 Browning semi-auto pistol, which was my service weapon. It was the most useless, inaccurate, prone to jamming up handgun in existence, but at this point, that was irrelevant. I reopened the door and shoved it in Fergus's face, and said,

'If I shoot you right now, you won't have to worry about going to jail, do you? So, it would be much better if you just went home and let things run their course.'

To my relief, he did just that and walked away. Eventually, acquitted by the jury, he resumed his everyday life.

At the time, the Vietnam war was in progress. As a result, US military personal were occasionally in St George, visiting other Americans engaged in cotton farming in the area. A year or so later, I heard that Gibbo, the previous number three, had forgotten about his experience and gone back to his usual behaviour of picking fights with random strangers. One Saturday morning, Gibbo spotted a stranger in the main street and promptly challenged him, but to his dismay, the stranger promptly gave him a dreadful hiding. He then grabbed hold of Gibbo's earring, by which he dragged him along the footpath. Desperately he tried to keep up with the bloke, who kept walking, dragging him along by the earring. Unfortunately for him, he'd challenged a United States Green Beret on leave. How unlucky was that, finding one of them so far from anywhere? Gibbo decided to lay low after that encounter, and no more was heard of him.

GROCERY RUN FATALITY

On my days off, I found that a good way of exploring the surrounding countryside was to go on grocery deliveries with my mate Brian, the local storekeeper. His delivery run involved several outlying local properties, covering several hundreds of kilometres, which took the more significant part of the day to complete. It was a win-win situation for the two of us, as I got to see outback places and various sheep properties, and Brian, in return, had company plus a "gate opener". With me on board, it meant that he himself didn't have to get in and out of the car every time he approached a gate. The opening and closing of the many station gates was a time-consuming exercise if you had to do it without the help of an offsider. The process repeated many times on the way in and again on the way out.

One night, a call came through to the station of an accident with a vehicle roll-over not far out of town. Upon hearing the details, I straight away knew that it was Brian who must've been on his way home from his delivery run. He had most likely travelled at high speed and lost control, causing the vehicle to roll several times.

Brian died instantly. For obvious reasons, I opted out of attending this accident where police retrieved the remains of Brian, who'd sustained massive head injuries. The miraculous thing about this incident was that of the survival of his five-year-old daughter, who was in the rear seat, unrestrained. She was held suspended inside the car when the vehicle rotated around her until it came to a halt, upon which she climbed out the window and walked away unharmed. Guardian angels sure come to mind in cases like this.

There is always the possibility when you are working in emergency services or in a hospital in a smaller community that you will know, or be friends with, people involved in tragic circumstances such as this, but there's nothing that can prepare you for it when it happens.

CROP DUSTER CRASH

I received a call that a crop duster had crashed on a cotton and wheat farm not far from town. Upon arrival, I found the light aircraft on the ground, showing some signs of damage and, other than the absence of its landing gear, seemed largely intact.

The pilot had been spraying a large parcel of land, which had power lines running alongside its roadside border. The shaken-up aviator told me he'd clipped the power lines and had come down in the paddock. I got a few required details necessary for an incident report of this nature and returned to the station. I furnished the relevant statement per the instructions contained in the Queensland Police Manual, which were not much different from a standard vehicle collision. That was pretty much the end of it as far as I was concerned until precisely seven days later when once again, I received a message to attend to the site of an aircraft crash. Unbelievably, it was in the same paddock, involving an identical crop-dusting aircraft colliding with the same set of power lines. Not hard to guess who the pilot was. It was the same man whom I had interviewed the previous week when he'd clipped the lines, and just like the first time, he was lucky to be uninjured. I could only agree with him when he said with true conviction, 'That's it. I'm giving the game away. I've been two times lucky, and I doubt I'll walk away a third time alive.'

It didn't take me long this time to furnish yet another report, which was an almost identical account word for word as the first. I was getting good at this.

EXPLOSIVES EXPERTS

During my police career, I came across offers presenting possible career paths of a different kind. One of them being an explosives "expert" for an earthmoving company. The other, a heavy vehicle driver. I was always happy to explore new avenues, and I decided to take a holiday job with a couple of blokes who had a contract supplying rocks for a railway line in Central Queensland.

I started together with "an also new on the job" ex-soldier. We received two days of instructions from a Slavic bloke who couldn't speak English and became explosive experts overnight. From there on in, for two months, there was no stopping us, blasting one cliff face after another using drilling equipment and explosives. One part of the job I liked was climbing down over a freshly blown cliff face with a small jackhammer powered by a Volkswagen motor, specially designed to make holes in the large pieces of rock created by the blast. I roughly estimated the depth needed for the secondary blast to produce rocks of the required size. I then embedded each hole with a length of cordtex, a type of detonating cord, and dynamite, followed by ammonium nitrate and a diesel mix. Once lit, every second counted in our getaway, so we'd jump in our car and hightailed it out of there.

Only once did we make the mistake of crawling under a tilted-up loader bucket. The noise of the blast reverberated like a gong through the steel bucket, followed by a shower of rocks pelting down on our place of refuge. We had learned our lesson, hence the "getaway car".

I had a great time working through the long days, earning the phenomenal rate of two dollars an hour. It might not sound much, but I was getting less than fifty bucks a week as a policeman, so a twelve-hour day for seven days was an attractive proposition. We lived in a small camp, all good knockabout blokes and always happy with a couple of beers every night, supplied to dissuade us from heading off to the nearest pub about an hour's drive away. At the end of each month, the bosses flew us over in their private aircraft to Brampton Island for a four-day break and some much-needed rest and recreation.

After my two months were up, the company gave me a twelve-month job offer that I found extremely tempting, but unfortunately, the commissioner wouldn't give me twelve months leave without pay, so, for better or worse, I didn't take the offer.

Another consideration I had was joining the Hong Kong Police as a sub-inspector. I applied for the position and was accepted, but at the same time, reports started to surface of alleged corruption on a grand scale by that police force, so in the end, I decided not to go. A couple of years later, I got a letter from the Hong Kong police advising me that the situation was a lot different now and that there was a job for me if I was still interested. I thanked them for the offer but decided to stay with the Queensland Police Force.

BRAVERY AWARD

My mate Ross and I happened to have a few days off at the same time, and as we both originated from Brisbane, we decided to head back there and meet up with family. We left in Ross's car, and as I had just come off a late-night shift, I crashed on the back seat for a bit of sleep. We were only twenty minutes into the trip, East of St George on the Moonie Highway, when Ross yelled out,

'Have a look at this.'

The urgency of his voice woke me up, and I sat bolt upright. In front of us was a serious car crash, a head-on collision with both utility vehicles on fire. Several twenty-litre drums of fuel were still on the back of one of the utes, while more of them lay scattered on the road near the second vehicle, which had rolled on its side. Most of the drums were on fire, and we knew that an explosion was imminent. A man was staggering around near the flipped over ute, so as soon as we'd pulled up, I jumped out and raced over. He was in shock and babbled incoherently about his dad, whom I could see was trapped underneath the burning ute. As every second was valuable, I wasted no time on words but put my foot on the man's back and gave him an almighty shove. It sent him flying towards a group of boof-heads who had started to congregate, not far away enough from the wreckage. Frustrated by their stupidity, I yelled loudly, in an attempt to shock the ever-growing crowd,

'Fuck off! The bloody car can explode at any minute!'

It must've gotten through to them because there was immediate action. With curiosity now replaced by panic, the thrill-seekers wildly scattered in all directions. I spotted a council truck that had pulled up, and I called out to Ross,

'Get in the council truck and back it up near the ute.'

The man pinned underneath was in grave danger, and I realised that so would we be if the situation was prolonged. Ross reversed at speed, and I was relieved to see a heavy chain and hook on the back of that truck. Grabbing it, I attached one end of the chain around the tow bar of the council truck and dragged the other end over to the burning ute, throwing it through the space where the front windshield had been. I climbed in after it, and once inside the burning ute, I placed the hook around the door pillar, yelling out to Ross,

'Start driving mate, take it steady.'

Slowly, the ute started to lift, and by doing so, the flames intensified. I genuinely became concerned there would be an explosion any second now. As it turned out, my unease was well and truly justified. My mind raced, and time seemed to slow. The bloke's body was trapped halfway in and halfway outside the vehicle. I soon realised that, due to the angle of the ute, there was no point trying to pull him out from underneath. This left only one way, I had to get him out through the inside.

As soon as the vehicle was high enough off the ground to allow me to pull the man clear, I grabbed both his arms and pulled him in through the passenger side window and out through the front windshield space. I then took off, dragging the man along the ground, knowing that I didn't have much time. There wasn't a fraction of a second to spare to stop and check the man's vitals.

I hadn't gone far when I heard an almighty blast followed by a big push of intensely hot air, which propelled me forward at an enormous speed. I only just managed to keep my footing and kept running. The fuel tank had exploded, and to add to the "excitement", drums of fuel started to explode, with some flying up to fifteen metres skywards. I spotted a young bloke, whose name I later learned was Phillip, running towards the fire brandishing a fire extinguisher. As I galloped past him, going in the opposite direction, I saw him flattened by the blast. I didn't know how far I had gone, but I kept running, with the injured man dragging behind me.

It was when I felt that I had distanced myself enough from the burning wrecks that I stopped, and I allowed myself to look back, behind me, at the fiery scene. It was then that I spotted a third person sitting in the front seat of the second ute. I had no choice other than to stand and watch the inferno run its course. At this point, the flames well and truly engulfed the ute, and we knew that any chance of another rescue was non-existent.

Ross and I stayed on the scene and took a few notes while waiting for police and an ambulance to arrive. It was a miracle that Phillip, who bravely ran in with the fire extinguisher, was uninjured other than being knocked over by the blast. After the medical evacuation to St George by ambulance was complete and everything wrapped up, Ross and I continued our trip to Brisbane as planned.

Upon our return to the station a few days later, we learned that the post-mortem examination of the incinerated deceased man indicated that he had suffered heart failure. The heart attack had most likely happened before the collision and was the probable cause of the crash. I also learned the name of the fifty-seven-year-old man we had rescued from the burning vehicle. The sergeant in charge of the police station asked me to furnish a report on the collision's details to which I included Phillip, the brave young man with the fire-extinguisher. Following this, Ross and I were recommended for Bravery Awards.

A couple of months later, the man, whose life we had saved while risking our own, came into the police station at St George. Incredibly, as it was, he came looking for the battery out of the utility he had been driving. The car, however, was a molten wreck, so he was out of luck. You would think that if someone had just saved your life, you would at least have the decency to say, "thank you". The man knew who I was, but he never said a word. This attitude, however, was something I sadly would become accustomed to over the next two decades.

I was given a favourable record by the police force and was flown to Brisbane to receive a Bravery Award, along with Ross and Phillip, by the then governor Sir Colin Hannah. I took my mother with me, and together we went up to Government House in the Brisbane suburb of Bardon for the presentation of the award. Mum was delighted as she got to meet the governor, and I met the new police commissioner. The ceremony, which included several other people recognised for bravery, was televised and covered by the Telegraph and Mount Isa North West Star newspaper.

THE YOUTH CLUB

I was approached by a group of young people asking me if I'd be willing to have a go at getting the old St George Youth Club back up and running. It had ceased operating a few years earlier and, even though I wasn't fussed about the idea of getting involved with this, I could see the value a youth club would have for young people in town, so I agreed. Upon checking the books, I found a dormant connected bank account with quite a tidy sum of money in it, which made for a great start. There also was no shortage of volunteers to help run the show, and it didn't take long to appoint office bearers and adopt a plan for a myriad of activities.

A couple of recently released boofhead crims stumbled in offering to teach youth club members how to box. Having crims teach at the youth club wasn't a good start, so I diplomatically headed them off. The club kicked off and became a great success.

As I wasn't in St George for much longer, the second in charge sergeant of the station put his hand up and took over the organisation. I later heard that it went onto bigger and better things, including a representative football team. Not bad for a small town.

I immensely enjoyed my time at St George, but I wanted to get further into the interior of the outback. Upon hearing of my transfer, my sister Mary and her husband Jim drove six hours from Brisbane to see me, knowing that my next posting was Mount Isa. If they had to come and see me there, it would add an extra fourteen hours to their trip. We had a great couple of days together, sharing a beer or two and catching up on family news.

After fourteen months of service, it was time to pack up. So, I got into my much loved, red 1967 MGB, four-cylinder, soft top, two-door sports car, purchased with the proceeds of my holiday explosives work, and headed off on transfer to the mining town of Mount Isa in the far northwest of the state. The MGB, I found later, was an excellent little sports car but totally unsuitable for the environment into which I was taking it.

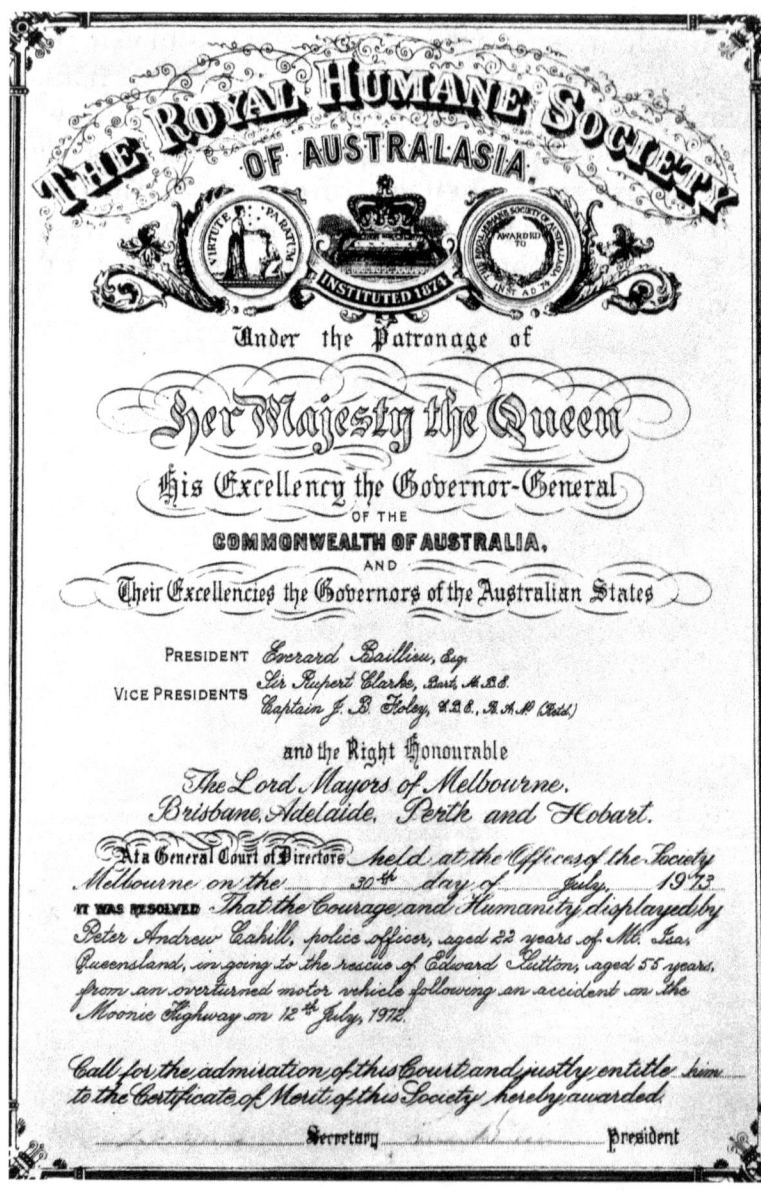

ST GEORGE

Queensland Police Force

Favourable Record

CONSTABLE PETER ANDREW CAHILL,
REGISTERED NUMBER 8013,
MOUNT ISA POLICE STATION,
IS AWARDED A FAVOURABLE RECORD FOR
COURAGE AND DEVOTION TO DUTY IN
CONNECTION WITH THE RESCUE OF AN
INJURED PASSENGER FROM THE BURNING
WRECKAGE OF TWO VEHICLES WHICH
COLLIDED ON THE MOONIE HIGHWAY NEAR
ST. GEORGE ON 12 JULY 1972.

R.W. Whitrod
Commissioner of Police

Brisbane, 24. 1. 1973

CITATION

AT 12.10 P.M. ON 12 JULY 1972, A FATAL ROAD ACCIDENT OCCURRED ON THE MOONIE HIGHWAY, 6 MILES FROM ST. GEORGE. CONSTABLE PETER ANDREW CAHILL, REGISTERED NUMBER 8013, MOUNT ISA, AND FORMERLY OF ST. GEORGE, WAS OFF DUTY AT THE TIME AND PROCEEDING ALONG THE HIGHWAY WITH DETECTIVE CONSTABLE 1/C R. LANG, WHO HAS SINCE RESIGNED FROM THE FORCE. THE MEMBERS IMMEDIATELY ATTEMPTED TO RELEASE A PASSENGER FROM ONE OF THE VEHICLES, WHO HAD BEEN PINNED BENEATH THIS VEHICLE. THEY WORKED AT GRAVE RISK TO THEMSELVES, AS FLAMES HAD ENVELOPED A UTILITY INVOLVED IN THE ACCIDENT, WHICH CONTAINED SOME FUEL DRUMS IN THE BACK. WITH THE ASSISTANCE OF A PASSING COUNCIL TRUCK AND OTHER PERSONS THE VEHICLE WAS LIFTED FROM THE TRAPPED PERSON, WHO WAS THEN CONVEYED BY AMBULANCE FOR MEDICAL ATTENTION. THE PERSON WAS JUST RELEASED BEFORE THE FUEL DRUMS EXPLODED. THE EFFORTS OF CONSTABLE CAHILL AND OTHERS WERE MOST COURAGEOUS AND COMMENDABLE, AND AS A RESULT THE INJURED PASSENGER WAS SAVED FROM ANY FURTHER SERIOUS INJURY FROM THE EXPLODING FUEL DRUMS, AND WAS ABLE TO RECEIVE MEDICAL ATTENTION AS SOON AS POSSIBLE.

MOUNT ISA

THE TOWN, THE STATION

I left St George in November, and with the outside temperatures up to thirty-six degrees, it wasn't the optimum time to be driving a British sports car around in the outback. I found out early in the piece that the MGB didn't like the hot conditions to which I was subjecting it. Halfway on route to my destination, I had inevitable engine problems, and taking it steady with the old girl, I struggled on and made it to the small outback town of Longreach. I knew an old mate there who'd quit his job as a detective, and after buying the old servo, he'd gone back to his original trade as a mechanic. It didn't take my mate long to find the fault, and he told me that he needed to order parts. It meant that I had to hang around town for a few days, so making the most of a bad situation, we had a few beers at the local pub. The parts arrived a few days later, were fitted, and once again, the MGB was back on the road, causing me no further trouble.

Mount Isa, known for its vast mineral deposits of lead, silver, copper, and zinc, has one of the most productive mining operations in world history. At the time, forty police were stationed at Mount Isa, commissioned to look after a population of twenty-five thousand.

Old wooden barracks, located directly behind the station, were utilised by a couple of policewomen, with the single men's accommodation at the end of the reserve. Twelve rooms were separated by a hallway, with a communal bathroom at one end and a kitchen, dining and lounge room combined, downstairs at the other end. Single police had the option, one man to a room with no air conditioning or two men to a room with air conditioning. Naturally, all went for the "two to a room" option if you expected to get any sleep during the hot months when on night shift. The system worked well if your roommate worked the same shift as you. It wasn't easy to get young police officers to go to a remote city such as Mount Isa, which, although it had most of the amenities, was a long way away from anywhere and where things could get rough.

When I worked there in the seventies, anyone employed in any business sector outside the giant Mount Isa Mines with its six thousand employees received the "lead bonus", a profit-sharing payment. This handout amounted to about twenty-six dollars per week, and, as I was grossing forty-nine dollars a week as a constable, it would have been a great bonus. Also, had we been given the lead bonus, I probably wouldn't have worried so much about moonlighting as a hotel bouncer or as a casual truck driver. As it was, the police department mucked Mount Isa Mines around so much that the offer was withdrawn, along with the generous offer of the provision of married police accommodation.

DEAD HORSES

The day following my arrival, I went to the outback town of Cloncurry, one hundred and twenty kilometres east of Mount Isa, with a detective from the Stock Squad. On arrival, I learned that we were to drive around looking for carcasses of several horses, shot a couple of weeks earlier. If that wasn't enough, we were required to dig around in the decomposed bodies and locate the projectile from the firearm, which had killed them.

We drove around in the Landcruiser while I had my head out the passenger side window trying to pick up the odour of decomposing horses. The stench, intensified by the summer heat, came wafting in on the breeze, and it didn't take us long to find twenty-three cadavers. We poked inside the corpses with a long stick, working on the assumption that the spent bullets find their way to the lowest side of the dead animal and onto the ground. The theory worked, and we managed to uncover nearly all the projectiles. Upon finding more horses, the story started to unfold as to what had happened. The shot animals were geldings with not a mare amongst them. The owner of the herd, a contract musterer, had been running forty quality stock horses. Someone had decided to take only the mares, obviously for breeding. Stealing the mares was bad enough in itself but killing the geldings in the process was unforgivable.

I burned the overalls I'd been wearing for the last few days, as the smell was terrible. It wasn't only in my clothing but now was also embedded in my memory. It was impossible to carry out a job like this without getting decayed flesh all over you, and I guess I should be thankful we weren't examining decomposing pigs instead. Now, they do stink. I went back to Mount Isa, pleased that I was able to be involved in something different, even if it meant digging through horse corpses that had been decomposing, in the thirty-six-degree Celsius, hot November sun of Cloncurry.

THE ELEPHANT AND THE ORANGUTAN

The Mount Isa magistrate, a well-liked, competent and impartial man, enjoyed relaxing with a few beers and one late Saturday afternoon, he called the police station.

'There's an elephant in my front yard', he said.

The cop taking the call thought it was hilarious and laughed heartily into the receiver, then hung up. We all agreed that the magistrate must have had a few too many when the phone rang again. This time he reported that the elephant was ripping out his ornamental trees, and if we thought the first call was hilarious, this one topped it. Gales of laughter followed the call, and just as we settled down, the phone sprang alive again. The magistrate, now extremely irate, complained about the elephant and accused us of ignoring his call. He said,

'Did you all score free tickets to the circus in return for ignoring the elephant?'

'Circus? What Circus?'

None of us had heard of a circus coming to town, so we trooped out with several off-duty blokes from the barracks joining in to see what was going on. It was hard to miss the enormous elephant standing in the magistrate's front yard, and it was hard not to laugh, as it looked very comical, holding and waving an ornamental tree about in its trunk. We were twelve strong, but it became apparent that the pachyderm wasn't going to take any notice of our efforts to move it on. No one was keen on getting too close just in case the elephant decided to replace the tree in its trunk with one of us.

The circus had set up camp on the flat on the other side of the Leichhardt River from where the big animal must've escaped and decided to wander across the dry riverbed to the magistrate's yard. So, one of us went across and informed the circus blokes and watched them herd the big beast back to the circus encampment. I couldn't help but wonder at what stage they would've noticed their "one" elephant missing. It wasn't as if they had a dozen or so to keep an eye on.

The encounter with the elephant reminded me of another hilarious incident my Uncle Mick told me, involving a circus animal, this time an Orangutang who belonged to a travelling family circus. During the season's break, the performing circus animals stayed on the large family acreage near Townsville. A large orange primate, a retired orangutan named Billie, didn't travel with the circus anymore and resided in a bedroom in the house. Occasionally parties were held at the house, and this night everything was going well with all the guests pretty much inebriated and having a good time. It was around four that morning when someone said that he felt sorry for the orangutan, who had been locked in his room all this time and thought he should be let out for a bit so he could mingle with the guests.

This bloke, obviously very much affected by the booze, went into the house to release the large primate, who seemed annoyed that he had been excluded from the gathering. The giant, hairy, orange creature charged through the now open door, grabbed his liberator and hurled him across the room. He then turned his attention to a dumbfounded supreme court judge and speared him out through the window, which, fortunately for the inebriated judge, was open. Pandemonium followed. Like all of his species, Billie possessed tremendous physical strength and charged around, flinging drunks all over the place. It all ended when the owner finally talked him down and took him back to his room.

In recent times, I met a CSIRO, Commonwealth Scientific and Industrial Research Organisation, retired scientist, who told me he had, back in the days, performed an autopsy on the orangutan. Unfortunately, he had died from a viral infection.

THE PAEDOPHILE'S DEATH

As soon as I walked into the office to clock in for my afternoon shift, the senior sergeant said, 'I just had word that a man threatened to kill his wife and two daughters.'

Living with his family in a caravan at one of the large van parks in Mount Isa, this man found himself barred from entering the van after his wife discovered that he was molesting one of their daughters. Following this, he had taken off down the road agitated and angry while making the threat,

'I'll come back and shoot the lot of you!'

The old sergeant told me to take up station at the caravan park to ensure the paedophile didn't return to carry out his threat. As police cars were limited, one of my colleagues gave me a lift, dropping me off at the van park. One might think that stationing a cop at the caravan was a good plan, and it would've been, though a vehicle, a radio, a portable walkie talkie and a decent torch would've been handy. Unfortunately, I had none of the above, nor a chair to sit on or a drink of water during what turned out to be a long shift. All I had was my useless .38 calibre, five-shot, short barrel Police Special Revolver. Seriously, one would probably be better off throwing stones. It wasn't unusual for a constable to be dropped off somewhere and be forgotten entirely. It had occurred before, and it looked like the trend continued.

The stake-out wasn't too bad while the sun was up, but as time went by, it grew progressively darker with the only dim glow provided by the waning crescent of the moon. Finally, as did most of their neighbours in the vicinity, the caravan occupants turned out the lights and went to sleep. The area became very dark, with many vans in the immediate vicinity providing a ready cover for any intruder.

I'd been on guard for over five hours when I heard a commotion. A dog barked furiously, not all that far from where I was. Lights came on, and I found that a cattle dog, living in a nearby van, had disturbed a man creeping around in the dark. I wouldn't have spotted him in the shadows of the night if the blue dog hadn't barked, making me an easy target. I immediately roused the caravan park manager and managed to ring the senior sergeant on the landline, which was a ludicrous situation. I had a few heated words with the sergeant, and next thing, a police car for my use and a heavy torch were delivered. The crew who delivered them stayed around for about half an hour and left. The perpetrator must have decided to lay low for the time being, and the remainder of the shift passed uneventfully.

The following day, two police officers on the morning shift drove around looking for the armed paedophile. They were lucky and spotted him driving through town in an old beaten-up Toyota. Upon pulling him over, they spotted a firearm on the seat next to him and, putting their own lives on the line, a desperate struggle for the rifle ensued. The paedophile tried desperately to take possession of his loaded and cocked firearm, and it was during this struggle, the rifle discharged, killing the man.

Fortunately, neither officer was injured, and to my knowledge, neither received recognition for their courage, which was common back then. I have had plenty of similar experiences. Police officers don't start a shift wondering how they possibly could achieve a bravery award nomination that day. Unpredictable things happen, where police-involved, should be recognised for their courageous actions. Fortunately, these days that recognition in most cases is honoured.

DEATH OF A SHUNTER

I was called in as part of an investigation team involving the death of a young German man who'd met his demise on his second day on the job. He was working as a shunter for Queensland Rail at Mount Isa. The young fellow and another shunter found themselves on one of several wagons, which were accidentally moved. There were also a couple of five-ton capacity concrete carriers on the flat top wagon, which weren't tied down. As the wagons gathered speed, travelling towards the barrier at the end of the line, the senior shunter yelled at the young German to follow him and jump off. Whether it was fear or poor language skills, we'll never know, but what we did know was that he remained in position and continued with the wagon until it hit the barrier. The sudden stop caused one of the concrete carriers to tip forward onto the young fellow, killing him instantly.

I went round to advise the deceased's partner, a young German girl, at the van park where they had been staying. And as we were leaving, I warned the sleazy van park manager to leave her alone.

WE FOUND A DEAD BODY

A dead body of a different kind turned up one night. There was a function at the single men's barracks, and late in the night, two newspaper reporters from the North West Star made their way in via the parking lot to join the party. As they walked past the Falcon paddy wagon, one of them spotted a still body lying in the back of the wagon. Straightaway, they came over to tell me about their gruesome discovery.

'We found a dead body. Come quick!'

A couple of us went out to investigate, with the uneasy reporters in hot pursuit, juggling cameras and notepads in the hope of scoring a good story. They held their breath in trepidation as we carefully opened the doors of the paddy wagon, and I'm sure that a sudden "BOO!" would've made them jump a mile high. It was tempting, but being the good sport that I was, I held back.

What we found, though, wasn't a deceased body but a straw man, as in a scarecrow, lying face down. One of the cops must have acquired him somewhere and was most likely going to rehome him in his veggie patch. Peering in from the window in the dark, you could be forgiven for thinking it was a dead body and, needless to say, the scarecrow never rose to fame and never made it into the paper, but it made for a good laugh.

THE DRIVING TEST

For a few months in between relieving duties at small stations, I worked in the driving licence testing section, a job I didn't like much, as I didn't think it was proper police work. One morning, a licence applicant had passed the required written test and needed to go out for the practical test. The job fell to me. I got into the passenger seat of the driving school car while the bloke going for his test climbed in behind the wheel. I never went out of my way to make things difficult for anyone and always remained calm, civil, and polite. That was until this bloke drove straight through a stop sign onto one of the busiest streets in the city. He hadn't been doing great as it was, but I'd continued as I figured that he might've been nervous. Running a stop sign, though, was a game-ender, so I said,

'I have to fail you. Best come back in a week or so for a second go mate.'

His reply came in broken English.

'I look to you; you look to me'.

I said, 'What on earth are you talking about?'

He replied, 'I give you money to pass'.

He didn't know that nothing angered me more than bribes, so I yelled,

'Get out of the fucking car.'

My roar left him in no doubt that he had become a person non gratis, and I knew he got the message when I saw him run-off at high speed. I drove the car back to the station, where the confused driving school instructor asked me where the test applicant was. I said,

'He offered me a bribe, so he's walking back. Don't bring him back in here again.'

I never saw that crook again and therefore believe that he must've opted for another testing centre.

MOTORCYCLE DEATH

At about nine one night, I was on duty on patrol in an unmarked police car. Driving up to the intersection of Miles and Marian Streets in Mount Isa, I pulled up at the stop sign, as did the motorcyclist in front of me. With his engine idle, he remained stationary on the white line while waiting for the right moment to enter Marian Street. I will never know why he decided to drive off at that moment because he rode straight into the path of a vehicle coming inbound on his right. Car and bike collided, with the rider thrown into the air before crashing down onto the bitumen.

I jumped out of the car and went over to the supine rider, who died a few seconds after I got to him. If only he had waited a few more seconds at the intersection, he would've still been alive. It is one of those incidents which come to mind, randomly, to this very day.

THE PRANK

On a regular basis, I boarded a commercial airline to escort prisoners from Mount Isa to Townsville's Stuart Creek Prison. I didn't mind the job because once the prisoner was safely ensconced in jail, I had a bit of "free time" until the return flight. It allowed me to have a few beers with mates living on the east coast. My uncle Mick had been a popular policeman in Townsville, and this stood me in good stead, as everyone seemed to know of him. Time went fast on those days away from the station, and it was usually around midnight by the time I arrived back at the barracks in Mount Isa.

I'd only been in bed a few hours when the inspector came in and shouted,

'Get up, you bastard, we are going for a drive to Julia Creek.'

I worked as his driver when the need arose, and this was one of those occasions, so I got up, showered, dressed, and grabbed a bite to eat on the way out. It was the wet season, and the usual roads were closed due to flooding, which necessitated a one-hundred-kilometre detour making it a three-hundred-and-fifty-kilometre drive. I was getting tired, having done a prisoner escort the day before, so, upon arrival at our destination, the boss left me at the hotel and said,

'Have a few beers and a feed.'

I happily obliged and ordered steak, eggs, chips, and a couple of pots to wash the meal down. By the time the boss returned, I was feeling completely buggered, so he ended up driving us back while I got a bit of sleep on the back seat of the sedan. We'd been travelling for about an hour when I felt a thump followed by,

'Wake up. We've hit a plains turkey.'

I jumped out of the car, but by the time I reached the injured bird, it had died. The boss yelled over his shoulder,

'Grab it. We're taking it with us.'

He told me that he had a liking for plain turkey stew. However, by the time we reached the Isa, the turkey had lost its appeal, so he said,

'Just get rid of it.'

That's when an idea came to me. Someone had once told me about a practical joke played on a constable who went to bed drunk. While asleep, his "mates" captured about thirty live rabbits and released them in his room, and as expected, he desperately needed to pee sometime in the night. An enormous scream reverberated through the barracks, followed by some unsavoury language, satisfying the pranksters.

I took the dead bird up to a constable's room, a notorious prankster, and, letting a few other blokes in on the hoax, placed it in his bed between the sheets. Hiding around the corner, we didn't have to wait long as our unaware victim wandered in after a big night out. Hardly containing ourselves, we watched him take his gear off and crawl into bed. The yells of consternation that followed were more than adequate, and quietly we crept off, leaving him to deal with the dead turkey.

I was the main suspect straight up, but the constable took it for the joke it was, and we all had a good laugh.

MORNINGTON ISLAND

The next day, I was off on a flight to Mornington Island to assist the relieving sergeant who had tried to settle a disturbance in the community. As a last resort to settle things, the sarge had to draw his firearm. Two of us went to the island to bolster numbers, but by the time we arrived, the disturbance had settled very much of its own accord. The argument had been between two different tribes who lived on the island. The main group was the Lardil Tribe, the other being Kaiadilt people who originated from Bentinck Island. Some of the Lardil blokes, like most islanders, were big men, while those belonging to the Kaiadilt Bentick group were smaller and rather lightly framed. They could speak little or no English, and before being brought over to Mornington Island, they had been living much as they had done for thousands of years.

We stayed around for a few days to ensure peace remained, and to kill time, we went fishing with the relieving sarge. We were catching heaps when the motor ran out of fuel. The sergeant had misjudged the fuel situation and, with no spare fuel on board, the fishing trip ended with me swimming the last thirty metres, towing the boat to shore, using a rope as a tow line. I must say that, even though the weight of the boat compromised me, it was a relatively speedy swim, as I kept a very wary eye out for the variety of predators which inhabited the waters.

The time on the island also allowed me to have my first encounter with community police, the blokes I would be spending a lot of time with during my police service. I thoroughly enjoyed the interaction with them, and when I left, I was surprised to see them at the airport waiting for me. The community police stepped forward before I had a chance to board the plane and solemnly presented me with a ceremonial shield and spear. The gesture touched me deeply, and I knew immediately that a great honour had been bestowed upon me. In addition, my interactions with the tribes of Mornington Island left a lasting impression.

PAYING RATES

I was tasked to execute a warrant to take possession of one of nineteen houses owned by a self-made old bloke named Barnsley, who was in the habit of not paying rates for his properties. The council seized and sold one of the houses to cover Barnsley's rates account from time to time. It took a few of us to deliver the warrant as he was an extremely aggressive man, and nothing ever went easy when it involved Barnsley. The exercise ended, as per usual, by having to lock him up for assaulting the police.

This bloke's mindset had me intrigued. One day, he fell out with a ringer who lived in the town of Camooweal, almost two hundred kilometres west of the Isa. To settle the difference of opinion, Barnsley decided to go and fight this bloke, and as he didn't have a car, he rode his old push-bike the entire distance. The days were hot out there, and the roads rough, with dirt and gravel all the way.

Now the robust and muscly ringer he was picking a fight with was "pretty handy" and gave old Barnsley a fair hiding. He left him a bruised and bleeding wreck outside the Camooweal pub. Sore and worse for wear, Barnsley crawled with great difficulty back onto his feet, mounted his bike and pedalled all the way back to the Isa.

MOONLIGHTING

I did a bit of moonlighting as bouncer and minder, looking after performers like Normie Rowe and Digger Revell. Being paid seven dollars fifty per hour was a phenomenal reward at the time, especially when compared to the forty-nine dollars for a forty-hour police week. Being a bouncer in Mount Isa was a hazardous occupation, with nightly fights being the norm. However, I mostly tried to settle the arguments amicably. A mate and colleague of mine, George, was similarly employed at the Barkly Hotel a bit further down the road.

There were only four pubs in Mount Isa at the time, and with a population of around thirty thousand, all four of them were in the yearly top ten for beer sales in Queensland. This fact was not surprising when one considered the almost nonexistence of single women, the intense summer heat, and the large percentage of single men. In addition, mine employees or ancillary industries were well paid for the difficult line of work they had chosen.

One night I didn't have much to do, so I decided to go out to the Barkly, have a few beers and hang around with George, who was working there that night. The time passed pleasantly enough until, near closing time at ten that night, a bloke staggered up to us. He was about my size and seemed to take a particular dislike to me. I ignored his aggressive language, and upon seeing that he wasn't getting anywhere with his abuse, he instigated a fight. He didn't leave me much choice, so I stood up in preparation to defend myself, and it seemed that the Barkley bouncers knew this bloke and knew that he was about to be injured. To defuse things, they grabbed hold of me, hoping that this was enough to calm this bloke down. However, he wasn't going to be defused and kept coming. It isn't easy to defend yourself with a couple of blokes holding onto you, so I said,

'Let me go, I won't hurt him,' and upon release, I said, grinning to the agitator, 'much'.

He straight away adopted his unusual fighting stance and yelled out,

'I was in the SAS.'

I replied, 'What does that mean? Shit After Shit?'

The blokes watching the proceedings roared with laughter. I thought enough was enough, and stepping forward, I hit this bloke with a tremendous right hook which lifted him completely off the floor and across the bar. This move left the gathered crowd impressed and comments like,

'He knocked him right over the bar!' were bandied about for a while. And the stirrer, who was never a member of our Special Air Services, was removed from the bar. I decided to give the bouncing game away and resolved to supplement my income as a casual truck driver, a much more peaceful job.

DAJARRA WELCOME

As the cop at Dajarra was due for leave, I was sent there for my next foray into a small station. Dajarra, a small outback town between Boulia and Mount Isa, was, back in its heyday, the largest cattle trucking depot in the world. Numerous head of cattle were processed here and trucked thousands of kilometres across the country from as far away as Western Australia.

I rolled into town in my police utility one late Sunday afternoon, and, as there was no one home at the little station, I headed off to the hotel. Several blokes hung around the doorway with a beer in hand. One of them was a well-proportioned bloke in his thirties, dressed in shorts and Jackie Howe singlet and I straight away assessed that this bloke might be able to fight. As soon as I pulled up in the police car, he yelled,

'I'm Rodrick Geer, and I'm here to fight the new constable.'

I was always on the lookout for useable fighting techniques from any source. At this point, I remembered a scene from the movie "The Magnificent Seven" with James Coburn delivering an unusual self-defence technique. I decided that now was the moment to put it to the test. I closed the car door, and briskly walking over to him, I said,

'That would be me, Peter Cahill.'

Like Coburn in the movie, I held out my hand to shake hands with Geer. This approach briefly confused him, and hesitantly, he held out his hand. I grabbed it, pulled him forward off balance and kicked him in the balls, sending him to the ground. The blokes at the pub door roared with laughter, and as far as they were concerned, the show was over. They went back inside to their beer while Geer lay defeated on the ground.

I dragged his still supine form over to the police ute, shoved him in the back, and transported him to the little watch house to lock him up. However, upon arrival, I found it was also locked and still not a person in sight at the station. I had no choice other than to tell Geer to get lost. I watched him hobble off in a hurry, still clutching his balls. He never gave me any more trouble.

Other than the usual mountain of bookkeeping involved in administering the affairs of the local Indigenous people, the actual police work was not at all arduous by any stretch of the imagination. The upside was I did get to see places I would never have been likely to, such as the small outback towns of Duchess and Urandangie and prominent properties such as Carandotta.

After his discharge from the army, my brother Tony came up for a visit and stayed for a few weeks. He spent that time working at the Dajarra hotel as bar manager, and when his time was up, I was sad to see him leave.

Upon the arrival of his bus that would take him home to Brisbane, we both had a good laugh at a southern male tourist who alighted the Greyhound bus. He was wearing mid-length shorts complete with a colourful Hawaiian shirt and sandals with long socks. There was no doubt that he would stand out like a sore thumb from the regular Dajarra crowd.

SETTLING SCORES

One incident I attended concerned a feud between two Indigenous families who asked me to referee a one-on-one fight between the two best fighters of each clan. One was a local, the other from somewhere out of town. I had a run-in with this out-of-towner bloke before, and it was he who insisted on holding the fight within the settlement. He believed that if the fight were outside the town's perimeter, I for sure would give his opponent a hand by punching him up, so in town, it was.

The fight was held early one Sunday morning, with me being the only White face in a crowd of probably six hundred Indigenous people. The two blokes facing off were excellent fighters, and I decided to let the bout run for a while. A good half an hour into the fight, I saw that both fighters started to tire, with neither giving in. I quite accurately gave the decision of a "draw".

Both combatants and the crowd seemed happy with that and dispersed, satisfied that the matter was settled.

TIME'S UP

One day, the weekly train passed through and left two railway carriages at the marshalling yards. Upon inquiring, I discovered that one carriage was a dentist surgery, and the other fitted out as accommodation for the train-dentist. In those days, dentists travelled and worked around the outback in towns and railroad sidings with suitable rail access. That service became redundant and discontinued because of progress and improved road conditions and transport. This was also the case with cattle trains. Dajarra, and other now almost deserted ghost towns, like Mingela near Charters Towers, were points of departure for thousands of head of cattle by rail each year.

During my time at Dajarra, I was offered a position as manager of a small pub in the Town of Duchess, and though I did seriously think about it, I decided that my police career was worth pursuing and passed on the offer. So my time at the small outback town came to an end, and I returned to Mount Isa, even more determined to spend my service in small police stations, like the ones I had worked in so far. Out there, you are more than just a cop; you become part of a community where everyone knows and supports each other, where and whenever needed.

SAM

The day I returned to Mount Isa, I received a phone call from a property owner, whom I had met a few times socially. We got on quite well, and during one of our conversations, he'd mentioned a large black curly coated retriever he had, named Sam. The breed was relatively rare in Queensland, with only four of them in the State. The cocky told me on the phone that Sam had started to get aggressive with some of the station hands and, as I had mentioned that I was thinking about getting a dog, would I be interested in taking him on? I didn't have to think twice about it and immediately said yes. Two days later, this black dog arrived at the police station.

Sam was a personable dog and quickly settled into the barracks lifestyle and was assured of a constant supply of pats from the blokes who lived there. He also was a good protection dog and perfectly capable of latching onto someone he didn't like. Bred as a retriever, he could carry a raw egg in his mouth at a gallop for one hundred metres without breaking it. One afternoon the inspector came over to the barracks and said,

'There's a RAAF Mirage fighter jet parked up for one night at the Mount Isa airport. So go out there with your dog and look after the plane.'

That suited me down to the ground, so Sam and I headed off to the airport to start work. I'd never seen one of those aircraft up close, and I was surprised at how small it was. My guarding duties during the night shift, with my canine partner by my side, passed without incidence. During the day, Sam followed me around, keeping an eye on things and at night, without fail, he slept next to my bed, and it didn't take long for us to become inseparable and great mates.

He was a young dog, and when I noticed that the persistent hacking cough he had developed didn't pass, I took him to a vet. He diagnosed an advanced stage of heartworm infestation, which indicated that it had started well before he became my dog. The big fellow was dying. Unfortunately, there was no cure available in those days, so I had no choice other than to have him euthanised. However, the canine love Sam had shown me led to a promise that I would get another dog one day, which I did, thus starting a lifelong passion for German shepherds.

AIRCRAFT CRASH

Late one afternoon, I received instruction to go out to the airstrip at the Lake Julius Dam construction site to investigate an aircraft crash. I'd flown in light aircraft before like the one I was in now, but none of them ever had to land on an airstrip we were about to attempt. On the way out to the dam, the pilot told me that it was an unusual strip. It was on top of a hill and had a deep dip in the centre which made taking off and landing something like an aircraft carrier with an upward-sloping flight deck.

As we were about to land, I spotted the wreckage of the light aircraft, which was the subject of my investigation. It lay on the side of the landing strip, and I figured that the crash must've happened when it attempted to land navigating the treacherous dip. As we were just about to do the same, us crashing also, was a consideration that hadn't escaped my attention.

The seriously injured pilot had already been transported to the Mount Isa Base Hospital, so basically, all I had to do was a preliminary investigation and stayed with the wreck overnight until the arrival of the federal investigators the following day. To kill time, I wandered down the side of a hill towards a low-lying creek and was greeted by a swarm of mosquitoes heading my way in anticipation of fresh warm human blood. So cutting my explorations short, I raced back up the hill, leaving the mozzies behind, down in the creek. The following day the investigators arrived, which meant that my job was done, and I could fly back to Mount Isa. After take-off, I was relieved when I felt the plane clear the tricky airstrip, and we were airborne. I furnished the usual report at which I was becoming quite adept with the practice I was getting attending aircraft crashes.

PERILOUS UTE DRIVE

Leaving the station in the open, standard-issue police utility, constable Fraser and I responded to a domestic disturbance call. The police car, a Holden ute, didn't have a canopy or cage and were common in these smaller outback places. The more suitable Toyota Land Cruisers started to roll out as the safer police vehicle replacements throughout the State.

Arriving at the well-attended disturbance, Fraser and I attempted to calm things down. It soon became apparent that, as long as this bloke named Ricko was involved, nothing would be resolved, so I arrested the stirrer and put him in the back of the "open back" ute. Climbing in next to him, I sat on the floor and kept him restrained on the trip to the watch house. He was a large individual who, if nothing else, knew how to fight.

We hadn't gone far when we drove past an operating radar crew, so I gave them a quick wave. It seemed that this second of distraction on my behalf was what Ricko had been waiting for. He seized the opportunity to attack me, and from that point on, I became engaged in a very desperate struggle with this giant, whose only objective was to push me out of the back of the mobile ute. I came close to falling out several times during the precarious drive, which would've meant the end for me. I wrestled with him as good as the small space of the ute would allow and accommodate, until I finally managed to place him in a restraining hold.

When we arrived at the back of the station, I still had Ricko in this hold while he screamed in an all-consuming rage. The racket he made as we drove up to the watch house attracted the attention of the police inside. I was relieved to see them appear and give a hand in transferring this bloke to a cell. He was charged and consequently forfeited his bail, which was the equivalent of a guilty plea.

Several times we'd come close to falling out of the back of that ute out onto the roadway. The idea of conducting an arrest in that manner, which at the time was perfectly legal, would now breach so many laws it would be ridiculous. Fortunately, I was never involved in an arrest of that nature again.

THE MOTORCYCLE GANG

A call came in that two police officers were being assaulted by motorcycle gang members on the footpath outside the Isa Hotel. As I drove up towards the melee, I could see two uniforms on the ground, being kicked by a group of up to a dozen assailants. I felt that using a firearm was out of the question as other people in the vicinity were at risk of being shot, so I had to think of a plan quickly. Taking on a dozen men in hand-to-hand combat wasn't an option either, so I decided to activate the lights and siren of the vehicle and drove straight towards the group on the footpath. I intended to intimidate and disorient the bikies, hopefully enough, to break up the fight. My plan seemed to work, and the mob dispersed immediately. Three of them were slow getting out of the road, and the nudge of the vehicle's bumper bar caused them to lose their balance. I immediately jumped from the car, and while my partner established that neither cop laying on the footpath was seriously injured, I placed the three men who had gone down in the rear of the police sedan under arrest. They were later charged with assaulting police.

What had happened was that the two assaulted police constables had been trying to arrest a member of the motorcycle gang on an outstanding warrant, and this was when the other gang members decided to attack the coppers.

On appearing in court the following day, one of them had a badly swollen eye. It was an injury he didn't have when he went into the watch house. A sergeant at the court was quite upset at this poor bikie's injury and went to great lengths to find out who was responsible, and have the alleged perpetrator charged. I was his prime suspect, but it wasn't me, and the matter died down. The bikie with the black eye got two months for his trouble, having entered a plea of guilty. As one of the regular prison escort officers, I took him on an uneventful trip on the plane to Stuart prison.

SEA SEARCH

Boarding the two-seater plane, I was off to Mornington Island in the Wellesley Group in the Gulf of Carpentaria. I loved flying and never tired of seeing the rugged landscape below gliding by. It took a couple of hours to cover the distance to the island, situated twenty-eight kilometres off the coast from the mainland. We made a quick stop at Burketown to give the local police supplies we'd brought in for them and to grab a dozen cartons of beer to take along to Denham Island. Upon arrival, I met Steve, who was only too happy to give me a hand to transfer the booze into the dinghy he had ferried over from Denham Island. I was to go there and conduct an extensive area search for two men who had gone missing in a fishing boat. The Island had a prawn processing factory, and I got on well with the owner whom I knew, as my late uncle Mick had played football with him.

As soon as we arrived, I started to get a search off the ground. I learned that the boat had left Burketown with three men onboard a few days ago. One man had appeared on Mornington Island, but no one had sighted the vessel and the two remaining men. The "survivor" said that he had swum several miles after the boat sank and didn't know what had happened to the others. I hired a couple of trawlers and worked out a grid type search over a large expanse of sea. I also hired a light aircraft to do an aerial search, though, in reality, we were more likely to find wreckage or debris, especially with the revelation that some witnesses had seen a "fire on the sea" at one stage during the night. A few days into the search, with nothing found, it wasn't considered practicable to continue.

The result of the inquest that followed was an open finding. There were allegations of the boat's fate and the two men, with the survivor questioned by a senior detective; however, there wasn't sufficient evidence to support any charges. The huge man had a reputation for having taken out blokes before, something like a hitman.

I did keep in contact with the prawn plant owner, who also had a pub in Townsville. I called in regularly on the various prisoner escorts I did from Mount Isa to Stuart prison. On one of those visits, it saddened me to hear that he had died in a vehicle collision involving his Jaguar.

CAMOOWEAL

CAVE RESCUE

One morning, the sergeant informed me that I was to be the relieving constable in the two-man station of Camooweal, an outer suburb west of Mount Isa's city. The 'suburb' is connected to the city by the main street, which is known to be the world's longest at two hundred kilometres. The small outback town of Camooweal, situated on the Northern Territory border, had around fifty Whites and a few hundred Indigenous people. It was very much like any outback town in that it had a small hospital with one sister, the usual pub, police station, school, a couple of service stations, a post office, and Freckletons' historic store. It was sweltering in that part of the country, with the lowest maximum for the previous six weeks measuring forty-five degrees Celsius. The police station, which once had been a shearing shed some ninety years earlier, came complete with authentic bullet holes. The old building had no air conditioning nor fans, which was a real bummer in the extreme heat. We ended up placing stacks of old files strategically on the floor to cover the large holes through which one could see the ground outside.

There was the distinct sound of white ants gnawing at what remained of the building. In contrast to the dilapidated station, the recently built new single man's accommodation, complete with air conditioning, was classed at the time to be the best of its kind in Queensland. I took up my position as the relieving constable for a few months after a bull knocked the permanent officer off a bridge when attending a cattle truck rollover. He ended up with a broken leg and was on sick leave recuperating from his injury.

After I'd introduced myself to the sarge and settled in, I left to check out the hotel as it was pretty much the only place to go. On Sundays, the prevailing liquor licensing laws allowed for two separate, two-hour sessions, being from eleven am to one pm and the other from four to six pm. Apart from the local blokes, there were teams of workers from Telstra and the Commonwealth Works Department engaged with the maintenance of federal buildings and the like. In addition, there were blokes contracted with fixing microwave dishes to the newly erected towers that started to appear around the country. The new microwave system was to provide phones and possibly television, linking the outback to the cities. The challenge was to get them in a direct line of sight as the microwaves couldn't pass around hills or mountains as lower frequency radio waves could. The blokes were good knockabout blokes and great company in the boozer and camp.

One Sunday morning, an unkempt young bloke came into the hotel and announced that his two mates had fallen down a hole somewhere. As he appeared to be very obnoxious, no one was interested in what he was saying. However, as it was closing time anyway, we decided to go and have a look. So about twenty of us drove out to where this fellow said he last saw his mates. It was an entrance to one of the many caves in the vicinity.

The Sergeant took command and directed me down a hole together with the microwave blokes, who were equipped with plenty of ropes. I'd never encountered darkness like that before; total blackness, a complete absence of light and the term "can't see your hand in front of your face" was the exact description of the cave. Someone produced a small torch which threw a bit of light on the situation.

The tunnel was narrow, and it was apparent that I was too big to go any further, so I waited on a ledge while the two, smaller in physique microwave blokes, went down deeper. Unfortunately, the trapped blokes had managed to fall into a chamber with sheer steep walls, without safety equipment. It was a relief to hear them call out that they weren't injured. The microwave blokes went about hauling them up one at a time from their entrapment and pushed them up to me. From there, I dragged them back up from the ledge and shoved them into the blinding daylight. As we emerged from the cave, the two inexperienced would-be cave explorers suddenly bolted over to an old Valiant sedan where the other turkey was waiting, they jumped in, and the three of them sped off in the direction of Mount Isa.

Once again, it would have been a nice gesture to say, 'Thanks for the rescue.'

We decided good riddance, especially as the publican had shown a lot of initiative by bringing a few cartons of beer to the site to quench our thirst and cheer the good ending.

CAMOOWEAL DUTIES

The most time-consuming duties involved the financial administration of the local Indigenous population, which numbered in the hundreds. Some of them added to the challenge as they couldn't speak nor understand English and only communicated in their language. As was the norm, in other small police stations throughout Queensland, community members lined up outside the station two mornings per week to receive their recommended food and clothing order. Police deposited the balance of their pay at the post office, which served as a Commonwealth Bank. The people then took their food orders to the local shop, where the shopkeeper filled them. Next, he sent an invoice to the police station, where staff debited it against the person's account. Pension, and paycheques for those working on a property, were posted to the police station with details entered into their respective accounts. Following this, the cheques were then banked at the local post office. All of this was carried out manually and involved a lot of bookkeeping.

The next most time-consuming activity involved issuing third-party insurance certificates to caravan owners from the Northern Territory. These people lived in their vans off-road and were required to buy insurance to cross the border and travel legally in Queensland. Never a day passed without issuing two or three of these certificates in our capacity as State Government Insurance Office agents. Following this, there always was the usual activity of locking up drunk and disorderly persons and writing out a few travelling stock permits. This was pretty much routine police work in small outback stations, where an officer often had to wear many hats.

I looked forward to the Monday to Friday daily ritual where the sergeant and I shared a six-pack in the late afternoon at the back of the station. Back then, both cops were in the office during the week and always on-call if needed on the weekends. Our fortnightly grocery run to Mount Isa involved the sergeant going first, and upon his return the next day, I'd meet him a few miles out of town, have a beer beside the road while relaying any relevant info, before heading off into town myself. No mobile phones back then, and usually, a once-weekly mail service was the norm.

I must've performed reasonably well, and with a lack of senior police, the then inspector wanted to send me as a relieving sergeant to small stations, even though I'd only done a few years of service. The suggested proposal was unusual as the average sergeant promotion occurred after about nineteen years. However, the police union had to veto it, not casting any aspersions on me personally, but felt it could create a precedent that could become a problem in the future.

THE SHOVEL MAN

It was pretty much the first time I'd worked by myself in the respect that, even though in places such as Brisbane, you were regularly by yourself, you had a radio with backup only a call away. Here that was not the case, but I was happy enough to work on my own. In the sergeant's absence, a fight started in a paddock down the road from the pub involving half a dozen blokes.

As soon as the call came in, I drove down in the old police ute, and upon arrival, I told the combatants to break it up and get going. They stopped, looked at me, and forgot their prior animosity against each other and decided to redirect their aggression towards me. They formed one solidified group, and I knew things could get nasty quickly, so I grabbed a star picket lying nearby as a defence weapon.

It proved very unwieldy, so I threw it to the side away from the mob and swapped it for a shovel which I grabbed from the back of my police ute. It proved to be a much more effective weapon. Approaching the mob, I gave the first few blokes in line a few good whacks across the shoulder blades with the flat of the shovel. It was enough to rattle the would-be-assailants, and in a hurry, the entire mob took off.

The story of the fight spread far and wide, and my reputation unfurled. As far as the city, I now was referred to as "The Shovel Man".

BOOTS THE DOG

On another occasion, of course, when the boss was away, a bloke started playing up in the hotel's bar. The publican, a mature aged lady and her barmaid grabbed their waddies, an Aboriginal term for sticks, which they kept under the bar for situations like this and started whacking the bloke, driving him out of the bar.

This bloke was strong enough to fight and injure these two women but opted out rather than facing the consequences of belting two women in a public bar. I know of an instance where a bloke stabbed a popular publican, and it was only the timely arrival of the police that kept that fool alive as a mob of ringers had gotten hold of him. Back then, hitting women or vulnerable people or using a knife in a fight were regarded as capital offences out in those places, and one could face severe retribution. I arrived on the scene and told the women to put their waddies away. I grabbed the bloke, put him in the back of the ute and drove up to the watch house, thinking that a few hours in there might be enough to calm him down, but the man decided that this wasn't going to happen.

Adopting a fighting stance at the entrance to the cell, he left me no option other than to fight him. I very quickly delivered a solid punch to his solar plexus and watched him go down. Unbelievingly he scrambled back up unto his feet, ready for another go. As I was squaring up to deliver another of my signature punches, I heard a bark. Over the fence came Boots, the sergeant's large pregnant blue heeler. She seemed keen to help and grabbed the man by his ankle, causing him to lose his balance and fall to the ground. At this point, with the odds stacked up against him, he got up and walked quietly into the cell pulling the door shut behind him, probably to make sure Boots didn't have a second go. A few days later, Boots had a healthy litter of five puppies.

Another bloke who had a shot at me was reputedly a good boxer. He seemed to disagree with everything and anything, and I saw him lining me up. I had no choice other than to get in quick, and the short tussle that followed ended when his head slammed into the toilet door. It was enough to knock the fight out of him. The reinforced door now had an indentation which was there as a reminder for several years.

SLIM DUSTY

The outback came to life when country music entertainers with their travelling show rolled into town. One of those concerts was by Slim Dusty, who in his lifetime covered many miles over rugged Australian outback roads to entertain in remote areas. I went down with a couple of other police to one of his concerts to keep an eye on things.

Slim was extremely popular, and his shows were well attended, especially by the Indigenous people who were very much in the majority in those towns. I did not meet the great man personally but remember that he always bought a carton of beer for the police in attendance.

STOCKMEN ON LEAVE

In Camooweal, older ringers or stockmen employed permanently on the various large cattle stations in the district, spent their four weeks annual leave at the Camooweal pub. Upon their holiday's arrival, these blokes gave the publican their paycheques which she then cashed, placing the money in the pub safe.

The ringers and stockmen stayed in the old sheds at the back of the pub, where the publican always insisted they first eat their breakfast before coming into the bar. She kept individual bar tabs and deducted their daily expenditures while stashing a bit of money away from each cheque. This way, she could give these ringers the few dollars she had saved for them when they headed back out to work. It made her feel better knowing that they would not be going back to their respective workplaces, totally broke. The old blokes had been doing this for decades, and it suited them down to the ground as an acceptable lifestyle.

FROM CAMOOWEAL TO BEDOURIE

I was sent to Bedourie, seven hundred kilometres south of Camooweal, for a few months of relief work. After having the usual rounds of farewell drinks, I headed off in my sports car. A courthouse clerk came with me for a run in the MGB up to Boulia, as far as the sealed road went. Unfortunately, the dirt roads that followed were unsuited for a low-slung vehicle like mine. I wondered if I should consider selling the MGB as it became apparent that its design wasn't meant for the harsh north-western country.

The cop stationed at Bedourie picked me up and took me on the last leg of the journey over dirt roads heading towards the Simpson Desert. It was all new country to me. In Camooweal, I had often peered out over vast treeless flats from atop the back of my ute. The plains stretching as far as the eye could see, along the horizon where land met the sky, and the only trees were those that bordered the, primarily dry, creeks.

All this changed driving up to Bedourie. It was like turning a page in a book, from treeless plains to endless rolling red dunes.

Bedourie, a small town halfway between Birdsville and Boulia in the Channel Country, had a population of about fifty. The only communication with the outside world was via the Royal Flying Doctor Service radio located at the shire office. The town was aptly named after the Indigenous word for "dust storm", of which, during my time there, I experienced several. These storms left me shovelling red dirt from the floor of the tiny police station and quarters. With visibility severely restricted during those storms, it made me often wonder how the old-time drovers had fared under those conditions.

The town itself was on a slight rise, obviously planned that way, for, with the arrival of the wet season, the transformation from desert dunes to an island surrounded by brown water as far as the eye could see was incredible. Travelling during the wet was by boat, a great variety of birdlife, including sea birds, appeared like magic and filled the trees and water.

Again, the transformation was magical and was something I'd never seen before. The pelicans arrived in their thousands along with other species, starting their breeding season under perfect conditions. Once the young were hatched and had grown strong enough to make the arduous flight back to the coast, the birds left, only to return the following year.

THE SNAKE

Police work at the tiny station consisted, typically for the outback, of an office connected by a fly screened walkway to equally small living quarters and was minimal at best. During the dry times, the fortnightly practice was to drive to a suitable, continuously shifting in the winds, nearby dune to assemble the three-piece radio aerial. After disconnecting the battery of the police Toyota, I connected the HF radio and put a call through to the police in Longreach to let them know all was good.

One morning, while I was in contact with the Longreach police, I saw something move rapidly, coming up the dune towards me. On a second look, I identified a sizeable two-metre snake, which I realised, meant business. Not wanting to wait around to see what happened next, I dropped the mic and took off and raced around to the other side of the Toyota with the snake in hot pursuit, relentless and determent to bite me. On the second time past the back of the car, I grabbed a long-handled shovel, turned to face the snake, and gave it a couple of good whacks across the head. The blows did the trick, and somewhat relieved, I looked at the now-dead snake.

Retrieving the radio mic, I called back to re-established contact with the Longreach police station. The bloke on the other end jumped in with,

'What happened to you, mate? You disappeared on us.'

I told the bloke what had transpired and described the snake that had tried to attack me. It was about two metres long, green on top and yellow underneath, with evenly spaced brown rings, along its entire length. It also had a particularly pointed tail end.

'Does it have a large flat head?' he asked.

'Well, it does now!' I said.

He signed off laughing. I took the dead snake back into town to see if the local Indigenous blokes could identify it, but they had never seen one like it. I've never been able to ascertain what breed it was and assumed it to be a hybrid of some sort. All I knew was that it was extremely aggressive towards me. I most likely had entered its' territory and nesting area. From that day onwards, I picked another dune to make my fortnightly radio call from, just in case that snake had relatives living in the vicinity. I thought I might not be as lucky next time.

THE FLOOD BOAT

I found that there was almost next to no police work to do other than completing the required monthly returns and issuing the odd driving licence, so to be asked to go and help recover the council flood boat provided a bit of excitement. Someone had left it on the wrong side of the swollen Diamantina River.

To get to the other side of the river, one of the local cockies and I grabbed an inflated truck tyre tube each and walked about five hundred metres upstream along the riverbank. Finding a safe enough spot, we entered the flooded river and drifted out, angling our way across. The strong current increased our speed dramatically as we raced along, and by grabbing hold of a low hanging branch on the opposite bank, we pulled ourselves up the bank near the boat. It was great fun, if not slightly dangerous. Then, feeling exhilarated, we boarded the flood boat and returned it downriver to the waiting group of council blokes. I liked the action as it was more my preferred kind of police work.

MISSING HORSES

There was an incident involving stolen horses, and even though the great wet was still on, the waters had been receding, making movement around some of the country possible. The complainant named Bill came with me, and together we headed out of town to where he had seen the horses last. Because of the wet terrain, it was quite a circuitous trip to get to the location. Our efforts delivered no results in finding out how or where the horses had gone. It was time to head home as it was getting dark, and we were still some way out of town.

The police vehicle at Bedourie was one of the first Toyota Landcruiser series, six-cylinder petrol, three-speed four-wheel drives and was used for "extreme off-roading". To get from one place to another involved charging at the sand-dunes, and once on top of the dune, the vehicle slid downwards on the other side, which was scary enough in the daylight, but it wasn't something I'd ever attempt in the pitch dark. There was the possibility of reaching the top of a dune, starting the downward slide, only finding the water almost level with the top as you began the descent, and this was enough for me to decide to stop and wait until daylight before continuing.

Bill, who liked his beer, had taken the precaution of bringing a "cut lunch" of several stubbies, and so we sat on top of a random dune having a few beers. It wasn't all pleasant as we were eaten alive by swarms of biting midges. Bill eventually fell asleep, and I sat and waited until dawn in the deathly silence that you can only experience in the outback.

In the days that followed, the horses reappeared. There seemed to be no explanation as to where they had been. Their return was a relief to all the cockies and managers in the area as none of them wanted to have the Stock Squad involved. There was no way of knowing what they would uncover if they started checking a few freezers. It was the "done thing" ever since there have been cattle and sheep properties that a bloke would always grab a beast from next door if he wanted to fill his freezer. I learned this truth during a lunch conversation where I complimented on the excellent quality of the beef. The reply was,

'It should be. It's from next door.'

Occasionally plains turkey appeared on the dinner table. It instigated a comment from one of the blokes regarding the drumstick on his plate,

'This must be the biggest chook I've ever seen.'

The transformations out in the Channel Country, from sand-dunes to floods to the sudden appearance of beautiful desert wildflowers covering the entire country, is something one can only fully appreciate by witnessing this incredible phenomenon. Even the most professionally taken photographs cannot capture the beauty and uniqueness of this landscape. The true essence of the bush, I was rapidly falling in love with, was becoming part of every fibre of my being.

During my time in Bedourie, I occasionally drove a four-hundred-kilometre round trip to the historic town of Birdsville to call in on a mate who managed a cattle station near there. He was kind enough to give me basic instruction in horse riding. I believed that having some rudimentary skills in riding a horse could very well come in handy in the future in the event of any outback bushland searches. A few months later, the permanent cop's leave was over, and when he returned, I returned to Mount Isa.

BACK TO THE ISA

I spent a fair bit of time associating with members of the public and met many good blokes with whom I remained friends for years to come. At times, police went from Mount Isa to the copper mine in the small outback town of Gunpowder, which didn't have a police station. I went with another cop to escort seven blokes to a waiting aircraft following their dismissal from the mining site. They had been involved in a brawl the previous night, and as in common with other mines, that meant instant termination regardless of position. Getting into an argument with one of the cooks was also a sacking offence in the mines at the time. The blokes at Comalco Weipa on Cape York had the term "Fokkerised" for the dismissed because they left under police escort on a Fokker Friendship aircraft.

Life in the single men barracks was good, and I lived with a good bunch of blokes. But, of course, when you have a group of primarily young blokes residing in one place like the police barracks, you tend to get many high jinks and practical jokes. The following occurred just before I arrived at the station, and as I wasn't averse to pulling the odd practical joke myself, I wouldn't have minded having been there.

A senior constable, who resided at the barracks, worked in a "Monday to Friday" office hours position. One night after he had a few drinks, a couple of wags snuck into his room with a pink feather duster and pot of glue. When his snoring became loud, they knew he had fallen asleep and plucking the fluffy pink feathers from the duster, they stuck them to his face with glue, gave him a bit of a shake to wake him up and raced out the door to watch, along with the rest of the mob, to see what would happen next. The heavy-headed constable got up and stumbled down to the communal bathroom in which was a long mirror designed to allow a few blokes to shave simultaneously. Looking into the mirror, he spotted this dreadful apparition staring back at him, giving him an awful fright. The reward could not have been better for the pranksters, as the constable ran screaming from the bathroom, out the door, and onto the road, naked. It was hilarious and entertaining for the pranksters who thought it better to contain the merriment to the police reserve. They immediately gave chase and managed to catch him and bring him back to the barracks amid continuing laughter. On finding out what they did to him, the senior constable went and grabbed his gun and came tearing out, sending the pranksters racing everywhere. They all had a good laugh, and the constable calmed down, and that was the end of that.

THE GARBOS

I had been in court giving evidence in an insurance and compensation hearing concerning a collision. I could barely remember the incident as it had happened at least five years earlier. When it finally finished, in the early hours of the following morning, I booked into the Isa Hotel and ended up having a coffee with Mac, the night porter. He had, for some reason, a down on the garbos who were in the habit of taking their smoko break on the front steps of the hotel. It was none of my concern, but he had me fascinated.

As soon as the garbos made themselves at home on

the front steps, Mac produced a horror mask that sent cold shivers down my spine in its unique ugliness. It was one of those rubber masks that fitted entirely over his head and was frightening, to say the least. He then retrieved a rubber hand from the fridge, which he slipped over his hand and donned an oversized parka type jacket. Following this, Mac made his way out of the pub kitchen to the front door, with me watching from the kitchen window.

He suddenly somehow materialised next to the three men who were making themselves quite comfortable on the steps. On seeing this "thing" appear next to them, two of them jumped up in terror and ran screaming down the road. The third unfortunate bloke froze in fear and crouched further into the corner. As the "thing" advanced on him, pawing at his face with the cold rubber hand, he started to scream,

'What do you want? What the fuck do you want?'

I watched in disbelief at what I had just witnessed. Mac slowly turned to make his way back inside, and with a big grin, he said,

'That'll fix 'em. Don't think they'll be back in a hurry.'

He took off his gear and returned to his, by now, cold coffee. He didn't mention the garbos again, and I decided to leave it at that.

SEARCH AT MASSACRE INLET

I was asleep in my room at the barracks when the Inspector came in and said,

'Get up Cahill. I've got a job for you.'

We knew each other well enough for this sort of banter. The job turned out to be a plane trip to Massacre Inlet on the Northern Territory border to check out the disappearance of a woman. She had walked off an outstation a few days before and hadn't been seen or heard of since. The country where this happened was rugged Gulf country, swarming with crocodiles. To top it off, it was also the wet season, with large tracts of land covered by water. The woman's husband had taken ill about two weeks earlier and been airlifted to the Mount Isa Hospital. She had been there alone, and her only means of communication was via the Royal Flying Doctor Service radio channel. There was great concern for her as she hadn't been on air for a few days, so they sent me up to investigate.

After landing at the outstation, I walked around the buildings and looked around the accommodation. Everything looked tidy, and finding nothing of interest inside, I went and checked out the back. There was a creek bank with steep sides, and looking over the edge, I saw at least half a dozen crocodiles who, in an instant, leapt up out of the water. Fortunately, they were too far down to grab hold of me, and I didn't hang around long enough to find out what they had planned for their next move. I seriously entertained the idea that the missing woman had met a dreadful end and had become a meal for the crocs.

Not equipped for a full search, I flew home to Mount Isa and, on the inspector's instructions to get an investigation going, I returned the following day. I landed near the main homestead, where the station owner picked me up. He looked at my 1898 vintage .308 Mauser carbine and asked,

'Can you use that thing?'

In a fleeting moment of confidence, I raised and aimed the rifle at a star picket some forty metres away and snapped off a shot knocking the picket down with a loud clang. It was a hefty rifle and how the original carriers of this weapon ever fired it from horseback was beyond me.

The manager spluttered,

'Jesus Christ!' and said no more.

I thought the same thing and knew that I could never do that again in a month of Sundays.

The Northern Territory police had stations at the Territory borders on major access roads, and the plan was to liaise with the cop in the one-man station at Wollorgorang and get a search underway.

I accompanied a search party of four Aboriginal trackers and a couple of ringers on horseback and started looking. Now the lessons my mate had given me in saddling a horse, putting the bridle on, and how to mount up and ride, came in very handy. I doubt you could call it "riding", but it was just enough to get me by. A detective arrived from Mount Isa to help with the search, and I met the two serving Northern Territory police trackers and two retired trackers. Never having had anything to do with trackers, I would find out just how skilled at their art these blokes were over the next few days.

We split up in pairs, and I teamed up with an eighty-four-year-old tracker named Gerry. After riding around for a couple of days without result, I knew that time was running out for this woman. She had been gone for nearly a week under appalling conditions in flooded country, crocs everywhere and millions of mosquitoes; the odds were heavily stacked against her. So on the third day, I rode out with Gerry, the tracker and the two ringers when Gerry raised his hand.

'Hold up.'

Pointing, he said, 'Do you see that constable?'

I got on well with this old bloke and was in awe of his tracking abilities. I peered into the space at which he was pointing and replied,

'I can see water about calf-deep on the ground. That's about it, Gerry.'

He said, 'I'll show you.'

With that, we climbed down from our horses, and Gerry continued his findings,

'The woman sat down here and removed her shoes, and these are the slide marks from her bum when she took them off.'

Looking at that which Gerry pointed out, I thought, 'How on earth did I not see that.'

But of course, you are looking at forty thousand years of tracking as a survival skill. These Australian Indigenous people are second to none in the world. So, we continued on foot, leading our horses.

'Not much further along now,' Gerry said.

'We're close. See here. She climbed under the fence here.'

He indicated some stalks of grass which were bent over and bruised under the water and said,

'If it were a cow, the grass would be broken.'

We left our horses and walked over to a small creek not too far from the fence line, where Gerry pointed out the woman sitting in the creek with only her head visible. She did this to minimise skin exposure and give the mosquitoes less opportunity to bite. They were swarming around everywhere in huge clouds, thirsty for blood. The woman was exhausted and seemed very confused. We carried her out of the water and over to a flat big enough for a chopper to land. One of the riders was already on his way back to the station to arrange transport.

After having spent about a week in extremely inhospitable country, she was incoherent, covered in mosquito bites, and very hungry. Otherwise, she seemed in reasonable shape. It didn't take long for a small helicopter to arrive and to collect the woman, flying her back to the station to await the arrival of the Royal Flying Doctor Service aircraft, which was coming from Mount Isa. The RFDS, a truly amazing organisation, had been a lifesaver for many a bushman.

We collected the horses, and I mounted up at the same time the helicopter was about to take off. I asked the ringers,

'What is this horse like around choppers?'

They replied, 'No problem.'

I suspected these blokes might've been having me on, for as soon as the helicopter started to lift off, the horse bolted. It galloped at high speed through the flooded country, heading straight for the station. Being a novice rider, I thought the best thing to do was to let the horse run and concentrate on remaining upright in the saddle. I somehow managed to do this but lost my police slouch hat, which I never recovered. Nevertheless, I managed to arrive back at the station unscathed and was quietly pleased that I had stayed on the horse during the impromptu gallop.

Back at the station, I waited for the RFDS aircraft to arrive and accompanied the woman back to Mount Isa, where an ambulance was waiting at the airport for her. To my knowledge, the lady survived her ordeal but never returned to the outstation again.

I have worked with trackers at different periods in my service, and I never ceased to be amazed at the skill of these men. I would hate to see that ability disappear from their culture.

Before my departure, My Mum and youngest sister Fran arrived on the train to visit me for a few days. Neither of them had been to Mount Isa before, and it was great to catch up with them. Our primary source of communication back then mainly consisted of correspondence via letters and postcards.

CALOUNDRA

TRANSFER FROM MOUNT ISA

My time at Mount Isa came to an end, and as I didn't want to drive the MGB to yet another location, I decided to sell it. An old local bush pilot took a liking to it, and straight after the deal, I went and bought an ex-police Holden ute.

I received notice that my next posting was at Caloundra, about one hundred kilometres north of Brisbane. Even though I'd enjoyed my time in the North-West, I didn't mind getting back to the coast for a year. Police staff usually qualified for a coastal posting after having done a few years of outback duty. I decided to transfer by train for a change and took my newly acquired ute down to Mount Isa Rail for transportation to the Sunshine Coast. I boarded The Inlander, which at the time was a relatively new train. My allocated second-class sleeper cabin was comfortable if slightly spartan.

As the trip would take more than a day, I snuck an esky into my cabin, loaded with ice and a carton of Fourex stubbies. I had a camp on the provided bunk until the train pulled in at the first stop at the town of Cloncurry. There wasn't much action on the small platform, and it wasn't long before the whistle blew, sending the train on its way. I thought this to be the perfect time to have a beer when a bloke walked in wearing a railway inspector's uniform. He stowed his bag, sat down, and told me that he was travelling to Charters Towers. As drinking booze on the train was prohibited, I thought,

'Great. How am I going to have a beer now?'
After a few minutes, he asked,
'What's in the esky?'
I thought, "Here we go. This could be trouble." As it was too late to hide the evidence, I replied,
'Best part of a carton of Fourex'.
To my relief, he said,
'Well, what are we waiting for?'
At being given the green light, I grabbed a couple of beers and handed one to the inspector and said,
'Just help yourself, plenty here'.

I never had anything to do with Queensland Rail staff before and was thoroughly entertained for the remainder of the trip I shared with the inspector. He related hilarious tales woven around the time he was working as a guard on the trains many years ago.

He told me about transporting an expensive, well-trained, prize-winning Blue Heeler Cattle Dog as we enjoyed the beer. Apart from his working ability, this dog was also going to be used as a stud. He came on board at Townsville and was bound for the small outback town of Julia Creek. He travelled in a cage in the guard's van at the rear of the general freighter train, which continually stopped at the various sidings and towns, shunting off wagons and picking up others. A trip on one of these trains took a lot longer than a regular passenger-only service. I knew of those lengthy trips, having spent time on them while escorting prisoners from St George to Boggo Road jail in Brisbane.

By the time the freight train had arrived in Richmond, the dog had been in the cage for several hours and whilst at the station, one of the porters thought he'd let the dog out for a bit of a walk and to give him a break from the cage. The dog seemed to enjoy his outing, and all went well until it was time to get back on the train and back into his cage again. This was when the dog decided to take off and headed at a fast gallop into town with the porter in hot pursuit, with outstretched arms and ready to lunge.

Railway blokes were searching everywhere for this dog which had seemingly vanished, and after an hour of holding up the train, the driver said they'd have to go without the dog. It was an embarrassing position, but as luck would have it, a local stray blue heeler came wandering by the station. In a flash, the blokes hauled him onto the train and placed the substitute into the cage. Fortunately, the stray was an entire dog and was duly handed over to his new owners. They paid one hundred pounds for him, which was a considerable sum in those days.

The stray must've performed well in all that was required of him, as the railway never received any complaints. The following day my travelling companion reached his destination and departed. I continued my journey and eventually arrived at Caloundra, where I moved into a flat in a quiet area known as Golden Beach.

DEALING WITH A DRUNK

Caloundra, a quiet, sleepy beachside town on the Sunshine Coast, had a relatively low crime rate. On the late shifts, I went several nights without receiving even one phone call. Though from time to time, incidents did happen that required immediate action.

It was Friday night when the detective on duty and I received a series of 000 calls. The callers were panicked kids using a public telephone box, but every time they rang, they failed to tell us where they were. With no technology to trace calls, it was all we could do but wait for the next call. Finally, after the fourth call, we managed to calm the caller down, and after a bit of coaxing, I managed to get the address.

We jumped into the unmarked police vehicle, and it took us only ten minutes to arrive at the location. We soon spotted the kids in front of a Queensland Housing Commission style home with a fenced yard and heard yelling and screaming coming from inside the house.

Moving past the kids, who were visibly upset, we made our way towards the steps leading up to the front door. Here we were met by a thin, haggard-looking woman who appeared to have large clumps of hair missing from her head. We ascertained that her husband was inside the house where he had been on the booze for several days. In his drunken rage, he had ripped chunks of hair from her head. She and her children had been sheltering in an unoccupied house down the road. For reasons unknown, the man also had ripped out the mature veggies from the garden. The woman and her children were unkempt and looked very hungry after spending four days in hiding while the man rampaged, drinking flagons of cheap wine. The detective, who was senior to me, said,

'I'll walk up the steps first and have a word with the individual inside.'

But when he reached the top step, the drunk took the detective by surprise and rushed out. Driven by anger, he charged and pushed the detective, causing him to overbalance and fall back down the steps. Luckily, I was right behind him and was able to break the momentum.

I then pushed past the detective on the stairs and managed to grab hold of the drunken but very powerful man. He then attempted to shove me down the stairs as well, and though I overbalanced, I had enough warning to compensate. We ended up both falling down the stairs, and as luck would have it, he ended up underneath me when we finished the descent and hit the ground at the bottom.

His haggard-looking wife rushed forward, screaming abuse at us and immediately took sides with the man. It was a clear display of Stockholm Syndrome; I had seen it many times before, where battered victims form a bond with their abuser and protect them from whoever dares take a swing. We charged the man and took him into custody. In cases like this, you have to fight both, the husband and stop him from hitting his family, and the wife from hitting and clawing you, the protector.

The man lay there groaning and said he was in pain, so after we charged him, we took him to the hospital. Afterwards, he alleged that his arm broke on impact, but he had no one to verify this. Later he was overheard boasting that he had broken his glasses sometime earlier but would blame the damage on the police. This man then wrote a letter to the prime minister alleging extreme police brutality and having his glasses smashed.

What followed was incredible. An investigation was launched at the highest level into the allegations. Commissioned officers from Brisbane interviewed both the detective and me. When it became obvious what had taken place, the top police prosecutor arrived to act for the prosecution during the court proceedings, as the man had entered a plea of not guilty. The court proceedings were over relatively quickly, with both the detective and I giving our evidence. The woman then gave evidence for her husband, and his evidence was nothing more than a pack of lies. The magistrate found him to be a liar and guilty of all charges and asked us,

'Would you like compensation for the fabricated complaints made against you?'

Both of us agreed that any monetary penalties against

this man would have to come from money allocated for food for those children and not from his booze money, so we declined.

There were a few more calls from the same phone box over the next few weeks concerning his drunken performances, but there wasn't much point in getting too involved, and fortunately, they left the district shortly afterwards.

THE DEAD BODY

One of my first cases in Caloundra has always been a case I'd rather not remember but one I never forgot. Someone rang the station saying, 'There's a stench coming from one of the rooms. It smells like rotting meat.'

They added that it possibly could be a dead body in the building and if so, could we come and remove it.

The old, dilapidated building in question was a large low-grade flophouse with narrow hallways and stairways. The small single rooms contained no more than a rickety old bed, a cupboard that hardly held together, and a table and a chair. The one shower and toilet were filthy and had to be shared by the assortment of dwellers. Those who lived there were people down on their luck and a hotchpotch of substance abusers and criminals. Four of us decided to go down, and upon questioning some of the residents, we learned that the room with the permeating stench was that of an old single bloke. The stench alone told us that the individual that resided there had indeed deceased.

The establishment's culture was pretty much where everybody minded their own business, and it took a fair bit of questioning to establish when the man had died.

The general guess was about five or six days ago. It was only when someone saw bodily fluids and flies come out from underneath the door, paired with an ever-increasing stench, that they decided to call the police. After that, the residents unanimously disappeared from sight, and we knew that things were left up to us from here on in. It was a dreadful sight that greeted us in that room. All we had at our disposal was a gurney with shallow sides. As there wasn't a whole body to grab hold of, we lifted the thin and worn mattress and tipped that, which was laying and sloshing on top, onto the gurney.

In an attempt to keep the gurney level, I took position on the lower back end, with one policeman up the front and the others, one each along the sides of the stretcher and carried this up three flights of steps. But, unfortunately, the containing sides of the gurney proved too shallow to hold the fluid and, as I was at the lower point, I finished up with the stinking mess sloshing onto my uniform.

After delivering the body to the hospital morgue, I raced home and burnt all the clothing I had been wearing. However, the smell remained with me for quite some time. I found out later that the olfactory memory readily recollects odours, pleasant and unpleasant, and evokes the corresponding incidents, ensuring they'll never be forgotten.

THE DROWNING

I was out on patrol, and so far, it had been a quiet afternoon. This, however, was soon to change as a call came through that a man was in trouble and possibly drowning at Shelley Beach. I turned on the siren and raced off to the beach, pulling up at the top of the sand-dunes. The ocean here was notorious for its rips, currents and rocks, and only highly experienced surfers entered the waters here. The person reported to be in trouble was a Melbourne man in his late forties who was holidaying at Caloundra with his family.

One of his sons had gone for a swim, and shortly after entering the water, he had found himself in serious difficulties. The father had jumped into the water, intending to go to his son's aid. However, as usually is the case, he also got into difficulties and was drowning when I arrived.

I spotted a young surfer out there who, with great effort, managed to drag the son onto his board and was bringing him into shore. Fortunately for the man, and before I could do anything, another surfer appeared. I watched him navigate the waves and skillfully maneuver his board, pulling the man to safety. It was outstanding work by those two young surfers who had risked their lives performing these rescues.

As an ambulance couldn't come down the sandy dunes, it was left up to me to get this bloke to the top. Besides the surfers, who were out of steam following their rescues and were busy looking after the son, there wasn't anyone there to assist me dragging this large semi-conscious man up the steep slope. Dune climbing is hard enough without the added challenge of a heavy, uncooperative body.

The loose sand folded around my feet as I made my way up the slippery sandy rise, and with every two steps forward, I slid back one. Every muscle in my body burned and ached, and my legs were on fire. The top was never so far away, and I was starting to see spots in front of my eyes from sheer exhaustion and physical effort. I made it to the top at the same time as the ambulance arrived. The bloke was transferred to a stretcher and taken to the hospital.

As usual, I never heard a word from the rescued man. However, it would have been nice had he taken the time to say at least thanks to those two young blokes on boards as, without them, I doubt he, or his son, would be around to tell the tale.

FALSE IDENTITY

I was working by myself one evening when halfway through the shift, I received a call over the radio that there was a two-vehicle collision in front of the catholic church. The four young women occupying a Morris Mini Cooper were unhurt. The other vehicle was a Ford Sedan occupied by a forty-year-old male. Upon seeing that the women were alright, I went over to the male driver. I noticed that he smelt strongly of alcohol on reaching him, so I was obliged to follow protocol. However, the man had other ideas that differed greatly from mine. He told me his name and advised me that he was going into the catholic presbytery to speak to the priest who was his friend and wasn't interested in talking to me, so he was leaving. I told him that he was required to remain there, upon which he said that phrase I really didn't like,

'Do you know who I am?'

Well, that pretty much set the scene for whatever followed, and I replied,

'No, I don't know who you are, but the fact is you are staying here for the time being,'

The man responded that he didn't have time to speak to the likes of me and made the mistake of lunging at me, trying to push me out of his way. I grabbed him, applied a full nelson restraint, marched him over to the police car and put him in the back, locking the door. After that, I decided to take him to the nearest police station, where a qualified breath analysis machine operator could take a breath sample.

This bloke continued to rant and make all sorts of dire threats of "dismissal and transfer" because of his position in the community. Yep, he was the chamber of commerce president and had a couple of used vehicle and caravan sales yards. I pulled up outside the police headquarters, about half an hour drive away and opened the door to get this bloke out. He started resisting violently, and again, I put a restraint hold on him and walked him towards the main entrance. He bucked like mad, and we finished up going through the main door with his head going through first. As I went past the front desk, the bloke behind the counter said,

'That's the president of the Chamber of Commerce.'

'He did mention that.' I said and continued towards the designated analysis room. Long story short, he refused to supply a sample of his breath, and I charged him with two liquor driving offences of being under the influence of liquor and failing to provide a specimen. There was a fair bit of interest in this incident, with people thinking it would cause me some trouble. However, a detective mate of mine got involved of his own accord, as it didn't smell right, and he made some inquiries of his own regarding the man I had arrested.

The result was that, within a very short time, the man entered a guilty plea to his charges despite having made all those threats and left the court in the company of some South Australian detectives. They had a warrant for his arrest for serious fraud and other crimes in that state. In addition, there were similar matters for him to answer in Victoria following his release from jail in South Australia. Furthermore, the detective had unearthed his real identity. How this man managed to get the required identification for second-hand dealing, driving licence, and the like was beyond our comprehension.

Anyway, that was the end of it. If the man had gone along with the original drive under the influence charge, he would have gone undetected and only gotten a fine and licence suspension rather than years in southern jails.

STARING EVIL IN THE EYE

At different times in my life, I have encountered truly evil men, the one I'll never forget was charged over the death of a little girl.

In the outer suburbs was an old house that had been empty for quite some time, so this bloke went and installed a homemade bomb in one of the kitchen cupboards. He then made an anonymous call to the local drug squad, telling them that drugs had been hidden in the house. However, before the arrival of the police, two little girls had gone into the empty house to play. Tragically one of them had opened the kitchen cupboard door and, by doing so, detonated the bomb meant for the police. She died instantly while her little sister, though severely injured, survived.

I attended the circuit court and was instructed to guard the prisoner during the lunch break. He was in a locked cell, and I sat on a chair outside the door. Now I always watch the eyes, and this was one of the times when I looked at a man's eyes and saw nothing. It's hard to explain, but the eyes are black and devoid of any expression. That's when you know you've got a really bad bastard in front of you. So, when I handed him back to the court orderlies, I was more than glad to be out of his company.

He was found guilty and served his time at Townsville jail, and later, upon his release, he returned to his native New Zealand.

THE BURLY GARBOS

Some blokes are extremely difficult to lock up, and in my opinion, the shearers and wool pressers I have dealt with were among the strongest and fittest. That was, up until I had my first encounter with one of the old-style garbos. These blokes used to jump off the garbage truck, run into a yard and tip the contents of the household bin into a larger bin which they carried on their shoulders. They then ran back to the slowly moving truck, tipping the rubbish in over the side and repeat the process for the duration of the shift. Some of them jumped over fences carrying these bins full of garbage without falter. It provided excellent physical fitness and strength training for them, as I discovered on several occasions.

The first time I encountered a bloke of that profession was on a night when I was rostered on by myself. I received a call out to a domestic disturbance. Nothing was jumping out at me in the actual radio call that waved a danger flag, but I nevertheless had a gut feeling something wasn't right. So I decided to drop by the detective's place on the way, and he agreed to accompany me to the job.

It was just as well there were two of us because a large, enraged man confronted us as we went in. He attacked without needing a prompt, and it was only that both, my colleague and I, were big men that we managed to overpower him and place him in the back of the police car. Unfortunately, the cars back then weren't partitioned off with a mesh shield, and even though handcuffed, this man put on a hell of a turn all during the twenty-minute drive up the highway. I drove while the detective struggled to restrain the man. A few times, he managed to almost climb over into the front seat, leaving me no options other than to slam him in the face with back fists every time he came close to me. We were travelling at speed, with this bloke determined to cause a collision.

We managed to get him into the police station, where he was charged and placed in custody. I later found out on checking his criminal history that he was an extremely violent man with several convictions. A note was made never to attend a complaint involving this man unless there were two in attendance.

LANDSBOROUGH

MOTORCYCLE LICENCE

I had passed my first examinations allowing me to wear one stripe, I transferred to Landsborough, a two-man police station with a sergeant and a constable. Back then, the police and army had identical grades and ranks, albeit having different names. The station had a motorcycle attached to it for use by the constable, and I, therefore, was required to pass the relevant competency test. I went and borrowed a bike from a local farmer I'd become friends with and took a few riding lessons through a driving school in Brisbane. During my final lesson, the instructor made me practice a hill start on a very steep hill. The 400 Kawasaki I was riding went immediately into a rear-wheel stand for at least thirty metres up the hill. It felt like riding a horse gone mad but somehow, I managed to stay on the bike and bring it back down.

Finally, the time came for the competency test, which required me to keep up with two police mechanics on a track winding around Mount Cootha. It was easy enough, and I left for home, qualified to ride my KZ Honda 750 cc police motorcycle. With the bike, I attended to the numerous collisions on the Bruce Highway and took the machine home, reducing the response time to callouts. I liked the motorcycle, and even when on leave, I kept it at home.

The Landsborough division contained five small towns, and I never got sick of riding through the massive pine forests and bush areas. The most enjoyed duty required me to do a mail run from Nambour, the district headquarters, to Caboolture south of Beerburrum, delivering and collecting internal police and courthouse mail.

Even though traffic enforcement wasn't my main preoccupation, I tried to do a bit in that area because, over the time I was at Landsborough, I saw the carnage done by those who didn't adhere to the road rules. In eighteen months, the sergeant and I attended many collisions ranging from minor dings to triple fatalities. I was still young enough to think that issuing traffic offence notices for blatant offences, such as overtaking on double lines and disregarding stop signs, would make a difference. In retrospect, it didn't; people broke the rules regardless. I issued over three hundred traffic offence notices during that time, with none ever disputed.

UNINVITED GUEST AT THE TABLE

I was delivering mail one night to a neighbouring station when the police sergeant on duty said,
'You. Come with me,'
Handing me a set of car keys, he said to the two slightly built young constables in the office,
'You two would get eaten alive.'
I followed him out to a police car, and once I settled into the driver's seat, he gave me directions to an address in the town. He filled me in and said that he'd received a complaint from a family of eight who had been sitting down having dinner when a huge man had come lumbering into their house. He'd chased the family out and went to sit down, helping himself to the food on the table.

This bloke was still stuffing food into his mouth when

we walked into the dining room, and rather than comply with our request to leave the premises, he took umbrage at being asked. It's when we knew that we were going to have a decent fight on our hands. I was in good shape, and the sergeant, a fair bit older than me, was solidly built and had crossed a few dry gullies in his time.

We wrestled with this man from the dining room through the hallway and down the front stairs of the high set house. The fight to get him under control continued through the front gate and out in front of the police car on the bitumen. This bloke was getting more and more violent and tried hard to hurt us, so I commenced landing a few solid punches into him in an attempt to slow him up. It was dark, but we were making progress when suddenly, the lights of the police car came on. A family member called out,

'I turned them on so you can see what you're doing.'

The sergeant said to me during the struggle,

'Why on earth would he do that for?'

We continued to grapple with the man until I managed to handcuff him and push him into the back of the police car. He must've had enough because he finally stopped struggling and remained quiet for the entire trip to the cells.

After forfeiting bail the next day, he went home, and we never had any further dealings with him. I saw him jumping off the back of the garbo truck with his bin from time to time. If he recognised me, he didn't give any indication.

THE SQUATTER

For a few weeks, I had been getting phone calls of complaint, and later in person, from the owners of an old deserted house in the middle of a state pine forest. Regularly, on weekends, a car parked outside this old house, but no one had any authority to be there. The owners were becoming very persistent with their complaints, so to satisfy them, I decided one Saturday morning to go and have a look and see what the problem was. Even though I had more pressing matters that required police attention, I thought I'd better do something before the house landlord started complaining higher up. I didn't know the house's location within the forest, and Google Maps or a Global Positioning System was something found only in science fiction novels.

Fortunately, there was a young bloke named Charlie, who was a regular visitor to the station. He had an intellectual disability but could hold a conversation and had passed a standard driving test. Charlie had a 1948 Holden sedan in mint condition, which was his pride and joy, and I ended up following him, as he knew where the house was. Unfortunately, it was drizzling rain, and being on one of those motorcycles at the time with crash bars, the first thing you noticed was your boots as they started to fill with water. Also, riding on wet bitumen roads, particularly after a dry spell, could be dangerous and slippery because of the diesel spills. Another problem on wet days was the two-way radio. It was mounted behind the seat and became inoperable because the rain always found its way into the unit.

Once off the bitumen, we continued onto muddy dirt tracks through the state forest and, after what seemed an eternity, the house came into view. Well, if anyone has seen movies such as The Blair Witches or any others set in hillbilly or swamp areas of the USA, this was precisely the type of house it was. It was an old, paint deprived, dried out and a forlorn-looking high set building. It was in the middle of, which seemed to be the only clearing in the forest and looked very uninviting. Out the front, parked up, was a late model gold-coloured Holden sedan.

As I approached the house, I observed that there was only one set of steps at the front, and as I got closer, I saw and heard the front door, which had been slightly ajar, slam shut. At the time, I was like many young blokes, ten foot tall and bulletproof, so I dismounted, removed my gauntlets, checked my revolver, and noted the registration number in my notebook. Nowadays, police can do a quick check on the spot and obtain the name, address, and criminal history of any registered car owner. However, no such facility existed back then, leaving me in a position where I couldn't call for backup due to an out-of-order wet radio and isolated location. There was only one option, and that was to handle things myself. It was an attitude that, during my time as a cop, served me well on a lot of occasions.

Having no idea of what I was going to face inside the house, I said to Charlie,

'Wait here and stay in your car. Then, if something bad happens, head off back to town and raise the alarm.'

I checked over the parked car and tried the doors, but they were all locked. I also noticed that it was well cared for and in excellent order. The thought crossed my mind that it might just be nothing more than a secluded spot for a clandestine tryst by a couple of secret lovers. As it turned out, it wasn't that at all.

I climbed the rickety front steps and knocked loudly on the door, announcing who I was. But, of course, whoever was there knew already it was a police officer when they'd slammed the door shut. I heard one set of footsteps inside, causing me to think this was something else and not just a couple of lovers.

I drew my revolver and kicked in the front door. Once inside, I found the usual "old house of its time" in floor layout with a built-in front verandah, hallway, and adjoining rooms devoid of furniture and fittings. Next, I heard movement, followed by the sound of a door carefully being locked, of a room down the hallway. After thoroughly checking the doorless rooms, I was now standing in front of the locked door.

The adrenaline had started to run as I didn't know what to expect. Again, I announced who I was and, on not receiving a reply, I kicked the door in and charged inside with my gun drawn. With the door hinged on the left, I anticipated any attack would be from that side, and as the door crashed crazily open, that's exactly what happened. What I saw before me was something I would not in the wildest imagination have expected.

There was a substantial individual behind the door holding a stick poised to strike. However, I immediately raised my left arm in an upper rising block, preventing the trajectory of the large stick from getting started. At the same time, I jammed my revolver into this person's mouth while simultaneously driving my knee into the stomach, taking the wind out of my would-be assailant. He immediately dropped his stick and started sliding down the wall to the floor. I can vividly remember the apparition which confronted me to this very day.

It was a huge male wearing a large woman's hat complete with plastic fruit and netting, as I had seen on some of my older aunties. In addition to this, he was wearing rouge, lipstick and a pearl necklace, a dress, stockings, and lady's shoes. I had barely time to comprehend what I was seeing when there was a commotion behind me. As I had already cleared the house, and there had been no one in the vicinity, it could only be Charlie, my young tour guide, who had shown me how to get there. Deciding that I needed help, he'd armed himself with a good-sized lump of timber, rushed in behind me and managed to deliver a few good blows to the cross-dresser before I could call him off. At this stage, the man had lost all inclination to fight back, and I was able to establish who he was and what he was doing there.

He told me that he had a fetish for cross-dressing and was reluctant to pursue this at home because he was married. One day he'd found this secluded old house to suit his purposes. I told him his fetish was none of my business or anyone else's but that the owners of the dilapidated house had been complaining for weeks and, as it was their house and didn't want anyone in there, he'd have to move on and find somewhere else to go. I added that if he had answered the door in the usual manner, instead of behaving like a criminal, we'd be having the exact same conversation as we were having now, without the dangerous action he had initiated. I suggested he'd change his attire, and I'd wait downstairs for him.

We left with him leading the convoy, and as soon as we came to the bitumen, he took off at great speed. After that, I never saw him again and figured that he must have found another place to go.

OUTLAW MOTORCYCLE GANGS

Early one morning, I drove down to the small corner shop to get some milk, and on walking in, I came across eight members of a notorious motorcycle gang. This mob was well known for their deviant behaviour, drug use, and violence and up close, they looked every bit the bad bastards they portrayed. Some of them with heads half-shaved, and another with long green hair, the obligatory tattoos and facial rings, and with the look of dangerous people in their eyes. I was wearing a pair of shorts, a Jacky Howe singlet and thongs and had my old Holden ute out the front. The old lady who was the proprietor of the shop said to the mob,

'The policeman is here, and now you've got trouble.'

Upon hearing those words, the mob slowly turned and looked at me. I thought,

'Now, here's some serious trouble.'

I glanced outside at my dog sitting quietly in the back of the ute. Zen was a large young German shepherd I had recently acquired from a hotel in Caloundra. They told me that he was in the habit of going into the bar around closing time to bite inebriated customers and saw no other option than to get rid of him, and therefore, he was offered to me. I had always been on the lookout for another dog after losing Sam, the black curly coated retriever in Mount Isa, and as I straight away took a liking to Zen, I said,

'Alright, I'll take the big fellow.'

One thing, he wasn't afraid of people.

I told the old lady to ring the Maleny police station and said to the mob,

'Time to leave, so get on your bikes and get going.'

They started laughing and seemed to find this very amusing. I looked at the group and said,

'Have a look in the back of my ute. He likes to bite people. Who wants to be first to have a piece ripped out of them?'

With that, I opened the shop door, showing my intent to follow up on my threat. Apart from the dog, I knew that I also had a waddy lying on the floor, just in case things escalated. There was a general shuffling of boots as the scum bags headed for their bikes. After mounting up and screaming obscenities, they rode off in the direction of the highway. They didn't seem at all interested in tangling with my dog, and I guessed that they had felt the powerful bite of a police dog before. I went back inside, rang the station informing them back up was no longer needed and grabbed my milk.

I had acquired a reputation for handling motorcycle gangs. I gained it when I had used a police vehicle to intimidate a mob who had been in the process of kicking two uniformed police officers on the ground a year earlier. That reputation extended to the instruction that a police car was to be sent immediately in the event of any confrontation by motorcycle gangs. Priority was to collect the detective or me, or preferably both of us, regardless of whether we were on duty.

The detective and I worked well together in a number of these confrontations with gangs. One I particularly remember was when one cocky looking gang member started his bike and drove straight towards us with the intent to ram. Fortunately, he hadn't accelerated to any great speed when he reached us, which allowed us to step aside and grab an arm each as he passed between us, causing him to remain there and heard the astonished scream,

'FUUUCCKKK!'

We watched amused as the motorcycle travelled on for a short distance before tipping over.

The, now not so cocky anymore, gang member finished up in the watch house for his efforts.

One night I was woken up by an insistent knocking on my door. It was a cop sent to take me up to Maroochydore. Word was that two lower-order motorcycle gangs organised a fight. On my arrival, the conflict was already in full swing, and I considered that it didn't matter whom I arrested, as everyone seemed to be committing an offence. I immediately got to work, and I had six blokes jammed in the back of the police car in a short space of time. I took my load to the local watch house to charge them and found among the mob a couple of extra ones I didn't arrest but were nonetheless attributed to me. That in itself wasn't a big deal, except for the fact that they pleaded not guilty. I spent the best part of a day in the witness box a few months later being cross-examined by one of the leading defence barristers in Queensland.

From that time on, I decided to attend these fights no longer, unless they were in my area and relevant to my colleagues and me.

THE OVERTURNED TRUCK

There wasn't much to do on my days off back in Caloundra, so I decided to pick up a bit of extra work as a casual truck driver for Banhams Caloundra Transport. The job consisted of driving furniture vans and the old International 1800 beer truck to Brisbane and back, with supplies for the local outlets. I got on well with the truck drivers on the highway, which came in handy when I attended a fatal truck rollover at Landsborough, at the Beerwah turnoff.

A fridge truck full of tomatoes had mounted the centre dividing section, which, sodden with recent rains, caused the heavy vehicle to overturn. The cabin of the new cab-over model was made mainly of fibreglass. It turned out that rollovers, which had been previously survivable in, for example, a steel B model Mack, suddenly became death traps. Once the cabin hit the ground, it bounced, and in this case, it was the second time landing that killed the driver. The truck cabin held him face down in the mud, causing him to suffocate.

Upon my arrival, I saw several senior police in charge, so I took a back seat to proceedings and watched on as they vainly attempted to right the truck using four small tow trucks. They had several goes at it with revving engines and lifting their front wheels off the ground like rearing horses. After about an hour, I went up to the senior bloke, seeing that he had run out of options.

'Would you like me to have a go?' I asked, 'I'll see what I can organise.'

To which he replied,

'Go for it. I'm out of ideas.'

I walked up the road and spoke to several truck drivers who couldn't get past the accident scene until the road cleared. The overturned truck was blocking the entire highway.

I got four prime movers to unhitch and replace the small tow trucks. As I knew from my days as a casual truck driver, these blokes knew what they were doing and, using heavy ropes and chains, had the overturned truck back on its wheels in a relatively short time. There now was room for the ambulance to move in and retrieve the body. The tow trucks moved the wreckage out of the way, and traffic flowed once again.

UTE BURNOUTS

The only departmental accommodation provided in Landsborough was the sergeant's residence. As a first-class constable, I had to organise my own accommodation, so I rented an old but comfortable house about two kilometres from the station.

Early one morning, I woke up from the sound of a car doing burnouts, complete with spinning wheels and screeching tires. I jumped out of bed, and from the window, I saw a Holden ute in full lock, causing quite a bit of smoke. I dressed as quickly as I could, grabbed my ID card and by the time I got there, the ute had stopped moving. I heard both occupants roaring with laughter, and the two of them were completely unaware of my approach. I reached into the driver side window and opened the door dragging the driver out and onto the road. I showed him my ID card and quickly ascertained that these two clowns had stolen the vehicle and had taken it for a wild joy ride.

After placing them both on the front bench seat, I jumped behind the wheel and drove the lawbreakers to the police station. I pulled up around the back, and this is where the offenders decided they'd make a break for it. The one closest to the door decided to run off towards the fence which separated the police yard from the sergeant's residence. Then, very unwisely, the other one initiated an attack, trying to punch me, but it was short-lived, and he very quickly regretted it, especially when I used his head to knock on the door of the police house to wake up the sergeant.

The second offender would have been better off staying in the car as when he jumped over the fence, in his ill-conceived escape attempt, the sergeant's little foxie dog rushed out and started nipping at his feet and ankles. It didn't pose much of a problem but was the catalyst that stirred up the kids' horse, who also lived in the police residence yard. Enraged, it made creditable attempts at biting the fool's back and head. It had the escapee screaming in terror and clambering back over the fence to the relative safety of police custody. Both clowns were conveyed to the Nambour police station and charged to face court the following morning. Both entered pleas of guilty.

The moral of this story is, "Never do burnouts in front of a police residence".

ANIMAL CRUELTY

I didn't get called out often to animal cruelty complaints, but it stays in your mind when you do. This one involved a harmless red setter dog who lived on a horse stud.

I rode my bike out to the property, where I found the injured dog who lay whimpering in pain. Someone had shot him through each of his four paws with a .22 rifle and left him to hobble back up to the homestead where the owners found him. The traumatized dog was taken to a vet in Caloundra and made a full recovery.

My investigations didn't turn up anything. Instead, it left me with the assumption that perhaps a couple of hunters had caught up with the unfortunate animal and had, had their "fun".

ACCIDENTS

By far, the most dominant aspect of being stationed at Landsborough was the involvement and investigations of road accidents. There wouldn't have been one you could describe as "a true accident" of those I attended. The causes were mainly inattention and the apparent breaking of road rules. Then there were the few heart attacks of which it was hard to say, if they were sudden or irresponsible, as in,

'Bugger it. I'm driving regardless.'

One of these collisions took place on a straight stretch of highway with good visibility. The driver of a wagon suffered a heart attack, lost control and drove head-on into an oncoming ute killing the driver instantly. At the scene, a distraught young man ran up to me who told me that he had been following his Dad and recognised one of the wrecked vehicles to be the old man's.

Trembling, he walked with me up to the dreadful sight in front of us, where his worst fears were confirmed. I couldn't do much for him other than place my arm around him. Because both drivers were deceased, no police action was required other than the standard procedures involving furnishing reports and postmortem examinations.

SECTION FIFTEEN OF THE TRAFFIC REGULATIONS

Riding a police motorcycle in a rural setting on the long stretches of highway at high speed was a source of excitement, and I loved every minute of it. Up ahead, I saw a car approach at just about the same time a large sedan swung out onto my side of the highway. It started to overtake several vehicles and headed straight towards me. Forced out onto the edge of the road in an attempt to avoid a head-on, I tried hard to stay off the gravel shoulder because I knew, if I lost control, hitting the ground at sixty miles an hour wouldn't be good. The road proved only to be just wide enough to accommodate two cars and my bike, therefore narrowly avoiding a head-on. The person driving the overtaking vehicle didn't even look at me as it raced past, so I turned the police bike around and gave chase. I switched on my flashing lights and siren, operated by a dynamo on the front wheel. The faster you went, the higher the pitch, until only dogs and cats could hear them.

I caught up with the car and made them pull over. The doors swung open, and five people emerged. The driver, a huge belligerent man, an ex-professional wrestler, was an unpleasant kind of bloke as was one of his passengers, a priest in his cassock and collar. Flanking these two were two unkempt, rough-looking women and a scrawny male. They formed a group and started to surround me in an attempt to intimidate me. One ill-tempered woman screamed,

'We are on our way to a funeral. Don't you have any respect for the dead?'

I replied, 'Another metre or so, and my family would have been going to my funeral.' Turning my attention to the driver, I said,

'Where is your driving licence?'

To my surprise, he produced it. I breached him under section fifteen of the Traffic Regulations in relation to driving a car without due care, following which he entered a plea of not guilty. However, by the time the court case arrived, he had entered a guilty plea, and I gave my evidence unchallenged. The magistrate imposed a suitably severe penalty which included a period of disqualification.

THE HUMOROUS SIDE OF THINGS

There were some not so serious incidents involving my bike as well. While writing out a traffic offence notice for crossing double lines whilst overtaking a line of vehicles, the female passengers started to chuckle while looking towards my police bike. I looked around and immediately saw the source of their merriment. It had been raining, and the shoulders of the highway were doughy.

The police bike had a very precarious lean because the spike stand had sunk into the soft earth. Fortunately, it had come to a halt before tipping the bike over in its entirety. I just grinned and handed over the ticket and went back to stand the bike up.

One day I intercepted a vehicle for a traffic breach. Because of the wet conditions, my biro wouldn't work, and neither would my backup biro. The offending driver was a pleasant bloke who realised he'd done the wrong thing. I didn't expect in my wildest dreams that he would offer me the use of his biro so that I could give him a ticket. I said,

'Thanks anyway, just consider yourself warned' and let him off.

The department commenced attaching microphones to police helmets so that you could speak on the radio by pressing a button on the handlebars. It was a great innovation but took a bit of getting used to. Often after a chase, my standard procedure was to park the police bike behind the intercepted vehicle, stand next to the bike, remove gauntlets, and grab the ticket book from the pannier. Then stride purposefully and professionally towards the offending vehicle.

Sometimes one forgot the critical step of removing the microphone from the helmet before stepping out, as it was attached to the radio mounted on the bike. A couple of steps forward saw you pulled backwards off balance by the attached cable. It was very difficult to recover that sense of professionalism you were attempting to convey a few seconds earlier.

DEAD BODY ON THE SUNLANDER

Late one afternoon, I received a call that a dead body was found on the Sunlander train heading north to Cairns and that the train in question would make a stop at the Landsborough Railway Station within the next ten minutes. My brother John was visiting at the time from Brisbane, so I said to him,

'I've got a call out. Is it okay if we use your car as all I have at my disposal is the police bike.'

He was more than happy to give me a hand, and together we drove up onto the platform where the Sun-lander was waiting. We saw railway staff near the door to one of the sitting carriages, and on pulling up, one of the Queensland Railway blokes said solemnly,

'Seat 23B.'

We walked up to the far end of the carriage and spotted an old bloke in seat 23B, next to the window. Even though he appeared for all the world to be asleep, he wasn't. Nobody knew exactly when, but he had quietly died during his nap somewhere after leaving Brisbane. When his two little grandsons, who were travelling with him, tried to wake their grandfather, fellow passengers in the immediate vicinity realised something was wrong and raised the alarm. I said to my brother,

'He's dead mate, and we've got to get him out of here and into your car.'

Even though it took John by surprise, it didn't faze him, and between us, we managed to get the old guy out of the carriage and into the back of John's vehicle. I took a few details and briefly spoke to the deceased's two little grandsons. I also questioned a few passengers in the adjoining seats and ascertained that there were no suspicious circumstances. The deceased had travelled down by train to Brisbane to get his two grandsons to return home for the school holidays. Queensland Rail staff and other passengers would look after the two boys until they arrived at their destination, in Bundaberg.

The incident was traumatic for the grandsons, but I believe that as far as ways of "checking out" go, this was as good as it gets. We transported the deceased to the police station, and as the local undertaker was already engaged, and, there was no place to keep the body, I had to put it in the garage and close the doors. Cops get plenty of unusual situations, and this was one of them. We waited several hours for the undertaker to arrive to take the body on its last journey.

HEAD ON TRIPLE FATALITY

One Saturday afternoon, I was on my police bike near Beerwah south of Landsborough when I got a call over the radio to the effect that there was a head-on collision close to Tibrogargan Creek on the Bruce Highway, Beerburrum. The vehicles involved were a Holden Sedan containing four elderly catholic nuns, and the other was a Ford station wagon occupied by the male driver and his elderly dog.

I parked the motorcycle, and, walking towards the scene, I saw an old seriously injured black dog lying on the dirt shoulder of the highway. As I reached the Holden sedan, I was confronted by the sight of three dead nuns, with a seriously injured fourth nun in the rear seat. As soon as the ambulance arrived at the scene, I left the injured woman in the care of the ambos. The unconscious driver of the second vehicle was a male in his thirties, and together with the nun, he was transported to the nearest large hospital at Caboolture. During all of this, the old dog quietly died on the side of the road.

Serious collisions, such as these, were investigated by the detective for the area, and

after we'd done the preliminary investigations, we took the necessary photographs and measurements. I accompanied the three bodies in the undertaker's van to the Caloundra morgue for postmortem examinations which I attended, and furnished the required relevant reports.

All three elderly women, although not bearing any signs of external bodily injuries, had suffered massive internal injuries, ostensibly from the seat belts that they had been wearing at the time of the collision. The crash's impact had been such that the Holden sedan, travelling south at about eighty kilometres per hour, had been brought to a complete stop by the Ford travelling north. Seat belts save lives, however in this case, because of the severity of the impact, they kept the bodies intact and inside the vehicle.

The collision occurred about thirty metres further along from where the double centre line began. The driver could not remember what had transpired before the crash, nor could the remaining elderly nun, so no criminal charges were laid against anyone. I haunted the spot for weeks following the crash and issued a few Traffic Offence Notices for overtaking on double centre lines hoping to get some sort of message across. Then, on being called to a single fatality vehicle rollover in the exact same place, I started to wonder if traffic enforcement was the answer.

MALENY RESCUE

Late one cold and rainy day, I was on patrol on my police motorcycle when I got a call via the radio that a vehicle had gone off the Maleny Range trapping a person. The spot where the incident happened was in the Maleny police division, not mine and with only one cop on duty, we frequently helped each other out when required. The area was enveloped in clouds when I rode up to the scene. Several people had gathered, including the Maleny cop and the Landsborough ambulance man. They quickly filled me in and told me that a fifteen-year-old girl lay trapped underneath the car. The driver had escaped injury and had managed to raise the alarm. I saw that the sedan had made its way well and truly down the side of the mountain. How it hadn't gone further down the wet slippery steep side and take both the driver and her with it is beyond me. They also told me that someone had managed to tie a couple of tow ropes to the back axles and had secured them to a nearby tree.

Being probably the physically fittest and strongest man there, I decided to go down and try to free the trapped young girl. I didn't know how long the roadside tree would hold the vehicle's weight, and I hoped that I had a bit of time. I grabbed a car jack and shovel and started my descent, trying to ignore the fact that I was soaking wet from the rain, and because of the low temperatures, I was freezing cold. I knew that I needed to keep moving so I wouldn't seize up and wasn't overly concerned for my safety, but more so for the girl's wellbeing. I knew I could jump clear if the tree gave way, but she wouldn't stand a chance and go down with the vehicle.

Over the next hour, I managed to dig, crank the jack,

dig, crank the jack until I could drag the kid out from underneath the car and carry her back up onto the roadway. Amazingly enough, she only had superficial injuries. The ambulance transported the girl to the Nambour hospital, and I rode up to the Maleny police station where I had a few rums and got a change of clothes as mine were drenched and covered in mud.

On this occasion, for a change, the girl's parents were extremely grateful for their child's rescue and wrote a letter of appreciation to the police department. There was also a commendation for the excellent work done rescuing the girl, but because it was in the Maleny division, it was assumed that the Maleny cop was the one down the side of the mountain instead of me. He came down to see me not long after the incident and said,

'They think I'm you with this commendation. What do you want to do about it?'

I knew him well, and he was a decent bloke but had managed to blot his copybook in recent months insofar that the local inspector became concerned. I could see he wanted me to let things slide so he could gain some desperately needed brownie points. I thought about it briefly and said,

'You can have this one. I'll keep the next one.'

He was happy with that, and away he went.

LANDSBOROUGH TO THURSDAY ISLAND

Early in 1977, I got a call from the personnel department at police HQ in Brisbane to see if I was interested in going to Thursday Island for twelve months. The entire Thursday Island staff, bar one, had been transferred, and they were looking for blokes like me who'd worked in smaller stations and remote areas. I'd been stationed in Landsborough for eighteen months and was getting tired of dragging dead bodies from fatal collisions. Also, having been on a police motorcycle during all that time, I decided I'd quit while I was ahead as far as a serious spill was concerned. So once again, I packed my bags for yet another transfer.

THURSDAY ISLAND

THURSDAY ISLAND, GETTING THERE

Thursday Island is one of the smaller islands found in the Torres Strait, north of Cape York Peninsula in Queensland. The island, which has an area of three and a half square kilometres, forms part of the Torres Strait Islands archipelago. Thursday Island is also known by its native name Waiben and the abbreviated nickname TI. During my years in the outback service, I learned that everything is more difficult when you live a long way away from civilisation, and even something as simple as finding transport for your dog, can be pretty challenging.

I boarded a train in Landsborough on transfer to my new posting on Thursday Island with my young German shepherd dog Zen. I managed to secure a cage for the dog and a double sleeper for myself on the diesel hauled passenger train The Sunlander. It wound its way along the track up to Cairns in far North Queensland, stopping here and there for an hour or so, during which time, I managed to let Zen off and take him for a run.

The trip up in the second-class sleeper was comfortable enough, and when, at one stage, I heard a commotion, I went and gave the railway blokes a hand, removing a drunk from the train after which I settled back in again.

From Cains, I flew with a Bush Pilots DC3 flight to Bamaga, a small township near the tip of Cape York. The DC3s was a prewar aircraft used extensively throughout the world, especially during WWII, and even though it was slow, it also was reliable. With Zen, the German shepherd, roaming around loose in the luggage compartment adjoining the seating cabin, it made an exciting flight. For the most part, the other passengers thought it a bit of a novelty having such a large dog for company, still, I was glad to touch down at the hot, dusty aerodrome at Bamaga, one of the main Aboriginal communities in the district.

Once again, I was lucky on my travels as a converted former pearling lugger was due to leave the next day on one of its regular twenty-six-mile trips across to Thursday Island. So, after a night at the Bamaga police single men's quarters, Zen and I boarded the lugger for the final leg of a long trip. By now I had been travelling with breaks between transport modes for about a week. The crew on the lugger were frightened of Zen even though he had no animosity towards them, so we remained up at the bow whilst they and a couple of passengers remained at the stern.

Riding on an ex-pearler through some of the most spectacular scenery I had ever encountered certainly made it an exciting and thoroughly enjoyable final leg of my journey. I arrived some hours later at the Thursday Island wharf, where a police officer met me. I would be working with him for the next twelve months. The old police Holden one tonner paddy wagon he was driving had seen better days. However, the rust had not completely taken over, and she still drove ok doing its intended job.

The police barracks, and the station at Thursday Island, were the one building and the typical old original police "station-barracks" combination. The building provided accommodation for five single officers, where we shared a communal kitchen and a tiny twin tub washing machine. There was no air-conditioning, and stoppages to the water supply were a daily occurrence. Thursday Island at the time had a limited water supply, but that hadn't stopped other government departments from moving in along with a hospital, post office and a school. In addition, traders set up businesses and thus, it became the population hub for the entire Torres Straits.

DISTEMPER

The moment I arrived on Thursday Island, I noticed the vast number of dogs who roamed the island entirely out of control. It was so worrying that I soon formed the habit of carrying my revolver when taking Zen for a walk. Outside the town area, the possibility or probability of dog attacks had the locals worried. Then Zen became crook, and the first time I noticed something was wrong was when he threw a fit. He roamed around the police accommodation, was disoriented, and became highly aggressive.

It wasn't looking good and had us worried enough to hide in the toilet, hoping that the snarling wild-eyed dog would settle down. One officer was still asleep on his bunk, and we watched from the toilet as the big dog wandered over to him and sniffed the sleeping figure. We kept quiet, not so much for the dog, but just in case it would wake our sleeping mate who, without a doubt, would be alarmed seeing the wild-looking dog. The fit lasted about ten minutes before he came good. The quarantine prescribed anti-epileptic fit tablets for Zen which seemed to help him.

I had to go to Brisbane to attend a court case, and while I was away, Zen had another attack. The alerted quarantine officer and two nurses snuck up from behind and managed to grab the dog. The chloroform applied was highly potent and resulted in his death. It was extremely unsettling.

The quarantine officer was worried Zen might have become infected with rabies, but this wasn't the case. It turned out that he'd contracted what was known as cerebral distemper upon arrival at the island. The only thing to do for the safety of the community was to eradicate the disease completely. I liaised with community police, the Department of Aboriginal and Islanders Advancement, the council, quarantine officers, and every other Government department, and after I received the all-clear, I organised a round-up.

Taking shotguns and the big council truck, we tracked across the island, rounding up as many wild diseased dogs as we could find. We collected nearly three hundred dogs that day, and to prevent further spreading, we burned their bodies. I can still smell the stench of their diseased burning corpses.

As for me, the whole episode and losing Zen left me devastated. However, I never forgot him, as it was through him that my love for the German shepherd breed was born. Since that day in 1977, I have never been without at least one or two shepherds by my side, and in each one of them, Zen's memory lives on. He was only a young dog when he died, but he had shown me immense loyalty and love in that short time we had been together. That unique bond irrevocably binds humans and dogs together forever.

CAUGHT IN A STORM

One afternoon, there was a severe storm in the Arafura Sea between Thursday Island and the Mainland, and a trawler had been washed ashore in heavy seas near Vrilya Point on the western side of Cape York. Jack, the TI harbour master, rang the station and asked if anyone was available to act as crew on the sixty-three-foot Tanu, the steel harbour master's boat.

He intended to go out to help the beached trawler, so another constable and I went down. Once aboard, we left immediately and headed into the storm in the direction of Vrilya Point. The harbour master said at the outset that it was doubtful that we would get anywhere near the trawler but that he had to give it a go. So we left the shore under extreme conditions, with huge waves crashing mercilessly around us, rocking the boat to an almost tipping point.

There was no seatbelt or tying point up near the wheelhouse, and as I was the wheelman, I heard Jack yell over the deafening sound of the relentless crashing waves,

'Keep the compass on South-West.'

That was easier said than done. Because of the tremendous jolting, I was thrown several times from the wheel and flung like a weightless toy to the other end of the wheelhouse. I remember spending a lot of time on hands and knees, crawling back to the wheel to keep the stern towards the waves. At one stage, the boat heeled too far to one side and driving into the direction of the wind, we thought we were also going to go down. Barely managing to hold on, we succeeded to regain control, and all I could see out in front of me in the gloomy dark was water, and Jack said,

'You're lucky it's dark because those waves are higher than our radar mast.'

They were something like ten meters high, and the situation felt absolutely horrendous! After several hours we had made very little headway.

Then we heard the crew of a second trawler talking on the radio to the harbour master. They'd attempted to reach the crew of the beached trawler but gotten into difficulties and were sinking themselves and were in the process of abandoning ship. They said,

'We have put on our life jackets and are abandoning ship'.

I heard Jack say,

'All the best, men.'

It was surreal. A third trawler then radioed in, stating the crew would try to reach the first two boats. Jack told them not to attempt any rescue as two boats had already gone down and, no doubt, their attempt would make it the third. But as the harbour master had already suspected, we didn't get anywhere near the beached trawler and were covering probably, one mile an hour. The engines screamed wildly, and after eight hours of navigating the wild sea, Jack had to do something to stop us from going down.

He maneuvered the boat towards one of the islands where we moored to wait out the storm. Once we hit the calmer waters, I turned green and felt terribly seasick. Thankfully no one had drowned, and it was nothing short of a miracle that the crews of both boats had managed to make it safely to shore.

BAKED BEANS

I was on duty with Bill when a call came through of a murder. It had happened a few doors up from the police station, with the offender hiding out inside. I grabbed my pump-action shotgun while Bill's weapon of choice was a police revolver, and it didn't take us long to run on foot the short distance to the nominated high set house. I noticed that a lifeless body lay sprawled across several steps at the top of the steep, narrow staircase leading to the front door.

With great difficulty, we clambered over the dead bloke up to the front door and to add to the challenge, it was dark as buggery. Usually, things like this happen on the night of a full moon. Somehow, it tends to bring the worse out in people, but not this particular night. Once on the landing, Bill and I kicked the front door open and charged in with shotgun and pistol at the ready. Our objective was to neutralise or take into custody whoever was inside. These jobs are hazardous as there is no knowing what we will find behind closed doors. The total darkness in which we had to operate added another dangerous element.

There was a bloke inside I had seen around the place, nicknamed, Baked Beans. He'd acquired the name during his employment as a cook at various locations. His employers were only too happy to have found a man willing cook, overlooking that Baked Beans' culinary expertise was limited to only dishing up many variations of baked beans.

Upon our entrance into the dimly lit room, Baked Beans immediately stood up and simultaneously raised his hands in surrender. We lowered our firearms as it was apparent that he had no intention of offering any resistance. He admitted to stabbing the man whose body was lying on the stairs outside. Hence, I issued the standard warning regarding making statements, which can be used in evidence. He was arrested and taken into custody, and that was just what he wanted before anyone else, like friends or relatives of the victim, could get to him to extract their retribution.

I had encountered similar situations before, where perpetrators just about handcuffed themselves and begged to be removed from the scene. The jail was a safer option, away from friends, neighbours, relatives, and direct family of the victim. Baked Beans had killed this bloke with a single knife thrust, either accidental or lucky, between the ribs, driving the blade straight into the heart of his victim. Either that, or he had maybe previous training, as in a military background, this I never found out.

CORAL POISONING

I had never heard of coral poisoning before going to Thursday Island, but that changed the moment an old fisherman with a weathered face stopped by the station one morning. The short run up the beach to the police station had him gasping for breath, and he told me that he had seen a bloke on a trawler who was looking worse for wear. He had tried to convince the man to come ashore with him, but the trawler owner refused. After discussing the flu and rash-like symptoms, the old fisherman was sure the bloke suffered from coral poisoning.

The boat was moored only a short distance from the shore, and using binoculars, I saw no movement onboard, so I decided to investigate. I thanked the old fisherman for reporting the incident and raced down to the beach where I "borrowed" one of the dinghies lying on the beach. Thankfully, the waters were calm, making the row out to the trawler relatively easy.

It was hard to miss the huge man lying unconscious in the wheelhouse, and I knew there and then that getting this bloke from the wheelhouse and over the side rails into a dinghy would be extremely difficult. I dragged the unconscious man by the arms out onto the deck and managed to heave the uncooperative body onto the side rails.

There was no time to fabricate lowering slings and straps, so I gave him a push, and with a heavy thud, he landed into the dinghy. I jumped in after him and started the row back to shore. Relieved, I spotted the waiting ambulance on the beach, and I silently thanked the old fisherman for alerting them. The coral poisoned victim was transported to the hospital in a critical condition.

The hospital rang me later to let me know that the man survived because of my quick action, and I learned that coral toxins could cause severe problems for human beings. He made a speedy recovery, and a few days later, was discharged. I had hoped to catch up with him but heard that he had left the island and realised that this was simply another one who hadn't dropped in to say, "thank you". I never saw him again.

FAMILY LOST AT SEA

During my time on Thursday Island, I gained experience across many levels of police work due to low staffing and the island's isolation. There were no experts on hand for everything that happened, and I realised from the beginning that, working in these out-of-the-way communities, I became the expert on all levels. It could get full-on most of the time, and as it turned out, this very day was no different.

Someone raised the alarm that a group of four adults and four children had left Thursday Island near sunset and had pushed off from the shore in a small dinghy. There was great concern as they had not arrived at their intended destination, Horn Island. These small dinghies had outboard motors far too small for the nine-kilometre trip. Lifejackets were not a consideration back then nor an Emergency Position Indicating Radio Beacon, known as "EPIRB". The local inhabitants possessed superior levels of seamanship, passed down the line throughout the generations. Dependent upon this ability to gather food, this inherited skill was necessary for their survival. Nevertheless, the situation outlined was a big ask, even for these experienced seamen.

I boarded one of the Torres Straits Pilot boats to join in the sea search looking for the missing group. I scanned the waters throughout the night with the powerful boat searchlight gliding over the water where it sometimes met the light beam projected from another boat. We also realised that if the lost group saw the lights, we wouldn't hear their voices because of the horrendous noise of the tidal waves. There was no doubt that the small dinghy, enveloped by darkness, had possibly overturned at some stage during their perilous journey, and if that were the case, the eight occupants wouldn't stand a chance in the shark-infested waters of the Torres Strait. We feared the worst, and hopes of finding the group alive diminished with every passing hour.

Then, amazingly enough, in the daylight hours, the group was located. Somehow, they had managed to grab hold of the overturned dinghy and place all four children on top. You've got to hand it to the adults for the action they took as they managed to hang onto the dinghy. It had travelled with the tide, first in one direction, and when the tide turned, in the opposite direction. For twelve hours, the dinghy and the survivors, sitting on top and clinging to it, were at the mercy of the racing speed of a Torres Strait tide reaching eight knots.

It was a relief to see them alive, attached to the overturned dinghy that had travelled about twenty-three miles since capsizing. They were pulled from the water and hauled on board one of the Torres Straits Pilot boats. All involved in the search realised that this was an incredible outcome of survival in what could have been a multiple fatality and tragic incident at sea.

PRISONER ESCAPE

Mondo was a big, aggressive bloke who escaped from the watchhouse when someone had come in to deliver his meal. He'd pushed past the unaware guard and taken off at speed, disappearing into the darkness. So, first thing at daylight, a team of police and I set out to start the search in the hills up behind the settlement. I knew of a quarry where some of these blokes liked to hang out, so I asked to be dropped off and decided to head up on foot towards the top. It was slow going as the growth was waist-high.

They must've been watching because suddenly two figures jumped out in front of me, Mondo, and his girlfriend, who was not your ordinary girl and was much bigger than me. Her worn out singlet of questionable colour allowed for the display of two strong arms, and when she grinned at me, I noticed that quite a few of her teeth were missing. Mondo flashed a large hunting knife, and his girlfriend brandished a massive lump of wood.

In my peripheral vision, I could see the police truck way down deep in the distance, turning around and driving off to continue their search on the other side of the hill. I felt very alone at that stage.

'You will have to come with me Mondo.' I said, 'If you don't, I have to shoot you.'

'You wouldn't shoot me.' he shouted.

I replied, 'Well fucking watch this.'

I pulled out my short-barreled, police thirty-eight Special and fired two shots into the air. The noise, smoke, and bits of flack that the gun produced terrified them both. Their faces went a grey colour, and slowly they dropped their weapons. It was a close call because this is where my revolver jammed up. The barrel had a slight visible bend to it, so I quickly put the thirty-eight back into my holster and said,

'The next one will be through your guts Start walking.'

Back at the barracks, in my rush, I had grabbed a handful of ammunition from my bedside table and loaded my revolver, not realising that I had taken the modified cartridges by mistake. They were like mini shotgun cartridges, quite lethal at close range but more for shooting snakes, and they obviously had too much powder in them. My mate from the Department of Aboriginal and Islanders Advancement workshop made them for me, and I really needed to have a word with him at the earliest opportunity.

I marched Mondo, followed by his girlfriend, down the hill, and at the bottom, I found another five massive blokes waiting for us. They were Mondo's gang. These blokes usually ran around in an old Jeep that had seen better days, so I said to one of them,

'Get your Jeep. We are going to the police station.'

Then I whispered in Mondo's ear,

'Remember any problems, and you will be the first man to die.'

Of course, they all decided to come along, so now I had five burley blokes, plus Mondo and his girlfriend and me getting into the Jeep. As we headed back towards the police station, I spotted the police truck, again going the other way! I thought,

'This is the second time backup is moving in the opposite direction.'

It was fortunate that one of the constables happened to look in our direction and spotted the blue shirt among all these massive island blokes.

The police truck turned around, and the officers looked quite bemused when the old Jeep creaked to a halt with these big blokes spilling from it. Myself, I was not as bemused but relieved that a very stressful morning had come to a successful end.

MURDER AT CLOSE RANGE

I had been called back to the mainland to attend a court case at Landsborough. I grabbed the opportunity to look for another dog and was lucky to find a six-month-old German shepherd for sale. I named him Shiloh and took him back with me to Thursday Island. My daily routine was an early morning run with Shiloh into the rugged hills behind the main settlement. The elevations offered a challenging workout for both of us and provided brilliant panoramic views of the island and the Torres Strait beyond. The altitude gave a clear view of the road below, and I knew there was trouble brewing when I sighted the old police ute winding its way up the hill. Trumby, one of the constables, pulled up next to me and shouted through the open window,

'A woman has been shot on Horn Island. Sorry to cut your walk short Pete, but you've got to come with us.'

I didn't hesitate and said to Shiloh,

'Get in the back.'

I jumped in next to Trumby, who first swung by the station, so that I could grab my shotgun and drop Shiloh off. Five officers and the ambo were waiting for us aboard the police boat at the wharf, holding the always reliable twenty horsepower twin outboards at idle. Though Horn Island had a sizeable well-maintained airstrip, manned by a Civil Aviation Authority employee, the only way to travel between the group of smaller islands was per boat. Once onboard, the driver skillfully navigated the seven-kilometre stretch of the Torres Strait that separated the two islands.

Upon arrival, a small four-wheel-drive bus was waiting for us, which took us across several dirt tracks. The driver drew to a halt in a clearing near an old shed that had seen better days. Most of the old, rusted corrugated iron sheets were barely holding on and very visible, even from this distance, were the narrow channels of mud that wound their way up along the timber posts, the tell-tale signs of destructive white ant activity. With their insatiable appetite, I had seen entire bush shacks crumble, and by the looks of it, this shack was heading the same way.

We sat there for a while, trying to gauge the situation, and it was hard to tell who was inside. Horn Island was inhabited by many cultures, including Papua New Guinea Islanders, Indigenous people, and some Europeans. Some people in this mix were of dubious character. It was eerily quiet, except for the rustling of windblown leaves and the occasional distant calls of seabirds. In the distance, a rickety old deck chair sat in front of the entrance to the old shack and on it lay a still figure. Experience told us that we could do nothing for this injured or possibly deceased person until the shed had been cleared. Therefore, it was imperative that we first neutralise and disarm the persons inside. Speed of action was paramount and potentially could save lives, and after a quick briefing, a plan was put in place.

Bill and I were to storm the shed and take care of whatever problem was on the other side of the door. The others would remain at the edge of the clearing waiting for our all-clear signal. Bill was a reliable bloke, the one you would want to have with you when things get rough. So, the two of us took off at a gallop towards the shed. I carried my Bentley twenty-inch barrel pump-action shotgun, my personal choice of weapon, and Bill his police revolver. To take a shotgun was not a problem back in the seventies, with the boss being aware and approving of the practice.

We were going flat strap. The idea was to jump over the inert form on the sunbed, kick or shoulder the door in, and arrest the person or persons hiding out inside. This plan almost came unstuck as, at the second we jumped over the body, the woman sat up, with eyes wide open. We almost went arse overhead trying to clear the extra height. Managing to maintain balance, we crashed through the door knocking it entirely off its hinges.

We found one suspect named Bernie inside, and it became very quickly apparent that he had no intention of offering any resistance. He had been waiting for us to arrive as he felt in desperate need of protection. To us, it was very understandable and with good reason that Bernie felt fearful. He was more than aware that the relatives of his girlfriend, whom he had just shot at close range with a shotgun, would be seeking retribution. He surrendered immediately, and we took him into custody. The victim, an Aboriginal woman from the Gulf country, drew her last breath and died as we were jumping over her.

An autopsy revealed that wadding from the cartridge had embedded itself in her liver, indicating that she was shot at close range. Bernie was duly charged with murder but entered a plea of manslaughter as he claimed that the lady had been "belting the shit out of him with a golf club". He'd grabbed the firearm with the hope to frighten her off when it discharged, and even though it was only birdshot, it was lethal at close range. Bernie was locked up and did twelve long months behind bars.

We were never sure why he returned to Normanton,

a small town on the Norman River in Northwest Queensland, from where his deceased girlfriend had originated. All her relatives lived there, and not long after arriving at Normanton, Bernie went missing, never to be seen again. The reason for his disappearance has always remained a mystery. Speculations made at the time were that he might've become a meal for one of the many large estuarine crocodiles that inhabit the Norman River, or perhaps payback, that we will never know.

THE PADDY WAGON SNAKE

One evening we received a call, that there was a disturbance up at the pub.
'A big fight's going on, and it's not looking good. Please hurry.' The caller shouted down the phone.'

As you can imagine, it gets crowded when five large police officers all pile up in the station's old one-ton police paddy wagon. We'd only gone a few meters when someone yelled,

'Snake!'

There weren't too many snakes on Thursday Island, so it was a mystery at first where this one had come from. We suspected that some of the New Guinea blokes who used to travel by dinghy at night from Horn Island had caught a snake and put it in the police van for a laugh. So, in order to get the five officers in the police car, they made the bogus phone call alerting us to a massive fight in the pub. We were driving up the road when that snake became very lively.

It must've been quite a sight to see with five constables jumping in every direction from the mobile vehicle, and it became a case of every man for himself. It didn't help that it was a moonless night, and as far as we were concerned, all snakes are taipans in the dark. From behind the bushes, the hoax callers were watching us thinking it was hilarious. They deservedly got a good laugh and story, which no doubt, has been retold many a time.

SCOTTY'S REVENGE

I got to know Scotty when he was a prison officer. He decided to quit his job to pursue his dreams and opened his own little hardware store. It was a success from day one, and Scotty became a very busy man. From time to time, I used to have a beer with him and his island-born wife.

Now there were whispers in town that his wife was seeing someone else on the side, making this a complicated situation, as it isn't a massive island and, to top it off, one where everyone knows everyone. Scotty became obsessed with this problem and wanted to get back at the bloke seeing his wife. Finally, one night he decided he had enough. So to get square with this bloke, he crept up to his white station wagon and set fire to it, burning it to the ground.

What Scotty didn't seem to be aware of was that there were two identical cars on the island, both white station wagons with one of them belonging to the bloke that was seeing his wife, the other to an unaware, innocent schoolteacher. On the night of the inferno, he got the cars confused, which resulted in him creeping up to the teacher's car and setting fire to it.

The following day Scotty came straight out with it and said with absolute satisfaction,

'I paid the bloody cheat back.'

I said calmly,

'Scotty, wrong car. You didn't do your homework properly.'

It took a while, but when the truth dawned on him, you should've seen the poor bastard's face. Unfortunately, this mistake cost him significantly, and Scotty got a few years behind bars out of it.

THE ESCAPED LEPER

There was an old building about a kilometre away from the main settlement. Nobody went near it as an unfortunate soul suffering from advanced leprosy, an infectious disease that causes skin sores and nerve damage, lived there. I had read about this disease in primary school, and there was still the stigma attached to it that leprosy caused flesh to rot and toes and fingers to drop off. There had been a time, with the need for a leprosarium, to isolate the infected people, as the disease was deemed highly contagious and untreatable. Needless to say, that I preferred not to go near the building or its sole occupant other than taking an occasional phone call informing me that the "leper had escaped".

I figured that obviously, the disease must have been contagious. Otherwise, no one would've worried about this bloke, and calls to re-capture him, would not have been made. Instead, every time the leper did a runner, the community police took off in a vehicle to locate the absconder and return him to his domicile.

Though leprosy, not as contagious as once feared, has not been eradicated, what has, is the stigma that surrounded it at the time.

THE FLOATING BODY

Police frequently receive calls to many situations countrywide. The location of a case has a significant effect on how that situation is approached and handled. In the 1970s, the facilities, equipment and resources were entirely different from what is in place today. Take the case of the floating dead body. One morning, a call came through that someone had seen a body floating down near the pier, so Geoff and I went down to investigate. The body was of a man reported missing and was last seen, not far from where we were now, which made it that he had fallen into the ocean about a week earlier.

When a person drowns, the body, as a rule, after the lungs fill with water, always sinks to the bottom. Generally, it resurfaces after two to three days due to the accumulation of gas produced during decomposition and floats away with the tide to turn up miles away from where the victim initially fell into the water. This couldn't have happened here as the body had surfaced at the same location as the man had been reported as last seen. Therefore, it had most likely been trapped by some underwater obstacle, thus avoiding being carried away by the strong tides that flow between Thursday and Horn Island.

Looking down at the floating body, we both knew that we had no choice. Somehow, we had to grab the corpse and lift it out of the water, which wasn't easy after a week in tropical seawater. There was extensive decomposition, and getting a grip on the body was extremely difficult as flesh came away in our hands each time we tried to grip the floating corpse. The smell was horrendous. Finally, we worked out that we could haul it onto the landing by grabbing hold of the available clothing left on the body. It was hard to contain the persisting rising nausea in my throat as the smell of rotting flesh filled the air. I don't know what Geoff did with his uniform, but I promptly burnt mine.

Routine police procedures involved the body's retrieval and transportation to the hospital morgue. Police were also required to attend the autopsy, followed by the relevant investigation and furnishing of reports. The location and nature of this situation had one further step which I had not experienced before and thankfully never did again.

The deceased was a resident and was known to the hospital ward staff. Some of the medical team were related to him and refused to assist in the autopsy. Not many guesses are required as to who exactly gets asked to put on the rubber apron and gloves and stand in as a post-mortem assistant. While the smell had not diminished, and with a large syringe in hand, I collected the required specimens of urine and blood samples. My concentration was broken when I heard the young doctor in charge of the examination swear loudly. He informed me that he had pricked himself with an infected needle. Ripping off his rubber gloves and with a high strength disinfectant, he repeatedly scrubbed his hands. The skin started to turn blood red, and I knew that a possible hepatitis infection was running through his mind.

After my investigations, I found that no suspicious circumstances surrounded this sad event, and it was classed as a "misadventure". However, as many police officers do, I did attend several post-mortem examinations over the years, but just as an observer.

WAYWARD BULLETS IN THE NIGHT

There were five of us residing in the barracks when, one late evening, we heard a loud report from a rifle, followed by the actual audible sound of a bullet zip past. The gunshot got our immediate attention, so I quickly donned my black overalls and grabbed my pump-action shotgun and waited for the arrival of the two sergeants, who lived nearby in government-supplied residences. Only seconds later, a phone call came through to the effect that a man named Harvick, who resided in the Department of Aboriginal and Islanders Advancement barracks, had a .303 rifle and had fired it in the direction of the police station. The plan was that the two sergeants and three constables would go into the DAIA complex and approach the room where the shooter was hiding out. Bill and I were to climb up onto the rainwater tank around the back, next to Harvick's room and from there, we would access the permanently open vent in the wall.

When we were ready, we left the police station and melded in with the dark shadows provided by the bushes and buildings. The DAIA quarters were in the same street as the hospital and police station, where a hedge bordered the yard of the manager's residence. I saw a slight movement up across the road from the police station, and dropping down flat on the ground, I snaked across, taking my shotgun with me. Upon approach, I could see the outline of a man concealed in the shadows. He was oblivious of my advancement, and when I sprang to my feet directly in front of him wielding a riot gun, he suffered a tremendous fright. I brought the shotgun up into a firing position, ripping the buttons off the front of his shirt as I did so, saying,

'If you move, I blow your fucking head off.'

He whimpered, 'I'm not moving.'
'Name?' I demanded.
'Frank Barlow.'
'What are you doing here?'
'I heard the noise, the gunshot, so I came out to help.'

I said, 'You have no idea what you're dealing with here. Get inside and fucking stay there.'

Barlow had a revolver on him, and fortunately for him, he didn't flash it. If he had, the situation could've escalated, and my response would've been quite different.

Covered by darkness, we snuck among the bushes and around the building, pinpointing the area where Harvick was hiding out. We split up with the other police moving to the front of the building and Bill and I climbing on top of the water tank around the back. From there, we moved to the skylight vent, purposed to let air in but not any rain. We could see Harvick inside and the .303 lying on the bed. Slowly, as not to make a noise, I brought the shotgun up and pointed it at him through the vent. The ceilings in some of these old buildings are very high, which was in our favour, because of the height and angle he couldn't see us. There was a loud booming noise at the front door, and I heard the sergeant yell,

'Open up! Police!'

From my position in the skylight, I saw that Harvick went for his rifle. I roared,

'Harvick! Leave the fucking gun alone and get on the floor now!'

I could see him whip his head around in the direction of my voice, and looking up, he could see the barrel of my shotgun pointing at him. Now that's enough to convince most people to do as they're told, and on having been on the wrong end of the barrel myself, I know it's quite frightening, to say the least. Harvick, not wanting to be blown apart, must've been thinking the same because he immediately obliged with my request and went to the floor. Upon my call,

'He's down, all clear.'

The police out the front forced the door open and took Harvick into custody. The revolver carrying individual, Barlow, whom I had encountered earlier in the hedges, turned out to be the DAIA manager. I had a few drinks in the bar one night and listened with interest as he recounted the 'gunshot night' story to a small crowd in the bar. I overheard Barlow say,

'I never learned who that cop was that ripped the buttons of my shirt with the barrel before pointing the shotgun at my head. But I have my suspicions.'

He looked over at me, implying it could've been me, but I never made any admissions. However, he had no animosity whatsoever and dined out on the story many times, including with the then Premier of Queensland, Joh Bjelke-Petersen.

THE BADU ISLAND RAPE

Badu Island, also known as Mulgrave Island, is one of the larger inhabited Torres Strait Islands. I had just finished my breakfast at the Thursday Island Police Station when I received a call from the senior sergeant.

'We've got a rape on Badu Island', he said, 'I want you to go over there Pete and investigate the situation. The sergeant will come with you'.

He added that the crime had happened thirty-six hours earlier and that a DAIA staff member had gone to Badu in an attempt to cover the matter up. DAIA's main concern was to get the nurse to withdraw her complaint.

If this occurrence became public knowledge, it would become even more challenging to recruit trained nurses for the islands in the Torres Strait. It was desirable to have a couple of trained nurses at every small first-aid post. These competent nurses could handle any minor problem, and if the injuries were outside their capabilities, they'd organise transportation to the better-equipped hospital of Thursday Island.

It didn't take long for us to cover the sixty kilometres in the small plane, and as the island came into view, I saw areas of basalt rock formations and open expanses of sparse vegetation. From the air, it was easy to spot the hostile mangrove swamps that ringed the island. Upon landing, three appointed community police who handled the island's disturbances, filled us in on the details.

The island had two competent nurses who were partners. At the time of the incident, one of them had left the island to shop for groceries, while the other stayed back to look after the medical post. Undercover of darkness, the three perpetrators waited for her. One of them went up to the nurses' living accommodation and knocked on the door, claiming to feel sick. So she took him down to the first-aid post, where, unbeknownst to her, two other blokes were waiting for her. The three of them had raped this girl multiple times.

I recorded the details in my notebook and took photos of anything and everything that could be used as evidence. But, unfortunately, most of the crime scene had been altered and disturbed by the DAIA staff member. So, there wasn't all that much to go on. The local community police had apprehended all three offenders and handed them over to us. We continued our investigations and separately interviewed the suspects. The whole affair took a lot of time as the interviews needed to be recorded manually in a notebook, and as darkness engulfed us, we had to content ourselves with a kerosene lamp. We also realised that it was too late for the small service plane to fly us back to Thursday Island.

'Looks like we are stuck on Badu for the night.' I said.

We finished the interviews with the three perpetrators and faced the problem of what to do with them? So we decided the best thing was to handcuff them together with two pairs of handcuffs, taking turns keeping watch, sitting across from them in the dark.

We sat there with a revolver at the ready, so if one of them tried to escape, they'd all suffer for it. It was a very long night, and at midday the following day, an aircraft came to pick us up and transport us back to Thursday Island.

The offenders were charged through the court and released on a five-hundred-dollar bail. After paying bail, these blokes thought that all was over and done with and went back to Badu Island. The nurse was interviewed at the Thursday Island police station and examined by a doctor and the Cairns Base Hospital. Upon her return, she came into the police station and said,

'I'm going back out to Badu Island.'

I said, 'I wouldn't do that if I were you.'

She replied flippantly, 'Oh no, that's fine, I get on well with them.'

Upon her insistence to go back there, I told her,

'I think you'll find that the situation is different now, but, as you are set on going anyway, there's only one way for you to find out, I guess.'

So, she left only to return the very next day saying,

'You were right. There's a great deal of animosity towards me now.'

As it turned out, I was going to Cairns on an aircraft, so I accompanied her and made sure that she boarded a connecting flight to Sydney. I didn't see her again until the court case sometime later.

In the meantime, there was a bit of political interference in the case. The government was more concerned to keep this matter quiet. Their main concern was that they might have trouble recruiting nurses for isolated communities if the story got around. But justice had to be done, so we went to court and were given a tough time. The prosecutor was a former policeman and set on a guilty verdict, and thus, the three rapists were convicted to five years jail each. However, there was an appeal against the sentencing, but it was to no avail as each of them was given an extra couple of years, so now they were sent off for seven years.

But unlike the three criminals, the nurse had been given a life sentence, as the trauma of the rape, undoubtedly, will haunt her for the rest of her life.

THE BAR FIGHT

Some blokes of the Torres Strait are huge, or for a better word, giants and as in any community, there's the good and the bad. My encounter with the bad that day is one I will never forget.

One of these giants weighed in at one hundred and sixty kilos, measured one metre ninety, and was therefore rightfully nicknamed Goliath. He was notorious for making trouble, and when he played up, it scared everyone; even the police tried to avoid him.

I was on duty that evening and received a call from the local hotel that Goliath was playing up. It was Saturday afternoon, and the hotels crowded with locals and government employees who worked on the Island. There was one other constable in the barracks, and, jumping in the police van, we left for the hotel. Upon entering, we see this giant of a man stalking around inside the crowded bar looking exceptionally dangerous. I wasn't feeling courageous, and everyone was watching what was going to happen. I was muscular and fit, but only half of the monster's weight. Standing immediately in front of Goliath, I stared at him and said calmly,

'Get out.'

He said, 'I throw you out.'

To me, this sounded like "game on". My evaluation of the big bloke told me that he must have had several drinks. I could also tell by his attitude that he figured this would be a quick and easy victory for him. Goliath had a cleanly shaven head and ming moustache and wasn't wearing a shirt. I could tell that he enjoyed the attention as he projected a terrifying spectacle by flexing his muscles.

He then took a mighty swing at me, but I managed to deflect the blow, which would have been a decisive game-ender for me. However, in my opinion, he had made two colossal mistakes, one, throwing the first punch and two, missing his target. I caught him off balance and grabbed his massive left arm, using it to leap up onto his back. I then grabbed him in a stranglehold and locked on. If Troy Dunn, the bull riding champion, would've seen me in action, I would have been recruited on the spot. Riding on the back of this monster would be no different to riding bulls like Chain Saw and Hot Rod at the Mount Isa Rodeo. He roared and crashed around the bar of the hotel, scattering patrons as he went, while I held on riding on his back. He was huge, with not much experience in being strangled, but then not many blokes have, I suppose. After a short time, I felt his maddened struggles weaken as he fought for breath, and slowly, he dropped to his knees.

I immediately released the pressure on his throat, and he dropped to the floor of the bar. Game over. Not wanting to allow him to get back up to continue the fight, I grabbed him by the feet and dragged him out to the van via the front door to the sound of the crowd chanting,

'Kill the cunt! Kill the cunt!'

At the police station, however, Goliath came good, and when I opened the rear door of the police van, it seemed as though he was up for another go. However, Goliath wasn't as quick as he had been earlier, so I put him into a restraining hold and dragged him up into the watch house, charged him and put him in the cells. He entered a guilty plea and forfeited his bail.

I went back up to the hotel where the publican slapped me on the back, exclaiming,

'I've never seen anything like that before.'

He owned several pubs in Queensland, so he roared,

'You'll never pay for a beer in any one of my pubs again, my son.'

So did I managed to visit all of his four pubs? The answer is yes. I did so at different times over the next couple of years, and the publican was true to his word as every time again, upon hearing my name, the beer flowed generously and free.

I came across Goliath on several occasions after that. He was quite friendly, and he had no animosity towards me.

THE NURSE AND THE ISLANDER

One morning, a call came through to the police station advising of a suicide, so I immediately jumped into the police car and made my way to the site. The small crowd that had gathered surrounded a Holden ute and parted just enough to let me through. Peering through the window, I saw the deceased body of a young male slumped forward in the driving seat. In his hands was a .22 calibre rifle. One finger was inside the trigger guard while the gun barrel was resting in a bloodied, empty eye socket where his right eye once would've been. My investigations revealed that the situation was indeed what it appeared to be, the tragic suicide of a twenty-one-year-old male. After the body was transferred to the morgue, I continued my enquiries, and the story of what had gone on before slowly began to unfold.

The deceased had been in a relationship with a nurse who worked at the hospital, and she'd ended the relationship with him for reasons unknown. Sometime during the night, the young fellow had driven out to the site, parked his car, and had shot himself through the eye. The incident was one of those tragic events where a young man takes his life over a failed relationship. I felt at the time that, as bad as the situation already was, when taking into consideration the interracial aspect, it could get a lot worse, and I wasn't wrong in my assessment. Back at the station, I pointed this out to my colleagues. We agreed that the priority was to obtain the relevant details to fill out the necessary paperwork, and the only way to get this sorted was to go and talk with the deceased family.

Since I'd been on Thursday Island, I made a few friendships. The result was that I was considered to be the sixth brother in the Akiba family from Saibai Island, and the adopted brother of David Musu. I also regularly socialised with men from the Mills family from Mills Island. With those 'credentials' plus the fact I was the oldest of the constables at twenty-seven and had one stripe, I was the logical choice to go out there and obtain the details. I heard someone ask,

'Are you taking your gun?'

This was an absolute negative as it would have been incredibly insulting. Not even to mention provocative to a grieving family, especially when we weren't in the habit of carrying firearms unless a situation expressly demanded it. I drove round to the family home, and the situation which presented itself upon my arrival was pretty much what I had anticipated.

Many grieving relatives and friends had gathered at the house, and upon my alighting from the vehicle, they went quiet. The silence was deafening. Hatred was too strong a word; however, the extreme hostility and resentment towards me were unmistakable. Like the young woman they obviously felt was responsible for their son's death, I was a White person.

I walked straight up to the deceased's father and briefly expressed my condolences for their tragic loss. I explained that I needed some details for my paperwork so their son's body could be released to them, and I could leave them to grieve and prepare for the burial. The father was civil to me, and as soon as the paperwork was in order, I made my leave feeling very relieved. I have never been so happy to walk away from a situation as I was that day. The hostility was palpable.

On my return to the station, the matron of the hospital wanted to speak with me. She was well respected in the community and had been living on Thursday Island for decades. I frequently enjoyed a beer or two with her at the Bowls Club, where the discussion often turned to the island.

'I like it here,' she'd told me many times, adding, 'Truth be known, I'll probably never leave.'

I went up to her office, and after a brief discussion, we decided that the young nurse involved had best leave the island, and it was to be done promptly for her safety.

The girl quite naively didn't think that was necessary, but matron told her sternly that her seat on the plane was booked for the following morning.

'The constable will escort you to the ferry, which will take you to Horn Island. A car will be waiting there to take you to the airport. Now go and pack your things.'

I kept my revolver in my overalls pocket as there was something I didn't like about the whole situation. The nurse was very aggressive and nasty towards me for making her leave. She wasn't at all happy about being railroaded out of place back to her hometown. She told me so several times, right up until I walked her onto the ferry.

Later that night, a large number of women stormed the nurse's quarters, intent on revenge. However, they were unaware that the subject of their grief and rage had already gone, and what could have been a dire situation evaporated. The women withdrew back into the darkness of the night. However, the tension on the island remained and was felt in the community for quite some time.

Some weeks later, I received a handwritten letter from the young woman. She apologised for her naivety and thanked me for what I had done for her.

CAIRNS

TRANSFER PERILS

After eighteen months on Thursday Island, I looked forward to a change of scenery. My dog Shiloh, my motorcycle and my luggage were all that needed transport. Transfers are often fraught with difficulties, and one from an isolated place like Thursday Island in the Torres Straits to the Police District Headquarters in Cairns in North Queensland was no different.

I planned to hitch a ride on a prawn trawler, but I got word that this was impossible as it would take too long. So instead, I would be travelling on the police Cessna from the Police Air Wing, but unfortunately, my dog was not allowed to travel on the aircraft. So instead, he was to travel by boat, and with mixed feelings, I booked him in and watched him disappear into the distance as he sat forlornly on the trawler deck. My motorcycle went on the barge while I boarded the police plane.

We took off and headed first for the small town of Weipa before heading south towards Cairns, along the commercial airline route. Unfortunately, the airport was covered in thick clouds, and we were forced to circle and search for a break in the cover. To top it off, upon touchdown, I felt a lurch and realised that the plane had blown a tyre. The pilot skillfully nursed the plane down the tarmac, and we got out unharmed, but it would be four days before a replacement tyre turned up. Unfortunately, it left me stranded in Weipa for the duration, with nothing much to do. I slept in the single men's barracks and had access to the mess hall. I've noticed during my life that if shit is going to happen, it invariably does so when I am in the immediate vicinity. Yet again, this was no exception.

I decided to work the evening shift with one of the local blokes, and within an hour of starting, we got a report of a murder where a domestic argument had gone wrong. A man had returned home to find his evening meal wasn't prepared. He wasn't at all happy about it, so he beat his wife to death with a pick handle.

I had minimal involvement in this tragic incident which led to the man being charged with the murder of the poor woman. He later pleaded guilty to manslaughter in the Cairns Circuit Court, where the accused was genuinely remorseful for his actions. However, I've never forgotten the circumstance of mitigation offered by his defence counsel. Which was, the offender had removed the head of the pick before striking his wife with the handle.

The replacement parts for the aircraft finally arrived, and the plane was made airworthy again. We took off and landed without further incident at the Cairns airport, where a sergeant was waiting for me, and after I'd settled in, I went around to collect my motorcycle. It looked scratched and worse for wear, and there was no doubt that they very obviously had forgotten to secure it, so it had slid back and forth along the bottom of the cargo hold for the entire trip down. My car was coming up by train from the Glass House Mountains and hadn't arrived either, and as my motorcycle had not been fitted with a sidecar to transport my dog, my only option was to hire a Mini Moke.

A couple of nights later, I wandered around town, and not far from the unit I was staying in, I came across my dog Shiloh tied up to a parking meter. I could tell by the noise and laughter spilling from the pub that the trawler crew were inside. They had taken a couple of days longer than they had expected, and after arriving and tying up, they headed with the dog to the nearest hotel. I joined them, and after sharing a few beers while listening to their tall tales, I thanked them and left with my dog.

It took a further fortnight of going back and forth to the railway yards before eventually my ute was found. Loaded onto a flat wagon which needed repairs, cargo and all had been taken to a workshop in Rockhampton, over one thousand kilometres South from where it was supposed to be.

I wasn't looking forward to starting work in a large station like Cairns. I was beginning to experience episodes of anxiety, which, at the time, I didn't know were early symptoms of Post-Traumatic Stress Disorder. The cause of my PTSD was directly related to the prolonged traumatic experiences and distressing events that came with my line of work.

THE FIRST SHIFT

My first shift started at midnight. I was to be the third man in a patrol car, not so much for weight of numbers, but more to give me an idea of the city's layout. I had been in small stations, but they were absolutely nothing like Cairns in terms of policing. Not being used to city living and policing, I was happy enough to sit quietly in the back of the car, looking out the window taking in my new surroundings. The two blokes I was with had a different mindset to mine.

They stopped the vehicle at the northern end of the

esplanade, which had a grassed area dotted with various trees, including coconut trees. Many of them had coconuts on them, and these two blokes stated an interest in getting some of them down. Now, these coconuts were out of reach for someone on the ground, and it was apparent that this was where they would stay. The useless conversation that was taking place about how to get them down was starting to irritate me, so I thought I'd put an end to it. Up to now, I hadn't uttered more than a few words, so I said,

'I'll get them down for you.'

With that, I reached for my service revolver, thus indicating that I was going to shoot them down. These blokes almost had a heart attack and somewhat panicked they said,

'You can't do that. This is Cairns, not Thursday Island.'

The next few hours, these two blokes surreptitiously kept looking in the rear vision mirror and over their shoulders, obviously concerned at what sort of wild bloke they had in the car with them. I just sat quietly in the back, looking out the window again, happy with my little prank, wondering how anyone could possibly believe I would start blazing away at coconuts on the Esplanade in Cairns.

After working in isolated areas, I was having trouble adjusting to policing in a large coastal city station. Although Cairns wasn't the biggest station in the state, it was for me, and even though the other police were good to work with, I still would rather be in a smaller place. The city itself was very laid back at the time, with a population of around fifty thousand. Nevertheless, it was a friendly place to live, the type where you walked around the city streets, and though not knowing people by name, you recognised their faces.

City police stations didn't have barracks like in the

outback stations, so instead, we were required to find our own accommodation, which I found at a hotel in the suburb of Redlynch, a cane farming community on the city's northern outskirts.

Living permanently at the pub in an upstairs room had many advantages. Still, these were overshadowed by the downsides, which besides the care of my large German shepherd dog, was the tendency for locals to wander upstairs to see, or I felt like a drink or two.

One of the kitchen requirements was collecting watercress for use on sandwiches, which grew abundantly around the railway station. Board at the pub included a daily cut lunch to take to work in addition to two other meals. All up, the cost for the week for bed and food was thirty-five bucks a week. It was a friendly little community, and I had plenty of mates, among them, a couple of old railway blokes who took me for a ride on the old, motorised railway motor-trolley. They used it to check the Kuranda rail line, used by the tourist steam train, which wound its way around the mountain through the world's oldest living tropical rainforest.

We travelled on the trolley to the halfway point to an unmanned station near a tunnel, and I was struck by the difficulties the railway-line gang back then would've faced with the initial construction of the line. Within the pristine world heritage listed rainforest, the terrain would've required, no doubt, a lot of men with picks and shovels. I have never forgotten the peaceful and breathtaking scenery I was so fortunate to have seen.

As the weeks passed, I was rostered on the counter, taking complaints interspersed with shifts in the patrol car. It was a little more interesting than waiting around, taking reports of missing wallets and the like. However, having been accustomed to being engaged in police work of a more serious nature, I became bored and started to wonder, or I could see a future in keeping doing this.

U.S. NAVY SHORE PATROL AND THE SHOWIES

As any cop knows, even mundane police work has its moments of excitement, and unusual situations arise when you least expect it. Back at the time, there was only one uniform car working during the night shift hours in Cairns. I was rostered on the night shift with another cop named Jim. We both trained in karate and didn't mind the odd beer or two on our days off. It was great working with him as he was very handy in a disturbance.

Two U.S.N. frigates docked in Cairns overnight with about seven hundred crew onboard. Most had "onshore leave" until midnight, and the uniformed sailors were everywhere throughout the city and were exceptionally well behaved. We had no calls to any incident involving them at all. When Jim and I were assigned two U.S. shore patrol petty officers each, we were told to use two patrol cars instead of the one. These Americans were good blokes and interesting to talk to, easy-going and, as it turned out, perfectly happy to give us a hand in whatever was going down.

The Cairns annual show was on at the same time, and more than a few side-show operators, referred to as showies, were wandering around in addition to out-of-town visitors. An hour of the shift passed without anything happening, but that wasn't to last. We received a call over the police radio that a group of men, thought to be showies, had surrounded the front door of one of the nightclubs in the city. For reasons known only to them, they had decided that no one was going to leave or enter the nightclub and, there were enough of them to see their intent carried out.

Jim arrived with his two shore patrol blokes at the same time as I did, and we pulled up directly outside the nightclub. I observed about fifteen men, none of whom looked particularly respectable. They had formed a rough semicircle around the main entrance, where I spotted several patrons inside the door who wanted to leave, but the showies simply weren't going to allow that to happen. As to why they adopted this stance, we had no idea. However, the arrival of the two police cars caught the mob's attention, and they turned to face us with even more belligerence and hostility. Even though the mob around the door heavily outnumbered us, I told the United States Navy sailors that the conflict wasn't their problem. However, both of them replied,

'Doesn't worry us Pete, we'll give you a hand.'

I found out a bit later that much the same conversation took place between Jim and his shore patrol petty officers. The six of us alighted from our vehicles at the same time. There was no doubt in my mind that the hostile mob would not hesitate to attack two uniformed cops, especially with their superior numbers, but the unexpected appearance of four U.S.N. shore patrol petty officers in white uniforms, complete with webbing belts and gaiters, certainly took them by surprise. The look of apprehension on their faces, particularly one tall, very overweight, unkempt, poorly attired, ignorant, and bovine faced individual, changed noticeably to one of fear.

In unison and in one fluid movement, all four shore patrol officers drew their very long batons. These blokes must have practised this before as all four batons were drawn with their right hands and then, in a perfectly straight line and in time, all started tapping the batons into the palms of their left hands while staring intently at the now rapidly demoralised mob. Both Jim and I began to step towards our erstwhile opponents, with the line of baton tapping U.S.N. sailors, flanking us.

It became abundantly clear to the mob that the situation wasn't going to end well for them, and without any visible communication between them, they simultaneously bolted. My last vision was of them disappearing as fast as they could run, or in the case of the bovine faced individual, lumber into the Cairns night. This sudden change of circumstances was hilarious and had Jim and me, the shore patrol blokes, and the patrons closest to the door laughing uproariously. After a few exchanged pleasantries with the patrons, we left in our two police vehicles.

'Matter settled. No further action desired.' I relayed to the radio room, and we continued our shift.

THE RUNAWAY TRACTOR

Cairns, which is a part of the wet tropics, lived up to its reputation that night, with a solid downpour that continued well into the very early hours of the new day. This didn't generally pose any problems, but at times it did, and this early morning was one of those occasions.

Earlier the previous day, a car had been reported stolen, with its whereabouts unknown, until a cane farmer in one of the outer southern suburbs had spotted a fire down in his paddock. Driving his tractor over to investigate, he'd found a vehicle on fire. The U.S.N. Shore Patrol and I had just finished a coffee when we got the call regarding the burning Holden sedan. It was around two in the morning, no longer raining and still very dark outside.

On our arrival at the top of a small headland, I could see the still burning, almost completely destroyed shell of a Holden sedan. The muddy slope to the top was too steep for the police sedan to drive up, so I parked at the bottom and walked up. The recent rainfall had made the rich red soil very slippery, and even a four-wheel-drive would've been hard-pressed doing this climb. The farmer's tractor was not far from the burning vehicle, facing towards the edge of the incline, sitting idle with running engine and headlights and spotlight on, giving us a well-illuminated crime scene.

After fully extinguishing the fire and taking a few details from the farmer, I walked back down to the police car where the American sailors were waiting. At the precise moment, I started the car engine, the tractor of its own accord, began moving towards the edge of the incline and down the slope. It was coming directly towards the police vehicle in which my U.S.N mates and I were.

Unsettling was that the farmer wasn't on the tractor but stood frozen, with an astonished look on his face. It looked there was very little he could do without running the risk of being run over by the large rear wheels if he tried to climb up into the seat. My options in the police car were also quite limited as I could see the tractor gathering speed lumbering towards us. The only way to escape an inevitable collision was to ascend the slope at an angle out of its direct path.

With wheels trying to find grip in the mud, I gunned the car and made way far enough to be out of the machine's trajectory. But, just when I thought we had avoided the rampant farm tractor, the steep slope proved too much for the police sedan. It decided to stop moving forward, and with wheels now spinning uselessly in the red mud, it started sliding, and there was nothing I could do to bring it to a halt. With a screaming engine, it slid directly back into the path of the oncoming and now very close tractor, which had managed to pick up a fair turn of speed.

The sailors, who had been watching this event quietly and with interest, suddenly realised that we weren't out of harm's way and although the one in the passenger seat and I were sort of protected, the man in the rear seat was not. Fortunately, most of the police sedans at the time didn't have barriers separating the front and rear seats, so with a startled yell of,

'Fuck, it's on my side now.'

He sprang over the seat into the front on top of us. The tractor then collided with the rear section of the police car, taking the back panel and bumper bar with it and reshaping the boot lid before continuing its way. It then crossed an access road into a large stand of cane, where it thrashed around for a few minutes until it eventually stalled. Relieved to be still alive, we spilled from the car.

It appeared the farmer had possibly not engaged the handbrake fully. Nevertheless, it was pretty much an insurance matter, so we drove the still mobile police vehicle back to the station, where we exchanged it for another one and finished the remainder of the shift uneventfully. At around five in the morning, I dropped the shore patrol fellows off at the US Marine checkpoint on the wharf near their ships and returned to the station to furnish the relevant accident report before ceasing duty and went home.

Well, the following day, the Inspector reading my report didn't believe a word of it and insinuated that the police vehicle was damaged another way. There was a strong element of doubt regarding the integrity of my report. Further inquiries, however, and statements from the farmer, plus the two shore patrol blokes, soon vindicated me. The worrying thing was that my story was in doubt when you couldn't possibly fabricate something like that.

WE NICKNAMED HIM POM

There was a weird sex deviate who used to roam around Cairns, particularly at night. On seeing him a few times, I asked my working partner,
'What's the go with this bloke?'
He said, 'That's Pom Jackson.'
Me, 'What? A Pommie?'
He, 'No, he did five years after he got sprung for bestiality with a Pomeranian dog.'
Me, 'Whaaat?'
He, 'Yeah, for a while driving past the grub, we'd howl like a dog. He hated it, and every time he tore off to the police station to complain. Eventually, the boss said we couldn't do it anymore as he was sick of the bastard coming in complaining.'
Me, 'That's a shame.' And both of us had a good laugh.

DEATH IN CUSTODY

One night, I was working a midnight shift in the watchhouse when two police brought in an obviously drunk person. This old bloke had the appearance of a derelict, and one of the constables said that he'd found this bloke asleep under some shrubs in one of the parks. I checked on this bloke several times during the shift along with the fifty other prisoners, and each time I found him snoring peacefully. When my time was over, I left for home. The next shift started, and upon checking the prisoners, found the old bloke deceased.

He had a sudden heart attack and died, so now it became death in custody. The old drunk died of natural causes, which was bound to happen after years of abusing his body. An inspector who had taken a dislike to me tried to get at me for misconduct, but I'd done nothing wrong, and he couldn't make it stick. I was starting to wonder if it was worth my while continuing with my current working arrangements, watchhouse, front counter, occasional patrol shifts and only on the midnight to 0800 shifts.

I wondered if there might still be a position available with the Hong Kong police I had been accepted for. Another offer came up a few nights later when I was having a beer with the Cairns manager of a global security company. Upon telling him what I was thinking, he said the position of manager for the Philippines was currently vacant and that I'd have no problem getting it if I was interested. I said I'd think about it.

I mentioned my considerations to the sergeant in charge of the Inspectors Office and explained why I was interested. Immediately he said that there was a relieving position at Port Douglas for a couple of weeks over the coming Christmas/New Year period, and he'd recommend I go up there. I'd always found this sergeant to be a decent bloke and said I would jump at the chance as Port Douglas was a one-man station in a coastal fishing village about sixty-five kilometres north of Cairns. This was far more suited to my temperament than a large station such as Cairns. So I decided not to worry about the Wormald's manager position and got ready to head off on the stint at Port Douglas.

Christmas approached, and not wasting any time, I grabbed a bit of gear together and jumped into my ute with my dog Shiloh. I planned to put my swag down in the small police station and use the watch house shower, which was rarely used and certainly wasn't when I was there.

PORT DOUGLAS

Port Douglas, a small fishing village with a couple of hotels and a courthouse, had, in my opinion, the best pie shop in Australia. The police station had an office, a storeroom, and a small, largely unused watch house.

Every morning I went for a run on Four Mile Beach, after which I grabbed a pie and newspaper. It was a small, quiet place, and the most significant decisions I had to make were largely at which hotel or fisherman's house I would go to have dinner.

Like most other long-term residents of North Queensland and the Gulf Country, I've experienced a few cyclones over the years. Most of them were lower scale, but there were a couple of scary ones. The weather reports had the cyclone thirty-five miles out to sea, but the local fishermen and trawlermen were adamant that the cyclone was right there on top of us. These blokes lived in an environment where knowledge of the weather was integral to their survival at sea. At that time, I knew where I'd put my money.

I drove up to the top of a nearby hill and turned on my police car radio. Communication with the Cairns police was impossible at the station because of the atmospheric conditions. The damaging winds and torrential rainfall were setting in, and I'd only just finished speaking on the radio when a large tree came crashing down, hitting the ground not far from me. My German shepherd dog Shiloh sitting in the passenger seat, looked at me as if to say,

'Did you see that?'

The vehicle had started rocking violently in the gale-force winds, and I said to him,

'Yeah, mate, I reckon we're outta here.'

I hurried down the hill and was more than happy to get safely back inside the station. After a few minutes, there was a noise outside, so I opened the door and was surprised when a grey sea bird flew in. It was looking worse for wear and was most likely trying to find shelter from the elements. Now neither the dog nor I had any problem sharing the office with this bird; however, it took exception to us being there. The seabird instantly went into attack mode, which took me by surprise. So in order to save us from being torn to shreds by its vicious beak, I grabbed the bird and shoved it back outside.

The cyclone passed without causing any serious damage to the town, but it brought a lot of rain, resulting in a flooded river breaking its banks and spreading up to two kilometres wide.

People never ceased to amaze me. I'd had been awake well over twenty-four hours by the time the place settled down and feeling completely buggered and exhausted, I fell asleep in my chair. The phone rang, and I woke with a start but didn't get to it in time, but it barely had stopped ringing when it sprang alive again minutes later. I picked up the receiver, and a male voice started complaining about how his first call wasn't answered and why wasn't it, and what if it had been an emergency and what if...? I interrupted him and said that I had fallen asleep after a long stint on the job with the cyclone, and therefore I had been a bit slow getting to the phone. He was pretty indignant upon hearing that police actually went to sleep. He then inquired about the navigability of the road to Cairns, and I said to him,

'The river is two kilometres wide and runs a strong current, so you can't get across'.

Incredibly I heard him ask,

'But do you think I can make it?'

I just hung up the phone. Sometimes, it is pointless talking to morons. Following the excitement of the cyclone, things pretty much went back to normal.

I'd befriended an old retired New Guinea patrol officer and occasionally had a few drinks with him at the pub. He told me about his German shepherd male dog who was becoming a bit of a problem, so he said,

'You want a second dog?' I considered it for a bit and said,

'Why not.'

A few hours later, I pulled up outside his back gate and saw this massive, big German shepherd with one lopsided ear. My mate told me it happened after being poked in the ear by a child with a stick. The kids were also in the habit of running up and down the chain wire fence with sticks teasing the big dog, resulting in his hatred of kids.

Now my mate, who had had a few at the pub, was a bit wobbly on his feet as we went through the gate, so I held onto him to keep him upright. The big dog, who didn't take much provocation, decided that I was attacking his master, and he rushed at me, showing me his huge teeth. German shepherds can outrun a Greyhound over thirty metres from a standing start, and here was this huge dog flying at me. Fortunately, I was agile enough at the time and was prepared to risk a bite on the arm rather than anywhere else, so I put up my left arm in a defensive move and grabbed the fence with my right hand. I was going over the top of the fence when I felt the sharp pain of teeth penetrating flesh. The dog had hold of my left arm and was, at the same time, viciously growling and biting me. I managed to clear the fence and pull my arm free ripping my skin in the process, and with plenty of blood flowing, my old mate was horrified.

Needless to say, I was no longer interested in taking over his dog, but he offered me one of the dog's pups which I decided to take and named him Sabre. Over time he grew up to be as good as his father. However, the problem still existed as to what to do with this vicious dog. I managed to get him into my ute and deliver him to a bloke who had trained one of my other German shepherds. This bloke made an excellent dog out of him to the point that he could be left unsecured outside the supermarket with the local kids crawling all over him.

The remainder of my time at Port Douglas passed uneventfully, and upon the arrival of the new appointee, a traffic policeman from Brisbane, I returned to Cairns.

YARRABAH

Back in Cairns, I started with the Traffic Branch as an inquiry officer, taking statements and the like arising from crashes and various traffic offences. I found it to be a good job, and on days where there was little to do, there was the chance of getting called in to assist other police with difficult arrests.

One night I got a call from the general duties' car on patrol asking for my assistance in arresting a large individual hiding out in one of the main streets' toilet blocks. On my arrival, I was informed by two patrol blokes that they had a warrant of arrest for this huge man locked in the toilet, but apparently, he wasn't having any part of it. I knew the bloke as I'd previously encountered this giant at Bedourie years earlier, where I didn't have reason to fight him. He was about two metres tall and weighed probably one hundred and fifty plus kilos.

The three of us went into the large toilet block, and without a word, I immediately put a stranglehold on him. It gave us enough time to handcuff him and take him outside to the police vehicle. One bloke in charge of the car said,

'Glad you turned up mate.'

I said, 'No worries' and headed off, back to my job.

Life passed uneventfully for a couple of weeks until I was at a send-off for a cop who was leaving on transfer. The function was held at the back of the police station with a fair amount of booze flowing. An on-duty cop came over to where I was and said,

'The boss wants you on the phone.'

Upon answering the phone, the inspector said,

'I need you to go to Yarrabah relieving.'

As I had a reputation for being able to get on with Indigenous people and Yarrabah being an Aboriginal community, I said,

'I'd like that. When do I leave?'

'Now', was the reply.

He told me that the relieving sergeant had gone on sick leave, and the Black police had all gone on strike. The inspector added,

'Get over there and see what you can do.'

I said, 'Had several beers, Boss, but I'll get my gear and head off.'

'Where's your dog?'

'Back doing some more bite training at Gordonvale.'

'Well, get him if you need him. Talk to you later.'

I grabbed my swag and a few uniforms and, having

replaced my old ute, I headed off in my newly acquired wheels, a Landcruiser to the settlement, which I knew was supposed to be "dry", but booze was taken in all the time. As there wasn't a point of purchase in the community, I stopped at the Hamilton pub in the small town of Edmonton on my way through. Here I grabbed a couple of roadies and a carton to take with me.

The constable, permanently stationed there, knew I was coming and drove out to the edge of the settlement on top of a hill that overlooked the small settlement. He was waiting in the police Toyota when I pulled up next to him and introduced myself. I was going to be an acting sergeant during my time there. Knowing that his shift was over, I told him to go home, and I went looking for the "on strike" community police.

There were fifteen of them, all pretty decent blokes. Two of them, a father and son, had been sergeants in the army, which was not a bad achievement for Indigenous men at the time. So the two blokes went and got the other ranks together for a meeting with me. After an hour or so of discussion, they all agreed to return to work.

The station left a great deal to be desired, not secure, dusty, and cluttered, but I was happy enough to be somewhere I liked, so that was ok. The quarters provided were pretty basic, but I didn't mind except for the lack of a fence, which I would need if I brought Shiloh back from school.

The settlement was filthy and muddy, with buildings in disrepair and the people living there were hostile and of mixed race. The police vehicle was a battered panel van that had seen better days. There was a fair bit of police work to do with a large number of assaults of various descriptions going on, and I tended to keep busy with that, rather than racing around with a ticket book worrying about drink driving. If someone was caught drink driving it meant, taking the offender to Cairns for breath tests about an hour and a half away in a shit police car. As the quarters were unfenced, there were always obnoxious drunks bashing at the door demanding police attention, and it didn't take me long to figure out who were the dangerous ones. One night, as usual, another one was yelling out at the door. It was getting very tiring, so I decided enough was enough, and I made up my mind to collect big Shiloh from the bite school and puppy, Sabre.

Each time after that, every time a drunk arrived at the door late at night, Shiloh, followed by Sabre, would rush to the door roaring in the manner that only a significant attack trained German shepherd dog can. After about a week of Shiloh answering the late-night calls for me, I took him back to school to continue his training. The community police were pretty much the only callers after that, as it should be, and things went a bit more smoothly after that.

One morning I was in the office taking a statement from a thirteen-year-old girl accompanied by her mother concerning a sexual assault. The three of us sat down at my desk when there was a big commotion at the front door to the office. This was followed by a desperate looking man, who charged in, ran past my desk and continued straight out the back door, yelling incoherently. There were about thirty men in close pursuit, and the whole mob charged through the office, leaving knocked over chairs, rubbish bins and the like behind, in their near cyclonic path. It was all over as quickly as it started, and the entire mob disappeared out along the roadway. I said to the woman,

'What was that all about?'

She informed me that the chased man had done something previously, and this was the payback call. As

I could see that this bloke was in real peril, I suspended the statement until later, got into my Landcruiser, and drove off in the direction the mob had gone. I drove a few kilometres along the waterfront, learning from locals on foot that the fugitive had been captured and taken in a vehicle. Some distance further, I came across the man lying on the ground in a large pool of blood with the lower half of his leg barely attached. I guessed that a machete was used, or perhaps an axe, but I didn't see it lying around. I was by myself, and this bloke was obviously in a bad way with his leg barely holding on. The only thing I could do was drag the unconscious man into the back of my vehicle and head to the small hospital where he could receive emergency treatment before transportation to the Cairns Base Hospital. The hospital staff took him in, and he survived his ordeal but wasn't interested in making a complaint. Consequently, along with the complete dearth of witnesses, the matter eventually fizzled out.

I continued my statement with the girl and her mother and sent the information to the detectives. It would have been physically impossible for two police officers to carry out the numerous investigations, arrests, and prosecutions of offenders in addition to carrying out regular general police duties.

The following day, the constable and I were in the police vehicle up on the hill when a call came over the police radio regarding a Holden driving dangerously around the township. The call came from Cairns because the phone had been switched through to them. In the distance, I saw a vehicle travelling at speed along the main street towards the banana plantation. By the time we got down there, the car was already tearing along the dirt road, leading away from the populated area. I saw the vehicle enter the plantation at great speed, flattening banana plants as it sped along. While in pursuit, we came to an abrupt halt as we sank to the axles in a deep muddy patch right behind the Holden, which had also hit the same patch of boggy ground.

Opening the Holden driver's side door, I walked over and pulled the driver out from behind the steering wheel, and this is when I saw six other blokes in the vehicle. As they alighted from the car, I noticed that they were full of booze, bravado, and aggression. So here we were, surrounded by an aggressive mob in the middle of a huge banana paddock, unarmed and without the slightest hope for backup. Not even my community police were aware of where we had gone. As the situation was dangerous, I handed the now handcuffed, apprehended driver to the constable and decided to follow my usual course of action by being the first to strike.

The one with the biggest mouth and displaying the most aggression was my obvious target. As he moved towards me with his fist raised, he screamed insults that I'd never heard before like,

'Snot sucking Jesus' cunt!'

I grabbed him in the customary stranglehold before he had time to think. He surrendered immediately, so I handcuffed him as well. Through nothing more than pure luck, a farmer of a neighbouring plantation happened to be driving his station wagon along the road. As he pulled up, the four other drunken passengers of the Holden decided to make a run for it and took off into the plantation. The farmer was decent enough to transport the four of us back to the police station where I charged the two men with assault, and I told the constable to lock them up in the watchhouse. The two men entered pleas of not guilty, and the hearing that followed was held some months later after I'd already returned from relieving at Yarrabah.

Incidentally, the magistrate was dumbfounded when he heard the various unusual insults that were flung my way. Apparently, during the time of his career, he had never heard anything like it. The men were convicted and fined, and I never saw them again. All in all, Yarrabah was not a great place to be, but then, I had asked for relieving duty. I learned a few things I didn't know and gained valuable experience dealing with people I'd not previously encountered.

There was one aspect about the time I spent there, and that was, I got into the habit of stopping at the Hambleton Hotel in Edmonton for a beer or a carton when returning from Cairns to Yarrabah. At the same time, a young Dutch woman was holidaying in Edmonton with relatives. We brushed past each other on a few occasions, without anything more than a 'G'day'. I was to meet her again some forty years later, under entirely different circumstances and in a completely different place, and as fate had it, she became my wife.

I kept in contact with some of the community police as we had become good mates. However, as the job takes you further away from places and people, staying in touch over time wasn't as easy as it is today, and those mates, therefore, slowly fade away. I always had a lot of time for the community policemen I worked with and spent more than half my service working with them, probably more than I spent with Queensland police officers.

FURNITURE COURT RIFLEMAN

Not long after my return to Cairns, I was involved in a serious situation. Now it is tradition for police to name a boat after officers killed in the line of duty, and during this incident, I could have quite easily, once again, managed to get one named after me. I was rostered on the afternoon shift when a call came through reporting that a man was seen, sitting in a utility, with a rifle. The location was the car park of a local furniture store.

The individual had absconded from the psychiatric ward and gone home to grab his ute and rifle. He'd then driven to the furniture store where his wife worked, intending to shoot her, himself and any police that got in the way. Three or four other police were already there when I arrived on the scene, including Neal and my mate Bill. We had a quick discussion and decided on smashing the windscreen to disarm the bloke who, so far, had refused to speak to us, and all attempts of communication had thus far failed.

Neal and I immediately looked for a suitable implement to smash the windshield and found a hammer in a nearby workshop adjoining the car park. At times though, communication can get a bit confused when serious shit is going down, and instead of going for the windscreen, Neal hit the side window. I was surprised to see it break as I had previously come across side windows that didn't, no matter how hard you hit them. I had intended vaulting over the bonnet and enter the cabin of the ute through the front windshield, boots first, but now, that wasn't going to happen. Neal had only been partially successful in breaking the side window, as a lot of glass had remained in place. This left him in the position of reaching in and make an attempt to grab the rifle by the barrel, which was in the gunman's hands. However, the jagged glass surrounding the small space in the window, through which he had to reach, caused some severe cuts to Neal's arms. In addition, the quantity of blood spreading onto the rifle barrel made it too slippery, and he was unable to get a decent hold of the gun. Neal had no option other than to let go of the weapon and jump back out of the way.

I moved in beside him, and reaching in, I managed to grab hold of the rifle barrel. However, the blood had made it too slippery for me to get a decent grasp of it, and the gunman was able to pull it out of my grip, cutting my finger with the front sight as it went. At this point, I realised that we had a psychotic armed man on our hands, sitting inside his utility and who was about to start shooting at any second now. I immediately yelled out,

'Look Out.'

I dropped to the ground, as did my mate Bill, who now was right beside me on my left. It was also at this point that I saw a sergeant, whom I had never met, running away as fast as he possibly could, out of the car park. It was one of those times when events seem to be occurring in slow motion even though they aren't. Both Bill and I drew our revolvers as we fell to the ground, intending to start shooting into the cab, but just as we were bringing our guns up to fire, we saw the white top of a helmet, as worn by traffic cops, enter the ute from the driver's side door.

Unbeknownst to us, Russel, a bike cop, had pulled up and had managed to get in through the door and land a decent baton strike on the gunman, causing him to relinquish the rifle. Bill and I jumped back up, reholstering our guns and managed to unlock the door with the smashed window. We dragged the now disarmed gunman out of the car and handcuffed him. The man was returned to the psychiatric ward, where he managed to take his own life three weeks later.

Back at the station, the shift sergeant furnished a report recommending that Russel, Neal, Bill, and I, be recognised for our actions in the car park. However, the Inspector, who didn't like me because I'd locked up his mate in the past, said,

'Just doing their job.'

BACK IN CAIRNS

The new inspector called me into his office one day and said,

'The police at Coen have been bashed up again. This has now been happening for the last five years. I want you to take your dog and axe handle and sort that mob out.'

'No problem.' I said, 'When do I go and for how long?'

He replied, 'As soon as the road opens and for as long as you like.'

Well, this was good news, I had never been to Coen, but I knew that it was five hundred and fifty-five kilometres up the road from Cairns.

I kept an eye on weather and road conditions, and when the months settled into the dry season, I was ready to move in April. I had a few send-offs with police and locals, and on the morning that I was ready to leave, a couple of my flat-mates, still half-drunk, decided to try me out for some reason or other. I told them to leave it be and that I was on my way on transfer. But they kept on insisting on a hand-to-hand fight, tried to challenge me further and, wouldn't take no for an answer. As they kept badgering me, there was just no way I would be able to avoid it, so I thought I'd end the matter quickly. So I grabbed a pillow from a lounge chair, shoved it into the first blokes face, and pushed him up against the wall. I followed up with a half-hearted low power knee strike to the stomach to slow him up. He went straight down, and as the other bloke didn't want to carry it on, I jumped into my Toyota where Shiloh and Sabre were waiting and hit the road.

I found out later that when I had applied the low powered knee strike to his stomach, he'd inhaled a lot of lint from the pillow, and therefore spent a couple of days in the hospital to get it removed.

COEN

GETTING THERE

The bitumen road leading north from Cairns ended after one hundred and sixty kilometres into the journey at the Wolfram Hotel at Mt Carbine. From here on in, I travelled the most appalling, bone-jarring, rough roads I'd ever driven. The gear inside the car bounced around with the corrugations and soon was covered in a fair layer of dust. It was rugged country. I turned off Lakeland Downs which had a little pub and felt that I was in a landscape that resembled parts of Africa. I drove through stretches of country used for peanut growing to the small town of Laura. The road conditions didn't improve, and the section that crossed the Desailly Range won it hands down for the worst bit of road I've ever been on. Occasionally I drove on the track under the power lines because it was partially better than the road.

After ten hours of rough bush roads, I finally arrived at the Coen police station, feeling tired and covered in dust. The single men's barracks were attached to the station with a separate residence for the sergeant. There were three other buildings, one of which was occupied by the police tracker. One was empty, and the other was used for storing coffins, as the police also served as undertakers in conjunction with the council bloke. With one narrow strip of bitumen making up the main street, the rest of the township boasted a pub, a school, one shop, a post office, a small hospital, and a boarding house for school kids attending the local state school. Several small houses lay dotted around, and about one kilometre out was an Aboriginal reserve where one hundred or so people from the Mungkan tribe, Edward River, lived, and that was about it.

Not an unattractive little bush town, I thought when I drove into the fenced yard of the barracks. I started unloading my gear with both my dogs running around inspecting and sniffing their new environment and busy lifting their leg to mark their new home and territory. At this point, two large wild dogs appeared from nowhere, jumped over the fence, and rushed at Sabre, who still was a puppy. Shiloh surged forward with raised hackles, ready to protect his little mate. I managed to deliver a few good kicks to one of the dogs whilst Shiloh tore into the other. Yelping, they took off, back over the fence. At the same time, a ranger drove past in his ute and seeing the wild dogs, he shouted,

'I'll look after this.'

With a roaring engine and dust in his wake, he took off after the fleeing wild dogs. Within minutes, the sound of two shots reverberated in the distance, and needless to say, I never saw those dogs again. The ranger came back the next day and introduced himself, and from there on in, we stayed mates until well after I left Coen a couple of years later.

After I had my gear squared away, I grabbed a beer and sat in complete solitude on the front steps of the barracks and watched the sun go down. To my absolute astonishment, in the fading light, the mountain range in the distance turned deep purple. In the next two years I spent there, I never tired of looking at the transformations the sunsets provided each night.

My duties started the next day, and with the sergeant in charge being away, I had a look around the office and decided to have, as soon as possible, a sliding door added, connecting the barracks internally to the office. It would save having to walk around the building to the station's entrance. I paid a visit to the local hotel. It was like the usual country pub with a few bushy looking blokes sitting around the bar. They all knew who I was, and generally, those places are well disposed towards police. One bloke, however, said loudly,

'If that big red dog of yours chases my stock again, I'll shoot it.'

It was like waving a red flag in front of a bull as far as I was concerned, so I said,

'I have been here less than twenty-four hours, and I don't have a red dog, especially one that's running loose. If you have any ideas of harming my German shepherds, you'd be best advised to give it a lot of thought as I will make sure you regret ever speaking to me.'

He immediately shut up and returned to his beer. Then another younger bloke off a property walked over and said,

'I've heard you're pretty good in a fight.'

I said, 'I get by.'

He replied, 'Well, so am I with my hands and feet. I will have to try you out sometime.'

So I simply said, 'How about now?' and added, 'Out the back.' I downed my beer, stood up and said, 'Let's go.' and walked towards the door.

This bloke went very pale in his face under the tan and stuttered,

'You're a bit eager, aren't you?'

I said, 'Your idea, come on, won't take long.'

He obviously wasn't used to this and skulked away muttering, accompanied by the muffled sniggers of the other drinkers. The following week he was in the bar again and was man enough to apologise for his antics, and we became good mates. He had a property not far out of town and, a few years later, after I had left the region on yet another transfer, he'd unwisely decided to go for a cash crop in the form of hooch and got caught. He spent five years in jail, losing his property in the process.

Upon my arrival at Coen, I got back into my physical training routine I had been neglecting the past few months. Before long, I was back, running up to twenty-five kilometres a day, half an hour bag work and half an hour weights, six days a week, and making sure that I was in the office by nine.

The sergeant left on a three weeks leave, and remembering the inspectors' words back in Cairns before sending me up here,

'The police at Coen were once again bashed up, so I want you to take your dog and axe handle and sort that mob out.'

So I used those three weeks to lock anyone up who looked at me sideways. There were some efforts at resistance, but it was twenty-six / nil in my favour at the end of the period. Establishing some sort of respect wasn't a bad strategy, and by the end of the three weeks, things had quietened down a fair bit, and I had fulfilled the duties I was sent out to do.

The local hard man even came around to the police station and asked if he could do some weightlifting training with me. I suspected it was a recon to find out how strong I was, so I set up a bar with heavy weights, which I had no trouble lifting, and straight-up did a dozen curls with no apparent effort. I then handed the bar to him. He held on to it, and I saw his muscles flex then tremble under strain, and after a few seconds, he dropped the weight bar with a heavy thud to the ground and decided to leave. Thus, his mission to gauge my strength was accomplished.

On pension days, there was an influx of blokes from Lockhart River coming into Coen. A canteen at the community centre opened for limited hours and filled with Kiaangi men who were sworn enemies of the Mungkan tribe. There were always fights going on requiring my intervention. I faced these situations on my own, as the sergeant had overturned the police vehicle on his way back from the city and now was on sick leave for the next twelve months. It was decided by the department that I could look after the job by myself, and therefore the sergeant was eventually transferred to Brisbane.

THE RACE MEETING

Once a year, the annual race meeting was held, attracting people from wide and far to the dusty racetrack, including a large contingent from the mining town of Weipa. Besides watching the races, a fair bit of betting went on to add to the excitement. Before my arrival, the practice was to send five extra police up from Cairns to assist at the races, and together with the two permanents, they all had nothing to do.

Once again, the annual race meeting approached, and as I was by myself, the boss rang to see how many blokes I wanted to come up to assist me during the two-day event, so I said,

'Just one constable will do.'

On the first night, as we patrolled the grounds, we ran into a couple of blokes from Weipa who were making complete arses of themselves by interfering with and insulting people outside the hotel, so my offsider and I locked them up. We then raced around to find six of the filthiest drunks and put them in with the two troublemakers, who, in turn, sat up all night huddled in a corner, and we had no further problems with the Weipa blokes.

On the night of the race ball, there were quite a few ladies on the dance floor, which was set up in the makeshift theatre. I was advised that a large unkempt drunk had gatecrashed the show, which had a "ticket only" entry, and he was on the dancefloor making drunken uncoordinated attempts to get the women to dance with him. I went over and grabbed him by the collar and marched him outside, straight into the back of the police Toyota and at that point, this bloke's mate came over to object. He had barely gotten the first word out of his objection when I grabbed him and shoved him in after his mate and locked them both in the watchhouse. When I let the pair out the following morning, they left town immediately and weren't seen again.

There was a serious sexual assault early on Saturday morning, and two detectives flew up from Cairns to handle the investigation, as we had enough on our hands policing the racegoers. The next day, after they had resolved the issue, my partner and I took the detectives to the airport. Once they'd boarded the Bush Pilots DC3 aircraft, a fight broke out near the little shed, which served as a terminal. The detectives viewed the disruption via the plane window. One of them, a mate of mine, told me later that it had been amusing to him and the rest of the passengers to sit back and see what happened over the next few minutes.

The plane was a ten-seater, and there were fifteen men in varying stages of drunkenness attempting to board the aircraft. They had started to attack the pilot, who in vain tried to deny them entry. We ran over to help him, and that's when the mob turned their attention to us. My offsider, who was also a big believer in keeping his fitness and training up, didn't hesitate and side by side, it didn't take us long to overpower the assailants.

The fight took place inside the small, corrugated iron shed with open shutters.

From the plane, as was reported to me later, all they saw were blokes flying out through the open shutter space, one after the other, with some flying out through the open side entry. There were no serious injuries but lots of groaning, shortages of air and clutching of genitals. We decided to lock up the ringleader so that he couldn't rally the troops back. They had become quite reasonable at that point as they finally realised that fifteen doesn't go into ten.

We took our prisoner back to the station and put him in the watchhouse. Later that night, I realised just how feral this bloke was. When I walked into his cell, I accidentally dropped the meal I'd prepared for him onto the floor, so I went back to get him another feed. By the time I returned, he had eaten the food straight off the filthy wooden floor and had licked the floorboards clean. I still gave him the second meal, which he ate with great vigour and let him go the following morning. He forfeited his bail, and I never saw him again either.

Some months later, a big bar fight broke out, which involved about fourteen blokes. Harold, the publican, gave me a call, so I went over with the police car and on my arrival, Harold, a big bloke, said he'd give me a hand. The mob, which included the "hard" man, who had wanted to lift weights and train with me, thought they'd have a go at us. The end result was that Harold and I grabbed the "hard" man first and shoved him into the paddy wagon, followed by as many blokes as we could possibly fit. The ones that decided to continue and fight lay within minutes of challenging us, sprawled out onto the deck. We then went and locked up our prisoners, and upon our return to the pub, we encountered a few tourists who had watched the incident. Amazed at the outcome, they said they had a newfound respect for country policemen in isolated places.

COEN TOWN POWER

When I first arrived in Coen, the town was dependent on a generator for power. It was housed in a little shed together with a windmill and several rainwater tanks for drinking water. Each night when the generator was turned off, a deathly silence descended upon the town, which, in return, was taken over by the pleasant night sounds of the bush. The quiet only lasted until the generator was cranked up again the following morning. The use of power pulling appliances such as toasters, electric fry pans and the like were out of the question, and sometimes even the cassette players would slow down and then speed up depending on the use of the generator.

The fridges were either kerosene or gas, as were the hot water systems and stoves. It wasn't too bad, and it made a massive difference once a large town-sized generator was installed. It was a case of "you don't know how difficult it is until the situation dramatically improves". The publican was an electrician by trade, so we already had someone in place to run the little power station, and just like that, the quality of life improved a fair bit. The water supply remained unchanged, and there always seemed to be enough rainwater in the tanks for cooking. The creek water was used for bathing, and as a plus, I did acquire some rudimentary knowledge on how windmills operated. I often thought about having a place with a windmill of my own one day, but, so far, that has not eventuated.

ROLLER SKATES

In isolated and remote towns fifty years ago, before TV, computers and such, people had to make their own entertainment. Coen was no exception, and apart from the local pub and an occasional movie, there was not much else to do for leisure activities. One day, about half a dozen of us decided to buy a few sets of roller skates and took them out on the tarmac at the airport, twenty-five kilometres out of town. We usually went on Sundays after the pub closed its morning session and returned in time to patronise the establishment for the afternoon. We had a lot of fun during those hours, with people often losing a lot of bark of arms and legs, scraping along the bitumen and concrete tarmac surfaces. It all ended when the pub was no longer required to close during those hours and the two sessions combined. Loyal to the establishment, the skates were relegated to the storeroom where they remained, collecting dust.

Another fun activity during the wet season was riding down the rapids in Lankelly Creek on inflated DC3 aircraft tyre tubes. We managed to score three of these huge rubber tubes, which we loaded onto the police vehicle and then drove along the road about one kilometre upstream. Upon reaching the small bridge on the airport road, we launched the tubes into the creek and jumped in after them. With two or three of us on each tube, we raced along with the turbulence, navigating through low hanging bushes and trees and ending up at the rear of the police reserve. Here we grabbed another car, loaded up the tubes, and repeated the process. In hindsight, it was quite a dangerous exercise, but no one ever got hurt other than scratches from the branches.

ILLEGAL IMMIGRANTS

I was in the office one morning when I received a phone call from the boss in Cairns. A group of thirteen men had been seen on the beach near Port Stewart, an inlet on the coast about sixty kilometres from Coen. It was highly unusual due to the sparse population in the area, which was pretty much confined to the caretaker/manager of the local cattle station and the odd fisherman or two.

When I was asked to accompany the pilot of an army helicopter to Port Stewart, I jumped at the opportunity to ride in a chopper of the type I'd seen in Viet Nam war docos, and I wasn't disappointed by the experience. The Bell UH-1 Iroquois, nicknamed Huey, is a military troop transporting helicopter and was known to be the workhorse of the Army. It is powered by a single turboshaft engine, with two-bladed main and tail rotors.

I boarded the aircraft at the racetrack close to the police station, strapped myself in and put on my headphones. From there, we flew straight to Port Stewart. Almost immediately, I spotted a group of twelve men waving from the beach. We descended and landed the aircraft near the group and found that they seemed to know very little English. I asked them where the thirteenth man was, and in broken English and somewhat agitated, they described the terrifying moment a crocodile had taken him. In a reasonably brief interview with the group, they informed me that they were shipwreck survivors and had been floating around at sea for what worked out to be nineteen days. They could not tell me what it was they had been floating on, and at strategic times during the interview, the "no understand" ploy came into play. Their story didn't add up, and I concluded it to be total bullshit.

My job was to collect the group and convey them to the police station in Coen, where they would have to wait for the arrival of immigration officials. All of them were healthy-looking young blokes of Asian appearance, wearing expensive clothing in good condition, and most of them wore gold necklaces and watches. They also had glass bottles with what I later found out were happy or lucky Chinese plants in them. In addition, they had in their possession expensive-looking radios and cassette players and two forty-four-gallon drums filled with fresh water.

I organised them into groups of four for transport to the Coen police station, which immediately sent them into a frenzied panic. They resisted and objected to moving. Then, alarmed, they glanced at the sidearm I was carrying, and it took quite a bit of convincing that I wasn't going to murder them. It required three trips to transport all twelve to the Coen watchhouse. I thanked the chopper pilot, and after he'd gone, the wait was for the arrival of the immigration people, which I knew was going to be a long wait. Eventually, they arrived in a large civilian helicopter. The group were to be transported to "somewhere", and the immigration blokes were less than forthcoming with any information.

Unbeknown to the so-called shipwrecked group, I happened to be outside the watchhouse during the wait when I overheard them converse in reasonably good English. The feds didn't seem interested in the thirteenth man who was allegedly missing. Instead, they seemed to be very accepting of the shipwreck story, which was believed without question.

It wasn't until early the following day that I had the opportunity to organise a search for the thirteenth man. I knew that it was likely that he never existed in the first place or may have left the area by other means. I conducted a thorough search accompanied by the council foreman and a couple of other local blokes but failed to find any trace of the missing man. Given the swarms of crocs in the vicinity, following the cessation of crocodile hunting some years earlier, he could very well have been the victim of these apex predators.

Some months later, the caretaker of the local property came into the station and told me he had found a twenty-one-foot dory, a fishing boat that is used both in coastal waters and in the open sea, hidden in the thick mangroves. The indicated location was a short distance from where I had initially encountered the group. I accompanied the caretaker to the site and found there was indeed such a boat fitted with a large binnacle compass for ocean travel. As far as we were concerned, this boat didn't exist as the twelve stranded blokes had been recorded as shipwrecked. Nevertheless, the caretaker, a part-time poor fisherman, got himself a beautiful big dory. I sent a note to the chopper's pilot that there was a binnacle compass for their army officers' mess in Townsville for collection when he had a chance. He came by a few weeks later on business and took me for another flight along the beaches around the port. I was pleasantly surprised when he flew over the wrecks of three wartime USAF Airacobra WWII fighter planes. They lay buried in the sand, their outline visible at low tide. The pilot was happy with the compass, and that was it.

Life returned to normal, and the erstwhile shipwreck survivors? As the feds did not inform us any further, I assume they happily settled in, unchallenged, into their new country Australia.

SUSPECT DRUG PRODUCER

Port Stewart came into my life again, only this time not concerning illegal immigrants but for much more sinister and dangerous circumstances. Over the period of about a week, I received a few anonymous phone calls informing me of a dangerous individual heading towards Coen with a herd of horses. I was advised to heed caution and to be very careful if I came across him.

The bloke in question was named Clyde and was the leader of a drug-dealing group known as the Pig Hunters. This group was suspected to be responsible for the disappearance of thirteen people in the Cedar Bay area, where he reputedly had large cannabis plantations.

I never learned who the anonymous caller was, but everything he'd told me was spot on. I came across Clyde with his horses, his old truck, and a four-wheel-drive vehicle as he came into the police station to get the truck registered. He was one of the few men I have encountered in my life who, when you look in their eyes, you see nothing, just emptiness and the strong vibration of being in the presence of a very evil man.

Clyde had purchased an isolated cattle property further north where he ostensibly intended raising cattle. If it concerned a drug grower setting up shop out there, the police work would've been simple enough; however, in context with other accumulating circumstances, it turned into a very dangerous situation in more ways than one.

Late one night, I was having a beer with a couple of blokes from Sydney who were in town to do a bit of work at the airport. We were talking about aircraft when a plane flew relatively low over town. I recognised the sound of the Pratt and Whitney engines, a Douglass DC3.

I had flown in them a few years earlier between Bamaga and Cairns on Bush Pilot Airways. At almost the same time, one of the blokes said, 'C47', which is the correct description of that aircraft used extensively for transport during WWII. It was highly unusual for that type of aircraft to be around at night and in this location, so I noted the time and date.

After a while, the subject of smuggling came up, and I learned from these blokes that if you receive information concerning the movement of protected fauna and advise the relevant authorities, you were entitled to a reward of ten percent of the smuggler market value of the birds. As the night went on, we downed a few more beers, and at midnight, they said their goodbyes and wandered off into the darkness with drunken promises of keeping in touch, and that was the last I saw them.

Over the next few weeks, reports surfaced regarding this aircraft being observed in the air and on the ground. The information came from airline pilots and other credible sources. There was a description of it being pale blue on the underside, with the top painted in camouflaged colours and was spotted on the ground not far from Port Stewart.

In the weeks before this, the American who owned a property near Port Stewart had been into town a few times, always accompanied by a tall menacing, powerfully built man. My attack dog, Shiloh, started to bark fiercely for no apparent reason when he saw these men. Like other dog owners who know their dogs well enough, I developed a feeling of suspicion as my dog had been right in his assessment before. As it turned out, the big man was the American's bodyguard and, before that, had been a sparring partner to some heavyweight boxing champs back in America. Whether or not the aircraft had been landing on the American's property,

I never found out.

As the weeks went by, more reports of sightings surfaced, including the setting up of perimeter guards every time the aircraft was on the ground. There was also a fishing trawler of some sort moored at the entrance to Port Stewart, which coincided with the plane's arrival. A fisherman who spotted the perimeter guards identified the weapons they were carrying as automatic light machine guns. The contemporary opinion was that the aircraft was flying from Daru in Papua New Guinea to Coen and was using the Automatic Direction Finder at Coen airport to get its' bearings before heading to Port Stewart.

Further information was also starting to circulate that the aircraft was bringing in drugs from Papua New Guinea, a relatively new activity following the Viet Nam War and the establishment of a new bank in Sydney purportedly for the laundering of drug money. In addition, the aircraft was suspected of taking protected fauna such as the various species of parrots in the area, including the Eclectus parrot found only in one particular area near Lockhart River where Clyde resided.

Despite reported sightings of the plane by airline pilots, nothing seemed to be happening regarding any investigation. I found it amazing that a good-sized aircraft could fly in and out of the country seemingly with impunity and was beginning to wonder why. Considering that the plane could do what it did, I decided that if the military hadn't become involved, there wasn't much point in my going down and confronting the men on the plane, especially by myself. So, I ignored the comings and goings of the camouflaged DC3 until, eventually, it ceased coming altogether.

THE MAN-EATER

It was Saturday around lunchtime when I walked up to the little store for some eggs. It seemed eerily quiet in the small town with a noticeable, distinct absence of local Indigenous inhabitants. The small community numbered about one-hundred and fifty, and on an average day, several of them hung around the area. I thought it very unusual, so I decided to drive out to the reserve to check what was happening. My first port of call, as always, was a reliable elder. I often spoke to him on matters of concern, so I asked,

'Where have all the locals gone?'

He replied, 'They have gone home. The Man-Eater is here.'

He must've seen the puzzled look on my face as he went on to explain,

'He came in from the bush, and he drinks human blood.'

Well, that answer sure made me none the wiser, so I said,

'I'd better go and meet this Man-Eater.'

The old fella called after me,

'Be careful, constable.'

I made my way to the hotel and immediately saw the Man-Eater. He was a bloke in his mid-fifties with disturbing prominent, bulging red eyes. I decided to watch him for a while before walking over as I wanted to find out why the locals were so terrified of him. He watched me like a hawk when I drew nearer. His voice was surprisingly low when I heard him mutter,

'Are you Peter Cahill?'

I didn't quite get to finish my affirmative reply as the Man-Eater punched me in the side of the face. It wasn't particularly hard but caught me by surprise. He was very obviously displaying his dominance, and I had no choice other than to place the man in a restraining hold and arrest him for his efforts. I took the Man-Eater down to the station, locked him up, and immediately noticed that the locals started to return to the little town square. It seemed the influence of the Man-Eater had evaporated as soon as he was locked away. Later that day, he was released on bail, which he forfeited. After that, I did spot him daily for a week or so, loitering around town before finally leaving.

There was a least one fair dinkum witch doctor in the area who had a young child apprentice. For me, meeting a blood drinker was a first. It wasn't particularly outlandish as many old customs and practices still existed, such as people who were made to cut off one of their fingers with a sharp stone. On one such occasion, a bystander had collected the severed appendage and hurried it to the hospital to be put on ice just in case it could be re-attached. Unfortunately, the owner of the finger never showed up at the hospital. That very night, the frozen finger was stolen, never to be seen again. At times like these, it was best to leave matters be.

OFF DUTY PERILS

Due to the longer than usual wet season and the lack of a temporary replacement cop, I stayed in Coen for eight months straight without a break. My only respites were a few trips to the small coastal Aboriginal community of Lockhart River, which lies about two hundred kilometres north of Coen. Finally, the opportunity to go down to Cairns, a six-hundred-kilometre drive down the road, arose. I was looking forward to finally doing a bit of grocery shopping and found that the trip was worth it to indulge in takeaway food and wander around various hotels to have a cold beer. The best part about being off duty was that I did not have to worry about anything, at least that's what I thought.

On my way down to the city, I travelled through one of the smaller towns, Mareeba and at the spur of the moment, I decided to pull up and stay the night. I booked into a motel, and after settling in, I went to check out the town. I walked around for a bit and satisfied my takeaway cravings in the form of a pizza, an absolute novelty when you never get the chance to do so. I enjoyed my time off, and when I walked past the hotel later in the evening, three men suddenly appeared in front of me. One was considerably taller and more robust than me, the other two were my size. Upon making eye contact with me, the largest one of the trio raised his hands intending to attack me and said,

'Give me your money. Now!'

They had intentions of rolling me for any money I was carrying. I was dressed and looked like any ringer or stockman from Cape York, and they had no idea who I was. It was a straightforward attempt of mugging, and unbeknownst to them, I had a couple of hundred dollars in my shirt pocket.

Without further ado, I stepped up to the big bloke, driving a solid palm heel into his chest, followed by a superbly executed foot sweep. My assailant finished up almost flying vertically through the air with his feet overhead. There was a substantial thud when his upper back hit the pavement. To avoid giving him too much time to recover, I followed up with a solid straight punch to the face. I hoped that this was enough to remove any inclination for him to get up for another go. Then, from the corner of my eye, I saw the second mugger approach. I landed a low kick to the outside of his knee and knew I had hit the spot when he went down screaming. The third man also wanted to have a go, so I gave him a decent roundhouse kick to the kidneys. So far, so good, I thought, admittingly slightly amazed at the successful use of the techniques I had been practising for so long. But it wasn't over. I regularly trained in unarmed combat, and I could somehow sense when someone was behind me. This was one of those occasions. Other men were starting to surround me. As I didn't want any trouble in the first place, I said,

'Peace brothers, we'll let this go.'

I instinctively turned around in time to see a man with a large beer bottle raised over his head. There was no doubt in my mind that he had the intention of hitting me on the back of the head with it. I managed to use an upper rising block to prevent the trajectory of the raised bottle and followed up with a tremendous kick to the balls of the bottle man. He went down. I continued my turn through until I was facing the same direction before the bottle attack. It was then that someone hit me in the mouth with a full can of unopened beer. I literally saw stars and knew that I was close to unconsciousness. Given the number of assailants, I knew that going down at this point could be fatal. I desperately fought off the effects and rushed towards the can thrower, who was standing about six metres in front of me, perplexed that I was still standing. A solid front kick to the attacker's stomach put him down with his mates already scattered around on the footpath and roadway. I said, sounding confident to the remaining would-be assailants and spectators,

'Next?'

Somehow there didn't seem to be any further contenders, and I decided to call it a night. I retreated to the motel where my attack dog was waiting in the old F100. I finished up with a few chipped teeth and a significant cut to my lower lip. It needed stitching up, but at that time, I was ten feet tall and bulletproof, so I didn't worry about it.

It was about a year later when I'd transferred to the Sunshine Coast. It was there that I met up with a mate of mine, who had an earthmoving business. As it happened, he was looking for someplace for one of his new truckers to bunk down, so I agreed to let him stay at the rental I had in the Noosa Hinterland. Upon arrival, the driver named Cam said,

'Hey, I know you! You were in that fight in Mareeba one night! I was inside the pub while it was going on.'

I said jokingly, 'Why didn't you come out and give me a hand?' to which he replied,

'You didn't need any help.'

We had a good laugh recalling the fight, and Cam and I became great mates. When his contract with the trucking company finally ended, Cam moved back to his hometown. After that, I never saw him again and wondered what had happened to him. He had a girlfriend named Brenda back home, and at times she'd come down to see him. They seemed like a great couple, and I was shocked when, one morning at work, I got a phone call from her. Brenda told me that Cam had committed suicide. She sounded very distraught and explained that they had a massive argument over something or other a few days earlier. Cam had disappeared and had taken his .303 Lee Enfield ex-military rifle with him and used it to end his life. There's no coming back after getting hit at close range with a weapon like that.

It was, as always, a tragic loss of life that was so avoidable. I have no idea what happened to Brenda after that, and I can't imagine what it must be like, carrying something like that with you for the rest of your life.

NIKKO THONGS

When you live in isolated regions such as the Gulf Country and Cape York, you get to meet various travelling groups such as Telecom, the Works Department and Main Roads. I always found them to be decent blokes and good company. One Telecom group was in Coen when I was there, and we became good mates. When I had gone to Cairns on a grocery run, it coincided with an RDO break for the Telecom blokes, so we arranged to meet for a few beers in Hides Hotel in the centre of Cairns. However, there was a problem.

A relatively new rule had been introduced requiring patrons in the public bar to wear footwear. Unfortunately, one of the blokes, nicknamed Jumbo, though I am unsure of the origin of the name as he was of average physique, didn't have any footwear. Not even a pair of thongs, so he was denied entry. We thought this was a bit of a blow and considered going somewhere else for a drink, but Jumbo had a plan.

He went into the newsagent adjoining the pub and emerged triumphant a few minutes later with a Nikko, a type of felt-tipped, black marking pen. He proceeded to outline a pair of thongs on his feet, and at a casual glance, it was sort of possible to think they were real. So we all trooped into the pub with Jumbo wearing his Nikko marker pen thongs, and amazingly, he was allowed in.

I doubt the staff believed they were real thongs, but I suspect his initiative and originality carried him over the line.

OVERSEER LOCKHART RIVER

My first trip from Coen to Lockhart River took me over two hundred kilometres of the most challenging roads I'd ever driven. Around the Northwest, I had travelled through desert areas and washed-out bush roads, but for sheer roughness, steep banks, and hill climbs, this was a first for me.

The Landcruiser was, in my opinion, one of the better "off-road" vehicles produced, and it was just a matter of taking it slow, and to be perfectly honest, I didn't mind it in the least.

I removed the revolving blue light off the roof as I found myself driving through a tunnel designed by nature. The growth of the rainforest canopy came down so low that it would have damaged the light. It was dark driving through there, and I was amazed by the numerous forms of wildlife that inhabited the area. A giant flying fox zoomed past my open driver's side window, and it looked in at me with big, startled eyes in its orange-coloured head. There were parrots, which are found only in that area named the Eclectus Parrot. This beautiful bird became, over time, a target for bird smugglers as they brought good money when sold overseas.

Upon leaving the foliage tunnel, I was confronted with the steep and rough pass which runs through Mount Tozer, known as Tozer's Gap. Just as I was about to start my way up, a small orange four-wheel drive appeared at the top of the hill. I was surprised as, so far, I had not passed a single vehicle since I left the main Weipa road. The orange car had no roof, and I waited for him to draw level with me. I was intrigued by the driver's physical appearance as the wild-looking bloke had long, grey hair and beard, wore sunglasses and a Jackie Howe singlet. He introduced himself as Mick and said that he was the overseer at the community and out to check the condition of the roads. I warmed to this bushie, and after a few minutes of exchanging pleasantries and enquiries, he said

'Do you feel like a beer?'

I replied, 'Is the Pope a Catholic?'

He laughed at my response and went back to his car to grab the beer, although there obviously wasn't an esky insight. I was horrified when I saw him reach under the front seat and come up triumphant with two hot bottles of "Brisbane Bitter" of all things. The beer had been rolling around in the car for who knows how long and tasted just as awful as I had anticipated. I somehow managed to get the booze down and keep it down.

Continuing, we headed off through the Gap towards Iron Range. I followed the orange ute for a while and found that the road conditions improved as we went. Mick pulled up at a cattle property as he wanted me to meet his mate. I was surprised to see a 25-pounder artillery gun in front of the homestead. I followed him inside into the large kitchen, complete with the obligatory slow combustion wood stove and was introduced to the owner of the property, a very affable man, and his partner. I couldn't help but notice the large stack of cartons of Victoria Bitter cans next to the woodstove. This time on being offered a beer, I wasn't anywhere near as surprised when Mick's mate grabbed four cans out of the top carton and handed them around. At least a hot Victoria Bitter, which has been stationary, was marginally better than hot Brisbane Bitter, which had been rolling around under the seat of a vehicle. Over the following years, I had further occasion to drink warm beer, but I rationalised that it was infinitely better than drinking lukewarm water.

After attending to police business the following day, I

was ready to return to Coen. Mick drove part of the way with me because there was something else he wanted to show me. We headed north towards a place named Portland Roads, where apparently ocean fishing vessels moored. We stopped and continued on foot. I followed him up a winding path that snaked up a steep hill, and on arriving at the summit, I saw the most beautiful small A-frame home perched on top of two WWII bomb shelters. Mick explained that his mate, who worked in a mine at Weipa, owned the place and had converted one shelter into a kitchen and the other into a huge water storage tank. Looking down from here towards the Pacific Ocean, Mick pointed out a small island. It was the property of the station owner I had met at Iron Range. The beauty of the island, surrounded by deep crystal-clear blue water complete with a giant shark swimming slowly around, left me speechless. I added it to my forever growing list of beautiful places I have been fortunate enough to have seen since I started my outback duties.

I said goodbye to my new mate, who remained so for many years, and headed back for my police station home at Coen.

NOT FEELING GOOD

I made several trips to Lockhart River as there was no state police stationed there in those days. I'd drive up there to attend to any problem that developed and never tired of the drive because of the incredible scenery, isolation and the two rivers I had to cross each time, up and back. These were the Wenlock and Pascoe Rivers. The Wenlock was like any other peninsula river and quite passable in the dry season; however, the flying fox, used to get across, indicated the high-water levels experienced during the wet. The Pascoe was a shallow, clear running stream and had a beauty about it that invariably made me stop for a break each time I crossed it. The dogs loved to splash around, and it was also the perfect place to bury a couple of beers in the clean sandy riverbed in the shallow, swift-running water. Fifteen minutes was all that was needed to make it pass for a cold beer.

I'd only made a few trips up to Lockhart River when, a week or so after returning to Coen, I became extremely sick. My fevers ran high, so much so that I couldn't remember three consecutive days of the week. I was crook. There wasn't a doctor closer than Mareeba, some five-hundred kilometres away, and the local nurse, who was rather good at her job, didn't know what I had contracted. To add to this, I was also by myself at the time with the sergeant away on holiday. The high temperatures continued, and I sweated the illness out until I slowly came good. I lost a lot of weight and was plagued with violent shivering sessions followed by hallucinations and unconsciousness. I'd wake up soaked in sweat, and the process would start again. Blinding headaches, yellow-tinted skin, teeth coming loose, a rash later identified in ongoing recurrences as shingles were some of the symptoms I experienced.

A few months later, I spoke to the overseer at Lockhart River, and on telling him about my illness, he said,

'Well, you weren't the only one. There were plenty more who became sick. So, when we reported our concerns, a team wearing hazardous material outfits, known as hazmat suits, were flown in.'

I was surprised to hear this and asked,

'What did they do?'

To which the overseer replied,

'They sprayed the inside of every building in the

community and paid particular attention to the walls up higher to the ceiling. When I asked this team why they were particularly interested in the high areas, they told me that this was where mosquitoes go after biting someone.'

As it turned out, this disease plagued me for decades and still does today, periodically destroying my immune system. However, the severity, duration, and frequency have lessened as the years roll by because I've gradually built some resistance to the disease, which I now know, is malaria.

CHECKING THE FENCES

One morning, one of the property owners who lived a fair way out of town asked if I could go for a flight with his helicopter pilot. He wanted me to have a look at an area of his station where fences had been cut. I climbed into the little Bell chopper on the racecourse in town, and we headed off towards the vicinity of the fences.

On the way there, we flew over the neighbour's property and spotted the owner, who was well known to both of us, riding one of his stock horses. This cocky was also a bit of a wag, so we lowered the chopper and circled close to the ground. From this position, I shouted insults at him over the loudspeaker of the helicopter. With him being on the ground, he couldn't retaliate, so he was pretty much restricted to making rude and obscene hand gestures at us from the saddle of his horse. After a few circuits of insults and obscene gestures, we laughed and waved each other off.

I examined the fences in question, but whoever had cut them had since been long gone.

THE DRIVING TEST

Early one Sunday morning, the only day of the week I didn't get up early and allowed myself a sleep in, I heard a large truck pull up outside the station. Although the arrival of a truck, generally a cattle truck, wasn't unusual, I got up, dressed, and went outside to see who was there. This time it was different as a young woman came walking towards me. As no one else was visible in the truck, I concluded that she was on her own. The girl stopped in front of me and said,

'Mum said to come and see you about a licence, and she said you have to cook me some breakfast before I leave.'

Upon checking her learner's permit, I saw that she was seventeen and that she was Toots Holzheimer's daughter. Toots is known as Australia's first female long haul truck driver.

The girl had driven this fully laden semi-trailer from Cairns to Coen over some of the most atrocious roads in Queensland. However, this wasn't particularly surprising as Toots's kids started driving the family trucks around the depot as soon as they were tall enough to reach the pedals.

I was pretty good mates with Toots, who was in the habit of occasionally pulling up for a cooked breakfast on her way to Weipa. So I duly issued a licence and cooked the girl a feed of bacon and fresh eggs. She then climbed back into the cab of the semi and headed off towards Weipa.

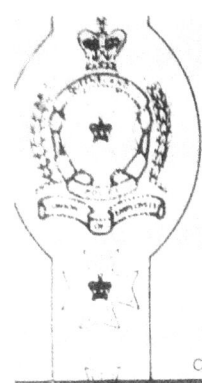

Queensland POLICE JOURNAL

NEW SERIES
Volume 23 No. 5 May, 1981

OFFICIAL ORGAN OF THE QUEENSLAND
POLICE UNION OF EMPLOYEES

Category B — Price 20c

SHORTAGE OF POLICE?
Constable Peter Cahill's German Shepherd dog "Shiloh" doing a stint of duty outside the Coen Watchhouse. Peter and "Shiloh" are now at Tewantin. — General Secretary

DRUG RAID

My German shepherd Shiloh was always keen and ready to go on road trips and do his duty should the situation arise. He was wildly ecstatic when he saw me grab my swag and his travelling kit. The inspector had called a few minutes ago informing me that two detectives were on their way.

'I want you to look after them and take your dog and shotgun.' he said.

Shiloh jumped in the back while I strapped my shotgun, in an upright position, to the dash and floor of the police Toyota. Upon arrival, the detectives filled me in on the details and purpose of the exercise. We were to investigate a large-scale cannabis crop production on a site near Weipa, a five-hour drive to the Northwest of Coen. The information had come from a reliable source, and we were to liaise with the local police sergeant in planning the raid.

In reality, these detectives didn't need any looking after as I had known one of them since the day we both started as police cadets. Stoll distinguished himself some years later, taking down a dangerous criminal named Mullins, who had shot and killed a policeman, and wounded a second one, on a raid named "Operation Flashdance".

Driving north, we traversed through country I never got tired of seeing, despite the bulldust and corrugated roads. Arriving at a relatively isolated site, we spotted a police Toyota parked in front of a large building which was the old Moreton Telegraph Station. The local police sergeant was obviously inside, so we walked up the stairs onto the open wrap-around veranda. They were built this way to provide shade and catch even the slightest of breeze. We found a few blokes sitting around a table drinking beer. It wasn't hard to spot the sarge we were to liaise with as he was in full uniform and was very intoxicated. The two detectives, my attack dog and I were keen to keep moving and to make a start staking out the cannabis crop. As the sergeant knew where it was located, we urged him to get moving on this. However inebriated, he kept rambling and slurring things like,

'You never know that what you hear is actually that what's going on.'

Other nonsensical utterings followed this. We knew that taking a drunk like him with us on the job, where firearms would be used, wasn't an option. So, we did the next best thing and unrolled our swags on the veranda and prepared to stay the night.

The following morning at first light, we followed the sergeant to a place about half an hour east of the township. Here we came across that, which was until very recently, like last night, quite a sizeable cannabis crop. There were remains of an extensive watering system. The people involved in this setup had obviously known what to do. All cannabis plants had been completely removed, leaving no evidence whatsoever. We were a bit put out and knew that we would have had a completely different outcome had we arrived last night.

It had been a wasted trip. The two plainclothes police, my disappointed dog, and I headed back to my station, and from here, the detectives continued to Cairns to brief the inspector. I didn't give it much thought until some months later when one of the detectives rang me and said there had been another drug raid. This time it was conducted by police from Brisbane. The mine's bosses had contacted senior police regarding the continuance of drug trafficking in the area. The southern squad conducted the raid and were taken to the location by the mine's bosses and found that which we hadn't, a good-sized cannabis crop. The perpetrators were arrested at the scene.

BARRY PORT

I hired a man named Barry Port as a replacement tracker for Roddy Short Joe, and I did not doubt that I'd made the right decision, even though it involved almost poaching Barry from another place of employment. He remained in Coen for the rest of his life which included thirty-six years as a tracker. He has been honoured for his excellent service, which included using his not inconsiderable tracking ability on numerous occasions. Barry and I were good mates with a few joint enterprises such as shared laying hens and veggie patch. Sadly Barry is no longer with us, having gone to his reward.

DRINKING AT THE CANTEEN

There were around a thousand residents living in the Lockhart River community, many of whom were prone to drinking at the canteen. The system was one whereby they had their drinking container measured, and from there on in, were charged accordingly as per the premeasured volume. On pay nights, there were a lot of domestic disturbances and fights involving large numbers of people. Often, they suffered serious injuries as a result, and that's when a yellow twin-engine aircraft was called in from Cairns to transport them to the Cairns Base Hospital.

One night the canteen was well patronised, with hundreds of individuals in various levels of intoxication and a range of corresponding levels of belligerence. A massive, big brawl spread throughout the community. It was very dark, the noise horrendous, and it wasn't safe for me or any of the half a dozen community police officers to venture into the arena. The local community police were invaluable when it came to settling domestic disturbances and more minor melees, but this night, they were all with me back at the shed, which we called "the office".

We decided to retrieve the injured and get them to the small hospital where they could be treated until the yellow plane arrived at Iron Range airport. The aerodrome, built for large aircraft, had been a wartime base for the Americans and was afterwards used as a commercial strip. We received a call that a woman had been struck in the head and was leaking brain fluid from her ears. So we mounted up the short wheelbase Toyota and took one of the two nurses with us. I drove while the community cops settled on the bull bar, running boards and on the back. The bull bar riders shouted directions of where to go, and I was given the choice of whether to reverse into the melee or drive straight in. I opted for the latter. Heaps of people suddenly materialised out of the darkness with one big bloke in the lead. There was another Toyota, similar to the police vehicle in the community, and it was owned by a White bloke named Phil. The only police insignia on my vehicle had been the blue light on the crossbar, which I'd removed because of the overhanging foliage in Tozer's Gap. To the casual or drunken observer, the vehicles were pretty much identical. This large drunk man armed with a large knife loomed out of the darkness and charged towards me screaming,

'Phil, you cunt.'

He was intent on settling a score and having a go, thinking that I was Phil. The last thing we needed was a pitched battle in the middle of this drunken, out of control mob, especially with the nursing sister with us. The cops on the bull bar jumped off as I drove the vehicle slowly towards this man, not going fast enough to hurt him if I was to nudge him. It was my only option, as we needed to get to the seriously injured woman as soon as possible. Adding us to the casualty list simply wasn't an option. As I reached the man, he was still charging, so I braked just short of the impact, but unfortunately, I still hit him with the bull bar and down he went. I felt terrible as I had a bad feeling that I'd hit him too hard, so I stopped and ran around to the front where he was lying spreadeagled on his back. As I went over to him, he said,

'Is that you Conjubal?'

I said, 'Yes, Neil.'

'I sorry for getting in your way.'

'That's okay, Neil, just don't do it again.'

'Okay, I won't Conjubal', he said, getting up and lumbering off back into the gloom.

We located the injured woman and delivered her to the hospital, where the nurses looked after her until the plane arrived. Unfortunately, there had been many more injuries, and I was at the hospital when several patients were transported to the waiting aircraft. I had the utmost respect for those nurses as they work in hostile environments and carry out procedures under instruction at times that would only be required of a qualified doctor.

I spoke to Neil, the man I had encountered with the police Toyota in the dark the previous night, but he had no knowledge of the incident and found it hilarious to find out he'd been "run over".

'I didn't know that.' he said, laughing.

The woman with the brain damage eventually returned to the community. She didn't know what had happened and neither did anyone else. That was not surprising, considering the severe levels of intoxication of a vast number of people that night.

TRANSFER TO THE SUNSHINE COAST

Promotions within the police department were given on a seniority basis and further determined by the date you were sworn in. As a senior constable, I knew that I wasn't due for the next jump to sergeant for quite some time, so I decided to transfer to the Sunshine Coast.

It was early December, the wet season started to announce itself, and it was time to leave the outback if I wanted to make it out. I farewelled the Coen community and stopped at Bamboo Station to say goodbye to the owners, as we'd become good mates. On hearing that I was at Bamboo, the property bloke of a station further north called me up on the radio, suggesting I get moving fast or be stuck in Coen until April. He said that in Fairlight Creek, a twelve-foot wall of water had just passed his place and was on its way down. I needed to cross this creek if I wanted to make it out, so I jumped in my ute and floored it, hoping to get across ahead of the wall of water racing down from the north. The thing is, with a wall of water that size, it travels at an increasing speed while picking up timber, dead cattle, and other debris and becomes impossible to cross.

I managed to beat the enormous rush of water by several minutes and only just made it across. Then, while trying to calm the adrenaline rush, I stood on the opposite bank and watched in awe as nature did its thing. Feeling relieved, I jumped behind the wheel and, with my dogs on board, started my travels south, looking forward to a change of lifestyle.

TEWANTIN

SUNSHINE COAST POSTING

I arrived at my new posting in Tewantin, a peaceful Sunshine Coast township on the Noosa River one hundred and twenty kilometres north of central Brisbane. I managed to rent a small cabin in the Noosa Hinterland on a twenty-acre block. It had a huge window that delivered impressive views of the surrounding forest and night sky. It was a peaceful place to live, which was good as I started to experience symptoms of PTSD more frequently. I didn't know anything about PTSD, and at that point, I didn't realise that it was this that was plaguing me. The first indication of something being wrong came when I was driving down a range, and while navigating the narrow roads, I felt gripped by an incredible sense of terror which made me pull over until the feeling passed.

I soon became acquainted with the rest of the blokes working at the station, and I settled into a busy but entirely different working environment. The police work at Tewantin involved a lot of attending to petty thefts, like stealing from supermarkets and stores, disorderly persons, drug offenders and the like. Between us, my permanent working partner and I were getting as many criminal arrests as any two pairs of detectives in Brisbane. I joined the karate club and trained up to five times a week, utilising the various dojos around the Sunshine Coast. The Noosa River provided an enclosure for swimming, and the various hills challenged my endurance.

With those provisions, I was in heaven and in top physical condition.

AIRCRAFT CRASH

One day I received a call to go to the Noosa airport in relation to a plane crash. The strip was unsealed and was used only by light aircraft. I didn't immediately see the downed plane, but on closer inspection, I managed to spot it amongst the trees on the other side of the strip. We also saw the pilot staggering around with facial injuries, losing a fair bit of blood.

Facial injuries usually produce a fair bit of bleeding, which sometimes makes it look worse than it is, and fortunately, this was the case. The pilot was taken for a check-up to the Nambour Hospital. The plane was a wreck. It had come nose down and tail up, and with a bit of wing damage, it stood vertical in amongst a stand of trees. How that pilot avoided serious injury is beyond me, it mustn't have been his time to leave. I furnished the usual aircraft crash report, a procedure I was getting quite familiar with.

IT'S ALL PART OF THE JOB

The Queensland Ambulance Transport Brigade, known as QATB, was often understaffed. It wasn't unusual for police to drive the ambulance when there was only one QATB bloke available. Even civilians have, on rare occasions, driven the vehicles.

I got in behind the wheel of one in Tewantin one Monday afternoon following a vehicle collision. The seriously injured, pregnant woman had been the driver of one of the vehicles involved and needed the undivided attention of the ambulance man. So I turned the F100, ambulances' light and siren on, and we were on our way. Incredibly, on the way to the hospital, a couple of fools in a white Volkswagen Beetle were in front of me, zigzagging. They were doing their best to prevent the ambulance from getting past. I eventually managed to get the big powerful Ford out beside them, wound down my window and yelled at the long-haired, bearded grub in the passenger seat,

'Get out of the fucking way, you maggots.'

On seeing a police uniform at the wheel of the ambulance, they panicked and veered wildly to the side of the road. I managed to get the rego number of the Volkswagen for future action.

The woman and her unborn child got to the hospital in time and made a full recovery. The driver of the vehicle involved in the collision with her, a young man who had been celebrating the Mad Monday tradition following the end of the AFL season, was also booked. I thought the whole incident resulted in a satisfactory conclusion.

SCHOOL BUS ROLLOVER.

One afternoon, I was working by myself in a car when a call came over the radio that a school bus full of kids had run off the side of the Cooroy Tewantin Road and had overturned. As did any other available police cars, I immediately headed towards the scene as quickly as possible. However, as I drove up the range, it was with much trepidation, as I feared the worse. Great was my relief as I arrived on the scene where I was greeted by the sight of a group of about thirty children sitting along the side of the road.

Other police and ambulances started arriving as well; the response was quick, but as it turned out that, apart from being badly frightened, the kids were okay, bar one who had a broken collar bone.

The bus was on its side, probably thirty metres down from the road, and it was very fortunate that it stopped there. One of the older boys had kicked out the back window, thus allowing the rest of the children to clamber out and back up onto the roadway. The injured child and driver were taken to the Nambour Hospital.

I made the preliminary inquiries and furnished an accident report. Later I also took a few statements from some of the children. The investigation was taken over by a member of the C.I. Branch in conjunction with the State Transport machinery Inspector because it was a school bus.

I don't know the final outcome, but I knew for sure that somewhere, someone was looking out for those kids on the school bus that afternoon.

THE VISITING DETECTIVES

Usually, there were two detectives at Tewantin, but both were away when two, New South Wales, detectives turned up. The business that brought them to Noosa was an investigation into drugs and money laundering. Police etiquette at the time dictated that these blokes were shown around the area and, in particular, the hotels. My partner and I were asked to do the honours.

The night went well, with one of the two detectives badly hitting the grog. He ordered cheese and salami platters and gave us a rendition of Danny Boy to show off his singing prowess. At closing time, he was starting to show signs of a big night out. He laughed at everything and anything and became extremely loud. Once outside, I opened the rear door of the unmarked police vehicle so he could fall straight in. At this point, he thought it extremely hilarious to yell out to the large mob of assorted drunks and ratbags who were swarming in the car park.

'Hey, you blokes. The coppers are locking me up.'

Now the large resident community of drug and booze abusers had started referring to my partner and me as "Four Eyes" and "Kiddy Cop", respectively. I had started wearing glasses, and my mate had a deceptively looking, young face but was capable of some impressive hand to hand ability when required. With my partner already seated in the front, and both visiting detectives in the back, I was left on my own outside the vehicle. I found myself surrounded by a herd of emboldened louts who, by their vast superiority of numbers and fortified by booze, decided to have a go at us with a view of rescuing the "prisoner".

As the circle of drunks around me drew in closer, I advised them to move away as it was none of their business. The drunken detective in the back of the car was in hysterics. Over the din of the herd making threats, I distinctly heard the click of the car door of the police vehicle, which meant that my partner got out to join me. Knowing that together we formed a force to be reckoned with, I immediately laid into my wannabe assailants leading with a good solid punch to the nearest stomach. I followed it up with a highly effective series of back fists, elbow strikes, foot sweeps and stamping kicks. Barely had I just landed the second strike when my mate hoed into the mob on my left with some beautifully executed kicks and strikes, and almost as quickly as it started, the mob dispersed in all directions, bar the half a dozen which laid sprawled out on the ground.

However, one turkey had an enormous big mouth right from the onset of the confrontation, and he was having great difficulty making his escape due to the press of the fleeing mob. So I grabbed him. I wasn't interested in locking him up or anyone else if I could possibly avoid it, so he was told to start running along the footpath and that if he stopped running, he would immediately get a hiding. I never saw a drunk run so fast.

By the time we dropped the inebriated detective and his mate off at their motel, he had gotten over the hilarity of it all. His only mention of the incident the next day to the local detectives was that,

'Those blokes are very hard on the hoons.'

SLEDGEHAMMER

One evening I was working with a detective who was investigating complaints from a building company. The company was engaged in the construction of a housing estate near Tewantin. Reported was that someone had gone to the area and shot out the newly installed upmarket streetlights, and the detective had a fair idea of who was responsible.

It was just after hotel closing time at 10 pm when we drove past one of the hotel car parks. Here we saw the bloke the detective was looking for. He was sitting in the driving seat of a large white Ford sedan, parked up on a wide footpath adjoining the car park. The man was also drinking out of a long-necked, tally beer bottle. We both got out of the unmarked police car and walked over to the driver's side door—the detective wearing plain clothes with me in uniform.

The detective tapped on the car's side window and motioned for the man inside to lower the window; however, the man simply laughed and took a big swig from the beer bottle. I went and got a breath testing device from the police car, which I handed to the detective, who in turn showed it to the man inside. This caused him to laugh even more, and once again, he took another mouthful from the bottle and was obviously, thoroughly enjoying the situation.

It was now plain that the man inside the car wasn't interested in opening the door, so the detective went and retrieved a sledgehammer from the boot of the police car. He then walked back over to the white car and held the sledgehammer up so that the man inside could clearly see it. The bloke inside the car thought that this was even more hilarious. He burst out in a fit of laughter and followed it up with another swig of beer. This was becoming a bit monotonous by now, so the detective then tapped on the car's window with the sledgehammer causing the man inside to erupt in gales of laughter.

However, the look on his face changed instantly to one of absolute astonishment when the detective swung the hammer with force and smashed the side window. The man's expression was priceless and was one of those rare occasions when you would love to have a camera handy. He had ceased laughing.

The man was charged with an alcohol driving offence in addition to the wilful destruction incidents involving the streetlights. We found a silencer in the glove box of his car, fitted to a small calibre pistol, used to destroy the streetlights. He admitted to being responsible for the damage, and after entering a plea of guilty, he was given a substantial fine along with the bill for restitution.

TANNUM SANDS

THE STATION

Tannum Sands was a small coastal town which, in combination with Boyne Island, an adjacent small town, had a population of about seven thousand people. Most of the people were employed at the large aluminium refinery on Boyne Island. A new temporary two-man police station had been opened on Boyne Island because of the growing population and the distance of the nearest police station being at Gladstone twenty kilometres to the north. I received a phone call from the personnel section asking me if I would be interested in transferring to the new station. Although I wasn't unhappy with my current position at Tewantin and had excellent workmates, I decided to accept the offer. I knew that I would be due for promotion to Sergeant Second Class Officer in six months or so, and as I had never worked on the central coast of Queensland, the situation suited me well.

After the usual send-offs, I hooked my boat up to my ute and headed north to Boyne Island. The name of the police station was listed as Tannum Sands because a much larger new station was due for construction there in the near future. The temporary station was a duplex, with one side used as single men's quarters and the other housed a small police station. There was an open area beside the station extending down to the incredibly blue Boyne River. As far as police work went, there wasn't much to do, and during the time I spent there, I made two arrests only. The bulk of the work was issuing Queensland driving licences to the refinery employees, who had moved to Boyne Island and Tannum Sands from other Australian States and New Zealand.

There was a sergeant in charge of the station, a thoroughly decent bloke, but I didn't see him much as he had a massive backlog of court cases to attend in Cairns after spending a couple of years in Yarrabah. On my days off, I occasionally did wide load escorts to one of the several coal mines to the west of Rockhampton. In addition, I had the opportunity to continue some serious training in my martial arts style at the local club. So, all in all, I spent a relatively peaceful six months at the little station until a vacancy for a Sergeant Second Class Officer in Charge of Burketown in the Gulf Country was gazetted. I successfully applied for the position and got my gear ready to move.

CARL THE GERMAN SHEPHERD

I was friendly with the bar manager of the Tannum Sands pub named Viv and often went around to his place on a social basis. He owned a large male German shepherd named Carl, a great family dog and an excellent natural protector. The dog had assigned himself the task of collecting the daily mail delivered by the postman. Big Carl would pad out to the letterbox as soon as he heard the approaching postal bike and waited on the footpath for the postie. The postie knew Carl, and each day, after pulling up at the mailbox, he handed the mail to the big fellow who'd take it inside to Viv's wife.

The postie had a few problems, early in the proceedings, if there was no mail to be delivered. The house didn't have a front fence, so the dog went and stood on the footpath to stop the bike, not aggressive but definitely requiring mail. So, the postie decided to make sure he always had a piece of paper, cardboard, or anything that he could hand over to the sizeable canine mail collector. It didn't matter to Carl what it was, all he wanted to do, was his job and take "the mail" inside.

FROM TANNUM SANDS TO BURKETOWN

It had been a long and hot eighteen-hundred-kilometre trip up to Burketown from Tannum Sands. I hit the road in my old Dodge 114-Series two-ton truck I had purchased from the army. It had spent its life as a military police vehicle at the Oaky army base. For thirteen years, the only serious work required of the old truck had been to transport beer for the military police mess. I had my two dogs, Shiloh, and Sabre, with me, and during the four-day trip, the heat was getting to them. These old trucks did not come with air-conditioning, and with daytime temperatures reaching up to fifty-two degrees centigrade, I decided to travel mostly at night. The going was slow because kangaroos and wallabies were out in force, spilling out onto the road. They were most active at dawn and dusk to avoid the heat, feeding on the green tufts of grass growing on the road verges. It stands to reason that this is when most kangaroo hits with cars and trucks happen. They're also a bit like rabbits in that they are attracted to headlights.

About eight hundred kilometres into the journey, I managed to hit not one but two roos, which were impossible to avoid. While collisions with animals account for five percent as causes of fatal car accidents, kangaroo and wallaby collisions make up almost ninety percent of those. They can do some serious damage to your car, and it was no different for the old Dodge, with enough damage to the radiator that it required repairs.

There is a severe lack of roadside telephones and passing traffic on bush roads, and I was happy to make it, at snail pace, to the small town of Alpha. I pulled up at the local police station, where I learned that there were no mechanics in town. The cop in charge said,

'No worries mate, we'll fix this.'

With that, he handed me a bottle of black pepper and told me to tip the contents into the radiator, guaranteeing that it would fix the leaks. Sure enough, it did the trick, and I decided there and then to have a bull bar fitted at the first opportunity and to carry a bottle of black pepper in the glove box just in case.

On my way again, I encountered a bit of rain, and when I was nearing Burketown, I hit a boggy patch of road. I knew that I was in trouble, and once again, on a deserted road. Just like that, the wheels lost grip and spun around uselessly in the wet black soil. I didn't have mud tyres fitted on the old Dodge, but, it being low geared in first, there is a way of leaving it to turn over, stand next to it and push it along. It is considered a dangerous practice, especially by yourself, so I was pleased when a bloke in a four-wheel-drive ute pulled up. He introduced himself as a local cattleman and was kind enough to tow me out of a boggy patch, and without further mishap, I arrived in the Gulf Country town of Burketown.

It was peaceful in town as it was still the early morning hours. I was ready to start my two and a half years of duty as Sergeant Second Class Officer in Charge.

BURKETOWN

THE NEW YEAR'S EVE TRAP

I met the young relieving constable, Dick and didn't get much time to settle in, as on the first night, there was a run-in with two half-drunk brothers, whose disorderly conduct resulted in their arrests. We locked them both up, and I got on with organising my gear into my new living quarters, the police residence, which was to be my accommodation for the next two and a half years.

On New Year's Eve, Dick and I decided to have a beer at the local hotel with some of the locals. We'd barely arrived when someone informed us of a fight going on outside down the road from the hotel. I saw that a disturbance was in progress a short distance away, and I should've realised something wasn't quite right. However, it was very dark, and the brawl was not far from the local store near a cluster of small Melaleuca tea trees, common to the Gulf Country.

It was the start of the wet season, and it had been raining a lot, causing the dirt shoulders of the one-lane bitumen road to be very muddy and slippery. When Dick and I arrived on the scene, several agitated men were very vocal, pushing and shoving each other. One of them was huge and would weigh in at least one hundred and forty kilos. He seemed to be the most formidable member of the group, and even though my weight was just eighty-five kilos, I decided there was no point mucking around.

I went over to him and told him to get going, and

when he didn't comply, I grabbed hold of his arm and pushed him away from the man with whom he was arguing. He turned and took an almighty swing at me, aiming for my right eye. Here my martial art training stood me in good stead, and I managed to see the punch coming. He hit me, but I avoided the worst of it, so I grabbed him and managed to put a police stranglehold on this massive bloke. My manoeuvre subdued him considerably, and soon I had him on his knees and followed up with a full nelson restraining hold that limited his movement from the neck, head, and arms.

While this took place, Dick had become separated from me and was now surrounded and trapped by several screaming, extremely aggressive men who had suddenly stepped out from the darkness of the trees and the back of the store. I knew then that we had most definitely walked into a trap. Dick had his back to me, and while I held the massive bloke on the ground, I called out to him.

'Don't turn around. Walk backwards towards me!'

Unfortunately, with all the screaming and mayhem that went on, Dick didn't hear my instructions. Fearing the worse, I watched him turn around as if in slow motion, and with his back now towards the mob, he walked towards me.

Immediately, the mob sprang into action, attacking Dick from behind and delivered several blows to his head, leaving him half senseless as he stumbled towards me. At this time, the bloke I'd been holding got his second wind and attempted to get up. He was ready to continue the fight, so while he was still on his knees, I applied a quick elbow strike to prevent that from happening. The huge man hit the ground again, and this was enough of a demonstration to make the other participants in the melee reconsider their next move. This also gave me enough time to drag Dick out of there and throw him into the front of the Dodge, where both guard dogs were waiting. I jumped into the driver's seat next to him and slowly reversed the vehicle away from the scene, then drew to a halt.

The fact that we were retreating emboldened the crowd once more; feeling encouraged, they moved forward together, united in one group, to where I had pulled up. If we were to salvage this situation, I saw only one option, so I shifted gears and accelerated the large ute across the slippery, muddy street towards them. I put the vehicle into a full broadside and braked in time to come to a screeching halt, just in front of the astonished group. At no stage was there any chance of anyone being run over, but my surprise stunt well and truly had the desired effect.

Once again, they were left to reconsider their moves and relieved, I saw them scatter in all directions. But still, it wasn't over. Some of the extremely aggressive men refused to settle down. I wanted nothing more than to return peace to the night so, I decided that enough was enough. I left Dick in the truck with my younger dog Sabre while I got out with my trained protection dog, Shiloh. Upon seeing this big German shepherd by my side, the aggressive men completely lost interest in carrying on the confrontation any longer. Several of them bolted into the surrounding scrub while another clambered in panic onto an elevated fuel tank to avoid contact with Shiloh. Dick, who had by now recovered, joined me and together, we rounded up and arrested the blokes responsible.

Things settled down after this initial confrontation. It seemed that an acceptable position, and an understanding of required social behaviour, had been established.

From that day onwards, the locals addressed me as

Sarge, Sergeant and shortly afterwards as Dad, or Our Old Dad, even though I wasn't that old, being thirty-two years of age. It was a form of address and a mark of respect and, other than a few outside visitors coming to Burketown, I had no more trouble with the locals.

HASHTAG'S DAY IN COURT

I had been in Burketown for about six months when I decided it was about time to go to Mount Isa to meet the new inspector. As is custom when living in remote communities, I would also do a big grocery run in the city as my sad-looking pantry desperately needed stocking up to see me through for a minimum of three months. The wet season was well and truly over, and the small local store only carried the basics. They simply couldn't stock the range of stuff you'd find in big supermarket chains. I allowed the other constables to go first and take a few days to do their grocery runs, and upon their return, I left.

The road to Mount Isa via Gregory Downs and Thorntonia was the shortest way. It was not the best road as the country dries out quickly and creates bulldust to replace the previous boggy mud. But, in my experience, it was a lot better than the rough road through Tozers Gap on Cape York, which I had driven before. I was approaching the Gregory Pub when I saw a heavy freight truck approach. It was enveloped in a massive cloud of dust kicked up by its many wheels, so I slowed and pulled up to let it go by. Several rocks were thrown up by the eighteen-wheeler, which unavoidably hit the police vehicle, but I didn't know at the time that one of the larger stones had hit the radiator. I resumed my journey, and when the motor started to fail, I quickly realised the probable cause. My suspicion was confirmed when I found a large hole in the now dry radiator and knew the engine was past redemption as it, well and truly, had seized up.

These were the days without mobile phones and police radios, and it was a nightmare to get the car towed to the pub for transport to Mount Isa. Organising a ride back to the police station for my dogs and me was another, but I was lucky and managed to organise a lift. Once back at the station, I fired up my old Dodge truck and headed off for the second time on route to Mount Isa, where my first task was to meet the new inspector. I wasn't particularly looking forward to giving him the "good news" about the damage to the police vehicle.

I knocked and entered through the open doorway, and after introducing myself, I relayed the bad news about the seized-up diesel motor of the police vehicle. You could expect to get yelled at back in those days, and I was ready for it.

'You stupid bastard. How on earth did you manage that, and what do you have to say about the matter?'

I explained what had happened and added,

'My responsibility, my fault. I was the driver and should've been more alert. That's about all I can say.'

The inspector went on a bit longer, saying how stupid this was and, if there was such thing as next time, I had better be more careful, and I said that I would.

I learned later that the inspector had informed his colleagues that there is no doubt about Sergeant Cahill, he tells the truth as it is. From then on, my credibility amongst the bosses was excellent. As I turned to leave the office, the inspector said,

'What are you doing at five today?'

I replied, 'Nothing in particular.'

'Well, you know where I live, come over for a couple

of beers.'

At five that afternoon, I wandered over to the inspector's house with my dogs, where I found him sitting underneath his high set house. He tossed me a cold beer from the well-stocked fridge, and we settled in for a yarn while the dogs ran loose in the fenced yard. We only just pulled open a second beer when there was a hell of a commotion coming from the front yard. One of my dogs was barking furiously at a scruffy, shabby-looking bloke with long unkempt hair and beard who stood on the footpath screaming and flailing his arms wildly at the dog, who in turn, badly wanted to eliminate what he saw as an intruder. The bloke obviously felt a need to provoke the dog, so I went over to the fence and said,

'You better get out of here before these dogs jump the fence and something really bad happens to you.'

I could see the threat registering on his face and watched as he walked off, and when he was well down the road, I went back under the house to finish my beer. You wouldn't know, but about ten minutes later, the commotion started up again. It was the same bloke screaming and agitating the big dog. I also knew that this bloke would be a direct threat to the community in his drunken and high on drugs state, so I called out to the Boss,

'I am going to have to lock this bastard up!'

'I'll get my station wagon!' he replied.

I called Shiloh over and secured him under the house so he couldn't join in by "helping" with the arrest. Out onto the footpath, I approached the bloke whom I learned was named Hashtag. I did not want to injure him, so I placed him in a full nelson restraining hold. True to word, the inspector pulled up with the wagon and opened the rear door. I was walking this bloke towards it when I noticed that he had a reefer between two of his fingers, so I said,

'Boss, he's got a cigarette in his fingers. Can you grab it?'

'No worries Pete' he replied, and in a flash, he reached up and tried to grab the cigarette, but this bloke would have none of it. In the struggle that ensued, the still-burning reefer ended up inside this bloke's tracksuit pants. Well, you should have seen this bloke buck and scream. I was laughing so much that I had to make sure I didn't lose him. I placed Hashtag in the back of the wagon and accompanied him on his short trip to the watchhouse. He continued to carry on and screamed when I took him into the charge room,

'I demand to see the inspector.'

He was visibly deflated when the Boss stood in front of him and slowly said,

'I am the inspector.'

We placed him in a cell and went back to finish our interrupted beer session. The Boss left a message informing the morning crew about the arrest and for them to follow this bloke once he was released on bail. They gave Hashtag a few minutes to settle back into his tent in one of the local caravan parks where he was kicking back, relaxing with his bong, when the two young cops entered his tent and arrested him on drugs charges. Hashtag was gobsmacked. Upon leaving the local courtroom later that day, he turned and announced to everyone present,

'After arriving from the Northern Territory, I've been in Queensland for only two days and never before have I met such a collective pack of bastards like you.'

Once he was released, he immediately moved back to where he had come from, and we never saw or heard of Hashtag again.

MORNING GLORY

A fascinating flat country interspersed with numerous stunted trees and termite nests. Waters of the Gulf of Carpentaria creeping in, morphing the ground into black tidal flats devoid of vegetation. Thick mangroves grow along the edges of waterways as they flow towards the Gulf. I have always been fascinated with the geography of the Gulf Country. The flat country extents at least one hundred kilometres inland from the Gulf, and in the early nineteen hundreds, the sea reached Gregory Downs. Unfortunately, several lives were lost, including that of the police sergeant's wife.

The wildlife is much the same as anywhere else in Northern Australia, but there is one spectacular atmospheric-meteorological phenomenon I was privileged to observe many times during my two and a half years in the Gulf. It's the cloud formation that's known as the Morning Glory. The phenomenon appeared in the Gulf of Carpentaria during August and September. The formation also occurs in the Gulf of Mexico, with similar characteristics to the Gulf of Carpentaria. Still, despite the wind movements being the same, it lacked the spectacular cloud formation.

It rolled in at around forty kilometres per hour from the Gulf towards the coast and then onwards overland, the cloud moved forward while rotating to the rear as it raced by. Sometimes there would be one long cloud stretching across the horizon as far as you could see, and sometimes, there were several following each other with the intensity dropping off with each successive "glory". One morning I got a call from the new matron of the local hospital who, at not ever having witnessed a Morning Glory or even knew of their existence, telephoned the police station thinking it might have been a type of nuclear attack.

HELICOPTERS GULF COUNTRY

The big stock camps of years gone by have pretty much been replaced by mechanised methods such as quad bikes and helicopters. Helicopter mustering requires a great deal of skill when rounding up a mob of cattle while trying to avoid collisions with trees and power lines. During my service in the Gulf Country, I came across a few of these pilots. Their aircraft skills were frankly unforgettable.

My private vehicle, the old two-ton Dodge utility, looked for all intents and purposes, especially with the canvas canopy, exactly like a light army truck. It was my day off, so I decided to go for a day trip to Normanton, about a three hours' drive east. An old travelling saddler who had conducted his saddle repair business out of the courthouse, and a professional barramundi fisherman, jumped in as well. They were both quite happy with the opportunity to have a day out.

The country we travelled through was primarily flat, with a few stunted trees and river crossings. The quantity of water in these rivers varied with the seasons. However, we were never disappointed by their beauty, albeit the dark brown flow of the Albert, the yellow clay colour of the Leichardt after the Wet and the deep blue of the Flinders and Bynoe rivers. The crocodiles in the Leichhardt River were yellow in colour due to the build-up of yellow clay on their massive bodies, whereas the Albert and Nicholson River crocs were covered in black mud. Despite the uncomfortable heat, especially in my old non-airconditioned truck, a dip in any of those rivers was out of the question. We were travelling along, yarning away, and enjoying a beer, when suddenly, in the distance, a helicopter appeared. It was flying very low and was following the road directly towards us. The barra bloke said dryly,

'Here comes a helicopter.'

The saddler and I both had to agree with him, and I just kept on driving. The gap between the truck and chopper rapidly decreased, and we unanimously agreed that the helicopter would lift in time. It was a road for vehicles, after all. Well, it did so at the very last second and only just missed my CB radio aerial by inches. The fisherman said,

'That was close.'

And once again, we had to agree with him. It was unusual, to say the least, but this was Gulf Country where anything could happen.

Suddenly it appeared again. This time it was flying low to the left of the truck and slow enough for us to see the pilot clearly. The barra bloke held up his beer so the pilot could see it, and to our surprise, he nodded and gave us a thumbs-up. The aircraft shot forward and landed some distance ahead of us at the side of the road. We pulled up next to it and handed the pilot a beer, who said he'd thought we were with the army seeing it was an army truck. He had not long been out of the military himself following a couple of tours in Vietnam as a pilot. When he spotted us, he'd figured he'd frighten the soldiers with his manoeuvre. It was good for a laugh, and after downing the beer, he climbed back into his aircraft and took off until he was no more than a speck on the horizon.

ENTERTAINMENT COMES TO BURKETOWN

As in most small outback towns, Burketown had a community hall. The town was abuzz because a couple of country music performers were coming to town. I had some court briefs to go through and was in my office when I heard a knock at the station's back door.

Upon opening the door, I was surprised to see a well-known country singer standing there holding a bottle of rum. He said he wasn't required to perform that night and felt like having a drink with someone and thought the police station would be an excellent place to start. I wasn't averse to a beer, and being off duty, I invited him in, thinking this was a one-off having a drink with a bloke I'd only seen on television. I put my paperwork aside and grabbed a beer from the fridge.

Probably an hour later of exchanging stories, there was another knock on the door, a very loud, angry-sounding knock at that. This time upon answering the door, I was met by an agitated man who was the boss of the touring group demanding to see my newfound drinking companion. He seemed to feel that I was responsible for his performer's absence, but I quickly told him the rum drinker's story of not being required to perform that night. Annoyed, the organiser of the show left right away with my erstwhile companion in tow.

Now the rum drinker was in a fair state of intoxication, and out of curiosity, I thought I'd go round to the hall and see what sort of effect that would have on his performance. I wasn't disappointed in that respect, he slurred a few rude comments to the audience, and I was amazed that none of them had gone up and punched him. However, out of politeness, I guess, no one did.

The group left the following day for Normanton, and I heard later that he had parted ways with the touring group altogether after an incident of him being drunk and vomiting on stage during his performance.

THE COP WHO OUTRAN A CHARGING BUFFALO

As part of my self-set physical training program, I was in the habit of jogging ten kilometres once a day along the Albert River and out to the bridge. One morning I decided on a whim to cross the bridge. After covering the extra distance, I noticed a movement well off to my left across the flat Gulf Country terrain. There was a bull standing there, watching me. At least, I thought it was a bull. I stopped jogging and had a better look at my visitor, only to realise that it was a large buffalo with an impressive set of horns. The situation didn't feel at all comfortable, as these buffaloes can be aggressive. Furthermore, I had difficulty comprehending how the buffalo had arrived where he was, considering his home was the Northern Territory, a good five hours drive away. I wasn't armed, so I decided my most prudent move would be to calmly turn around and start the walk back towards the bridge. I kept a close eye on the buffalo, who also commenced walking in my general direction.

Once I reached and crossed the bridge, I took off at a fast gallop towards the township, hoping the buffalo would lose interest, which he did. Once back at the police station, I told Dick about my experience. He promptly reported the location of the buffalo to the Normanton police, and as they happened to be on their way over, they soon located the buffalo and promptly shot him in accordance with disease control guidelines using a heavy calibre rifle. My M1 Carbine would have been about as useful as throwing a handful of stones at the beast, so I left it to them to handle. Unfortunately, those wild buffalo carried a lot of diseases that endangered the cattle.

By now, news of the buffalo had spread far and wide. The story was broadcast over ABC regional radio and featured in the next edition of Queensland Country Life News Paper and given the story a great deal of latitude in the description. As a result, I was a bit of a minor celebrity for a while and was known as "The cop who outran a charging buffalo in the wilds of the Gulf Country".

SHILOH GOES TO SCHOOL

Doomadgee is an Aboriginal community in the Burketown police division, about one hundred kilometres west of the town. Back then, it had a population of around two thousand people. It also had a state school with several teachers, one of whom, Phil, became a good and long-term mate of mine.

One day Phil asked me if I could bring out my trained dog Shiloh to give the school kids a dog obedience demonstration as a bit of a novelty. The exercise went down extremely well with the kids, none of whom had probably ever seen such a large dog, especially one that could do the things Shiloh did. A few brave kids came forward to meet the dog up close, with Shiloh, in turn, lapping up all the extra attention. All in all, it had been a successful exercise enjoyed by all.

THE STABBING

I'd established a good rapport with the locals in the Gulf Country, including the large community of Doomadgee where the residents referred to me as their "Old Dad". One morning I needed to travel out to the community in the police Toyota. I had a young relieving constable with me to give me a hand with inquiries regarding a minor incident that had occurred the previous day. Before we even had a chance to pull on the handbrake, a local ran up to the police truck shouting that Martin Cooper was killing people down near the eastern end of the settlement.

Leaving in a cloud of dust, I drove with speed to where the man had indicated this incident was in progress. On arrival, a dreadful scene was unfolding in front of us. Two males were on the ground, one badly bleeding, with a second male lying on the ground a short distance away. There also was a powerfully built male, I knew as Martin Cooper, bending over him, and he appeared to be pulling a large knife out of the man's back. A terrified woman stood close by, screaming hysterically. I did not doubt that she was going to be Martin's next victim. The young relieving constable had never seen anything like this before and had eyes like saucers as he was taking in the surreal event taking place in front of him. He started to do what any competent police officer would do under those same circumstances, especially in a city environment. He immediately reached for his service revolver, which he had sitting in the side pocket of the car door.

I knew the man with the knife well and never had any trouble with him previously. I decided to take a bit of a punt and asked the young bloke to hold fire for now. If possible, I wanted to avoid drastic action in the form of a deadly ending via a Ruger .357 Magnum revolver.

The shooting of a person, regardless of lawful justification, would only exacerbate the situation. It could create a riot involving the extended families both of Cooper and his victims. There would be other fallout issues following a shooting in communities like these by a police officer. Cooper looked up and saw the police vehicle. I figured I had only a few seconds to act to prevent any harm coming to the hysterical woman. I opened the door slightly and, leaning out, I called out to Cooper. He still had a large knife in his hand and looked at the hysterical woman who knew she was next. I said,

'Martin, drop the knife and get in the back of the police truck. Now!'

I wasn't surprised when Cooper dropped the knife, dripping with blood, into the dirt and calmly walked over to the police vehicle. He opened the door and climbed in the back, and sat down on the bench. The young constable was unquestionably more surprised by this than he had been on witnessing the goings-on after our arrival thirty seconds before.

At this point, two other people, a young couple, rushed over to the window through which I had spoken to Cooper. Both were visibly distressed.

The girl informed me that her brother had objected to their relationship and had started the process of having them both sung to death. It's often referred to as pointing the bone at someone. I knew personally of cases where this process had been highly effective in its intended outcome. The sum of the situation I now had was two blokes with severe knife wounds needing urgent medical attention, the offender in the caged rear of the police vehicle, and two young subjects of what could very well be a death sentence. The excellent level of respect I had within the community was more imperative than ever.

Buoyed by my success so far in this situation, with both

of them having their hand on my sleeve where the insignia of rank was, I told them to leave it with me, and I'll look after it, and that from here on in, they would be safe. They thanked me profusely and took off with speed. Now my offsider had a chance to check the injuries of the two men bleeding on the ground. Hospital staff had been advised and soon arrived on the scene. The injured men were treated and transported to the hospital. This left us with the prisoner, whom we took to the makeshift police office in the administration area of the community. Both stabbing victims survived their injuries, and Martin pleaded guilty and was sentenced to several years in jail.

Some years later, after being promoted and transferred to a troubled community on an island off the Queensland coast, I once again encountered Martin Cooper. He was released from prison at the expiration of his sentence. Martin was just leaving the local supermarket as I was entering, and when he saw me, he said,

'Morning Sarge.'

I replied, 'Good morning, Martin, how's life treating you?'

He said he was good, and it was apparent he had no animosity towards me at all. I saw him again a second time, on a trip to Burketown, not connected to police business. This time he was swimming in the Albert River close to the bridge near an area owned by a nineteen and a half foot long estuarine crocodile. The distance between the front paws of this beast was nearly five feet, and apart from taking cattle and horses, it once had a go at one bloke who was saved when his girlfriend screamed a warning. On seeing where Martin was swimming, I called out to him,

'Hey, Martin. There are big crocs in the water.'

He waved and yelled, 'No worries, Sarge, I'll catch one for you.'

At that, we laughed, and I drove off.

THE HELI-MUSTER PILOT

One morning, my truck was in the mechanic shop for a service, so I drove an old Toyota Landcruiser wagon out to the pier on the Albert River a few kilometres out of town. I had a large, twenty-one-foot runabout moored in the river near the pier, and I went out to check on it regularly. My mate came with me for something to do.

The dirt road was in fairly good condition, so I sped along at speed when suddenly, I could hear another sound over the noise of the old Toyota's engine. I recognised it as that belonging to a small helicopter they use for mustering. I couldn't see it and didn't know where it was until I felt a heavy thump on the vehicle's roof. I looked out of the passenger side window and saw the left-hand side skid of a helicopter. That's when I realised that we had a chopper on the roof, and I was moving along at one hundred kilometres an hour.

The situation got worse when my lunatic mate reached out the window and tried to grab the skid. He would've been successful in his manoeuvre if the passenger side door of the old car hadn't flown open. I immediately reached over and grabbed him by his belt, preventing him from falling out of the vehicle onto the road. The helicopter lifted, then disappeared as quickly as it arrived.

My mate was pretty good friends with the local Heli-Muster Pilots, and upon recognising the vehicle, the pilot had decided to have a bit of fun. Hilarious activity for him, perhaps, not so for me.

PILOT PAYBACK

One last close encounter with a chopper occurred one night when I drove the police vehicle out to the pier. I had Harold, a sandalwood getter, with me when up ahead, a red and a green light appeared some metres off the ground. I thought it unusual, as did Harold, and he suggested that they looked like the port and starboard lights of a boat. Due to its location, this couldn't be as we were still a fair way away from water. Our curiosity was soon satisfied when a helicopter suddenly appeared in front of us. It flew over the top of our vehicle, then raced around us in tight circles, engine roaring and kicking up clouds of dust and disappeared into the darkness. You can only experience these sorts of happenings on a moonless night in the outback. The remainder of our trip was uneventful, and we decided to return to the hotel for a few beers. Not long afterwards, a bloke I recognised as one of the mustering pilots also came into the bar. He wandered over to where Harold and I were sitting and said, laughing,

'Had a bit of fun out near the pier?'

I replied, 'What are you talking about? I haven't been out to the pier.'

A worried expression started to appear on his face, and he said,

'Weren't you in the police car out there half an hour ago?'

I replied, 'No, just told you I hadn't been out there. All I know is that the inspector went for a drive out there earlier, so it must have been him in the car.'

The pilot went a pale colour and said,

'Shit, shit, shit!' and promptly left the bar.

A few days later, he did find out that I had him on, but it must have worried him a bit as there were no more buzzing incidents involving helicopters.

SARGE, THE PIGS ARE OUT

The size of the police reserve at Burketown was an acre and a half, containing the sergeant's residence, police station, watchhouse and courthouse complex. The quarter-acre yard of the residence itself was fully fenced, and at some stage, someone had built a rough pen at the rear of the yard suitable for keeping pigs. I didn't have any pigs and hadn't thought about getting any either. However, one day, Mick, the constable, turned up with a couple of wild pigs in a cage on the back of a borrowed ute. These were young animals, grey and black, and neither had any tusks. A mate of ours, nicknamed "The One-Armed Bandit", lived in the property adjoining the rear of the police reserve. His wife had eleven dachshunds and loved this breed of dog. The first time I met The Bandit was not long after my arrival. He wandered into the station via the back door late one evening. I was in my office with both dogs asleep on the floor. Suddenly, they both jumped up and charged out to the rear entrance. I raced after them and saw The Bandit standing there with a six-pack of beer. He said,

'I thought they were going to take my leg off.'

Noticing he had one arm missing from the elbow down, I replied

'Christ, for a minute there, I thought they took your arm off.' He thought that was hilarious. Mick planned to rear these pigs for several months, worming them regularly with a view of eating them at a later date. Despite my misgivings, I agreed, so the pigs took up residence in the pen at the back of my yard. Mick demonstrated how easy it was to get these pigs quiet by tickling their stomachs with a long, light branch. It surprisingly worked with the animals lying down, enjoying having their bellies scratched. The pigs had only been there for a few days when the previously undetected flaws in the pen construction became obvious. I went downstairs one morning to find the pigs loose in the residence yard. Both pigs were out and had already started digging up the ground with their destructive snouts. Something had to be done and blazing away at them with guns simply wasn't an option. On the other hand, trying to herd those wild pigs back into a pen wasn't a good idea either, mainly because they were guaranteed to attack. My two German shepherds had taken a keen interest in the pigs, but as this breed isn't known for its experience in cornering feral pigs, I quickly called my neighbour, Terry the One-Armed Bandit, to come and give me a hand to re corral the pigs.

Terry arrived a few minutes later with the reinforcement cavalry in the form of eleven dachshunds of various sizes and appearance in coat lengths, all sausage dogs, nonetheless. So we now had a pack of thirteen dogs who'd never met but had no trouble forming a posse, a very noisy posse at that. We opened the pen gate to its full extent and let the dogs go with the idea that they would chase the pigs back into the pen. We figured that the weight of numbers might carry the day and stood back to watch what transpired. It's a shame that video cameras or mobile phones weren't around back then because the circus that followed defied description.

Immediately, as the posse of thirteen dogs entered the yard, they spotted the two wild pigs, and a pursuit commenced accompanied by a lot of barking and yapping from the pack. The combined noise of squealing pigs and barking dogs was incredible. As the yard was fully enclosed, the chase followed the internal perimeters, with the noise increasing several decibels as the race continued. Both my dogs were big powerful blokes and soon overhauled the fleeing pigs and attempted to grab them by the back of their necks. Unfortunately, this manoeuvre didn't turn out to be highly effective and only made the pigs squeal even louder if that was at all possible. The eleven little dogs were still racing along, screaming encouragement.

On the fourth lap of the yard, the three of us being spectators were on the ground, helpless with laughter and incapable of doing anything. The situation was pretty much in the hands of the dogs as we, because of uncontrollable laughter, we're unable to speak, let alone give any commands to the dogs, and the circuits of the yard continued. The pigs, I suspect, badly wanted to get back into the pen to escape the dogs, but the speed at which they were travelling prevented them from making the sharp change of course as they raced by the gate.

On the sixth lap, it was evident that all the competitors in the chase were tiring, and the pigs finally seized the opportunity to get back into their pen. At this stage, still laughing, I managed to get up and call off the big dogs. As luck would have it, as soon as their new pack leaders retired from the chase, all eleven little dogs trotted behind them back to where I was standing. Mick ran in to close the pen gate though I doubt very much the pigs were at all interested in venturing out again. With his eleven dachshunds trotting behind him, Terry returned home next door, and peace reigned again.

THE UNFORGETTABLE PLANE RIDE

Exciting as the encounters with the helicopters may have been; they totally paled in significance, compared to the terrifying, white-knuckled flight in a light plane, I was unfortunate enough to experience when the pilot thought he would impress his passengers with his skills. Undoubtedly, he did have superior flying abilities, having flown for years in the mountainous country of Papua New Guinea. I'm sure that without that ability, we wouldn't have survived the hair-raising flight he subjected us to. But to be honest, I would have been much happier living in blissful ignorance of his flying prowess.

During the Wet season, it had been customary for the shire clerk, his assistant, a couple of council roadworks foremen and the police sergeant to do an aerial inspection of the roads and bridges in the shire. The aircraft chartered was a six-seater owned by a local bloke who had moved to the area after some decades of charter flying in Papua New Guinea. It was also customary to deliver, where possible, mail and necessities to remote, isolated cattle properties. This flight was in line with previous ones, and I duly climbed aboard with the other passengers. I have spent time in light aircraft on previous occasions during searches for missing people and many times since that day. However, none of those flights came close, not even in severe turbulence, to what I experienced that day.

We took off and did some low flying so that the council blokes could have a good look at the flood-damaged roads from the air and make a couple of mail deliveries. After a particularly low pass on a mail drop, I leaned over to the pilot and only half-jokingly, I said,

'I don't think Australia Post expects us actually to

hand the mail to these people.'

This caused some nervous laughter from my fellow passengers. We spotted another property up ahead, and the plane started to descend towards a muddy landing strip. The pilot handled the aircraft very professionally and executed a smooth landing. We delivered the goods, had a yarn with the property owner and took off to the skies with a plane now completely covered in mud. We were flying over the western extremity of the shire on the Northern Territory border when the pilot said,

'I might show you, Gorge Creek. It's pretty impressive this time of the year'.

It seemed like a reasonable suggestion to us. None of us had ever seen this creek, and what could possibly go wrong? As we were approaching, what was obviously a narrow gorge with steep sides, at one hundred and ten knots, I thought it might be a bit challenging to see this "impressive-looking" creek from this position.

The gorge was not as wide as the wingspan of the aircraft. I was incredulous when, as we raced towards the entrance, the pilot did not suddenly fly upwards but turned the plane totally on its side so that the wings were perpendicular to the ground. This is how we entered the gorge at one hundred and ten knots. My mate, a foreman, had a dark complexion; however, at that moment, he could have passed for my brother. As the aircraft wound its way through the curves and bends of the gorge, the pilot said calmly,

'Up ahead is the water pipe. The plane needs a wash.'

We saw what he meant when we rounded a bend and spotted a hole in the vertical side of the gorge. The water was pouring from it much like a house downpipe in a big storm, only much more significant. As he flew the plane through it, the water cascaded over the aircraft as it raced through, removing the mud it had collected on our last landing, a bit like a car wash. Once past the water pipe, I could see daylight up ahead and sighed with relief when the aircraft burst out into the wide-open space and levelled up.

My mate, who'd slowly regained his colour, reached over, and with relief visible on his face, vigorously shook my hand. This pilot undoubtedly had a high degree of skill but displayed a very low level of responsible behaviour, regardless of how many times he'd done this before. I couldn't help but wonder what the first time would've been like when he'd done this manoeuvre.

The joyride seemed to have ended, and thankfully the pilot turned the aircraft for home. Everyone was quiet, reflecting on their experience, and as we were approaching the airport, the pilot announced that, before landing, he intended to wash the remaining bits of mud from the aircraft. He said that he would do this by flying low along the nearby Albert River with the landing gear slightly under the water of the heavily crocodile-infested river. Even if you survived a crash into the Albert and managed to swim, the chances of encountering a substantial estuarine crocodile or a highly venomous box-jellyfish were very likely.

I will never know if he really meant to carry out this last act of lunacy, but I leaned over to him and said quietly,

'I don't think so, not if you want to keep your pilot's licence. Now put this fucking thing down on the airport where it's supposed to go.'

He never said a word and did as I wanted. I never was so pleased to feel the ground under my feet as when I alighted from that plane. I let the whole thing go because we all survived and found out later that washing the aircraft in the Albert River was, in fact, something this bloke had done previously. He must have carried out those plane washes flawlessly because I heard that he lived to ripe old age.

CONFERENCE PERKS

As the officer in charge of a police station, I had to attend regular conferences at the district headquarters in Mount Isa, six hundred kilometres down the road. I didn't particularly look forward to these events other than that they provided me with a paid shopping trip. I always carried my swag with me and had a spot not far from the main road that led from Camoweal to Mount Isa, where I stopped for the night. After letting the dogs have a run, I secured them on either side of my swag before settling down. I never tired of spotting shooting stars and looking up from my swag at the brilliance the magnificent night sky provided. The clear winter nights were the best, with the Milky Way clearly visible as well as the many constellations of the Southern Hemisphere. I have never forgotten those magical nights spent in the complete silence you can only experience in the bush.

The following day, I'd attend the conference and the mandatory lunch at the Irish Club before doing a grocery run in the city. Like all country people, I always kept a good supply of staple foods in the pantry to last a few months. You never knew if, or for how long, you'd be isolated, especially during the annual wet seasons.

Once clear of the city, my next stop always was the small town of Cloncurry, where I was friendly with a publican. We usually had a cold beer out in the back yard with our dogs sitting on the tailgates of our vehicles. The next stop was the Quamby pub, where I occasionally stayed. They had given me a key to a disused room to stay in on my travels, but I loved rolling out my swag on the veranda for what was always a great sleep. Then it was on to the Old Burke and Wills Roadhouse, which was run at one stage by four ex-rodeo riders, all mad, and I never left there without a good laugh. Gregory Downs next stop, then back home until the next time.

BLACK SOIL BOG DOWN

Driving over bush roads wasn't always plain sailing, which came into play when I left to travel to Mount Isa for my First Class Sergeant examinations. I'd decided to travel in company with the manager from Gregory Downs Station who had to attend to business in the city as well. He was running late and left me a message that he would catch up with me at the creek crossing several kilometres south of the pub on the Thorntonia Road. It hadn't rained around Burketown, but, unbeknownst to us, it had rained, and a lot, further south and west of Gregory Downs. I headed off in the police Toyota until I reached the designated creek, and I hadn't been there long before my mate arrived. We noticed that the water was rising rather rapidly and within no time, became uncrossable, so my mate said,

'Shit, we have no choice other than to turn back, and if this one is up now, the dry one we crossed about ten kilometres back will be going up as well. It's a deep bastard, and if we don't get over it now, our cars will be trapped here for weeks.'

We raced back with the rain starting to fall heavily onto the black soil, which was all we needed. When wet, the black soil around that part of the country, turns notoriously into an instant glutinous, slippery sodden mess, impossible to drive or walk through. We hurried back only to find that the creek of concern was rapidly rising as well. We had no choice other than to cross it and immediately. The station ute and police car were both diesels, with the former having the benefit of a snorkel which lets the engine breathe even in deep water. We opened the bonnet of the police vehicle and undid the restraints holding the air intake, then stretched it up and tied it to the sun visor. I had done a few creek crossings before, but nothing this deep. The station ute made it across, and now it was my turn. The plan was if my truck faltered, at least the station ute could tow me out.

Tentatively, I drove into the moderately flowing deep creek with the windows up to help keep the water from flooding into the car. Fortunately, the deep creek wasn't w ide, and it was only for a matter of seconds that the water level rose four or five inches over the bonnet and up the windshield and somewhat relieved, I drove out on the other side of the river.

We weren't out of the woods yet by any means. We drove on in low-range, four-wheel-drive through the black soil towards the Gregory Downs pub. The rainfall was getting heavier, and as a result, the going was slow. The sticky black mud started to build up, sticking to the front wheels, making steering impossible. Many times, we stopped to remove the soil and move on if only metres. Eventually, about two kilometres from the pub, both vehicles were hopelessly bogged up to the running boards, leaving us no other option than to complete the last leg on foot, sinking knee-deep at times in the black mud.

What made it infinitely worse was getting my two large dogs through the mud. I grabbed them one at a time by the collar and rear end, giving them a massive throw forward. The dog then scrambled wildly ahead until becoming bogged again and waited for me to catch up and repeat the manoeuvre. Those might have been the most challenging two kilometres I have ever had to cover. It was hot and exhausting work, and the cold beer I drank immediately after reaching the pub was probably one of the best I'd ever tasted in my life.

Happy to have the dogs out, we still had to go back to retrieve the cars. My mate, the cocky, fired up the big shire council grader, which had been stationed there while I secured the dogs in the shade behind the pub where no one could get bitten. For some unknown reason, people often go up to large guard dogs and do things like holding their children or little dogs up to meet the "nice big doggies" or, in the case of one fool, who fired a cap gun at them.

We then rode back in the grader to the bogged vehicles, where we spent the next few hours, skull dragging them through the black soil to the pub. Back at the station, I put the garden sprinkler under the police vehicle for a few hours and managed to remove most of the sticky black mud and perhaps, needless to say; I didn't get to the police examinations.

CAR ROLLOVER

The annual Gregory Downs canoe races attracted a large crowd of spectators and the usual revellers from a wide area. The location was in my division which was about the size of Sweden. Usually, police from the district headquarters would be there as well because, in the case of more than one incident, we couldn't leave the event without police presence. There wasn't much trouble, other than a few idiots getting dropped off up the road a few kilometres for 'walkies' back. The headquarters blokes regarded the event as an outing, as did two inspectors who had come along for the ride.

The police had set up a camp down on the riverbank in a grassy area. However, it wasn't far from a steep embankment adjacent to a dirt track. At the site, I heard a vehicle at the top of the embankment beginning the trip down. Incredibly, a few seconds later, it drove off the road and overturned and rolled over a couple of times down the steep slope coming to a rest right in front of the police camp. The huge esky had burst open with numerous cans of beer spilling out on the way down. Some rolled down into our makeshift campsite, while others burst open when squashed by the vehicle in its trajectory. The four-wheel-drive ute landed straight back on its wheels and came to a rest just short of where we were, causing the police to scatter in all directions. The three occupants of the vehicle, including the driver, stumbled from the car very drunk.

Traffic Enforcement at the races hadn't been an issue in the past as the crowd was generally pretty sensible. Once they set up camp, no one worried about driving around until it was time to go home. I think that if the fools had turned the vehicle over in another part of the area, we never would've known about it, but they chose to do it right in front of a strong police presence. One of the inspectors said,

'Lock the bastard up.'

So, the driver was taken away to the Burketown lock up.

A COMPROMISED BATTLE

After the races, life returned to normal in the Gulf Country town. The only other significant event scheduled was the softball competition with several teams from various places in the Gulf set to compete. Now softball is a girls' game, but on the day of the competition, the pub team, comprised of two barmaids and three local girls, suddenly found themselves one team member short following an unexpected family illness of one of the girls. After a hurried meeting, they decided to amend the rules. In the interest of keeping the competition viable, they agreed that Police Sergeant Cahill could fill in for the missing team member only if he wore a full police uniform. I didn't have a problem with that and duly fronted up for my turn with the bat. Unfortunately for me, a previous back injury sustained in unarmed combat and again during grading for a brown belt in karate decided to reappear on the third strike at the ball. I hit the ball and sent it well off the field, leaving me in a great deal of pain and barely able to walk off the grounds. The injury took several months to come good, especially out in a remote area where treatment options were just about non-existent.

A couple of weeks later, I still hadn't fully recovered when I became involved in a dust-up. A couple of blokes from the Northern Territory were making complete arses of themselves, annoying the local women. Both my assigned constables were away on leave. I had a motorcycle kidney protection belt which I strapped on before leaving the station, hoping this would get me through. After the incident of capturing Hashtag, the inspector and I had become good mates, and he had taken a few weeks holidays to come up to Burketown with his wife. On telling him where I was going, he said,

'I'm coming with you and give you a hand.'

He was on his walking stick with his leg in plaster following a fall a few weeks earlier. I wasn't much better off walking very crooked, nursing my back injury, and I was more than glad of his company. Usually, if I found myself outnumbered in a disturbance, there were always plenty of blokes who were quite happy to assist me. But, as fate had it this day, the fishermen and council blokes were out, so we were pretty much on our own.

We both crawled out of the police vehicle close to where the two loudmouths were carrying on. They were yelling at a couple of Indigenous women across the road. I never met a decent bloke from the Northern Territory during my outback years, other than the Territory police in the border stations, and these two were no exception. The young fools seemed to find it hilarious that two policemen, one with a plaster cast and walking stick, the other with an apparent injury, were going to confront them. They sneered and laughed until I kicked the nearest one to me in the balls, and the Boss copied my move on the second one and hit him in the balls with his walking stick. Both competitors were down for the moment, and not wanting to find out, or my back was going to hold up, I told them they were getting a second chance. I said that if they took off now, they wouldn't be arrested and taken to the watchhouse, where they would be locked up for the duration of the weekend. Both men staggered to their feet and stumbled over to their vehicle. They took off in a cloud of dust in the direction of the Northern Territory border, and that's the last I saw of them. The old Boss and I were good mates. We remained in contact even after we both had left the Force until his death, twenty years after our respective retirements.

STARING INTO THE BARREL

It was late in the afternoon of Christmas Eve when I noticed two old utes, towing caravans, roll into Burketown. The backs of the vehicles were crammed to the hilt with a myriad of items, including fuel drums, timber, sheets of galvanised iron and the like. There also seemed to be several people of varying ages and sizes in the vehicles. The procession, which brought an image of the Beverley Hills Hillbillies to my mind, moved into the caravan park adjoining the police station reserve and set up camp.

Later that evening, as was our usual practice, I was in the hotel with my constable Mick and several other blokes having a few quiet ones. Most of them were Viet Nam Veterans looking for a peaceful life. We all looked up when an attractive but very grubby looking woman wandered in. She was in her early thirties and sauntered straight over to us, and all bar one, we recognised that this woman was trouble. None of us encouraged her to stay, but Gibbo, the shire council grader driver, thought she was lovely, so she engaged in conversation with him. We heard her say that her name was Elsie and that she was with a bloke named Ivo Nilsson, who was considerably older than her. They had rolled into town with their six children and the woman's parents. Elsie laughed when she said that Nilsson, an Austrian, had several firearms but couldn't pronounce the word "shoot" and said "hoot" instead. In later conversations with Nilsson in the ensuing months, I found that this indeed was the case. He liked going out "hooting". I also had a strong suspicion that Nilsson was, quite possibly, an insane and dangerous individual. I was to find out later that I was one hundred percent correct in my assessment.

Now Gibbo, the grader driver, was a single bloke in his forties. He happened to live in a van in the same caravan park as Elsie and Nilsson, and over the next few months, Elsie and her five children took up with him. The arrangement created a serious situation where everyone involved in this soap opera resided in the same van park. It was just a matter of time before it went bad, which it did, spectacularly, in the early hours one morning.

Mick and I were both single men and had been over at our neighbour's place for dinner. Gunther and Liselotte, both Germans, often invited us over, and we happily obliged. Gunther was a fisherman and Liselotte an excellent cook who, unquestionably, made the best meatballs in brown gravy sauce. After tea, we went back to Mick's barracks to have coffee when we heard a shot nearby followed by a scream. It all was quite loud, with the van park being right next door to the police yard. We both had a fair idea of what was going down, if not the exact details. It was just after midnight, and Mick had hardly a chance to note down the time, when Gibbo came tearing through the back door looking terrified, yelling in panic,

'Nilsson is trying to shoot me.'

Mick grabbed his .233 Ruger rifle, and I was unarmed as my rifle was away for repairs. My useless .38 police special was out of action, having exploded during operational work and with a new one on the way, I never had it repaired. While running out the front entrance of the police reserve and around to the Caravan Park, we started working out a plan. I was wearing my uniform shirt, which might've been quite impressive with stripes and badges, but presented a problem as the streetlights' glow would reflect off those badges and give Nilsson a target and chance of hitting us both. The best we could do in the situation was to split up. The area was quite dark, with a few stunted trees in the immediate vicinity, and the only light came from the streetlights on the road adjoining the park. I don't know if it was a great plan because the result was that I ended up confronting the gunman.

Here I was breaking the cardinal rule of going to a gunfight and not taking a gun. The situation I found myself in now was being unarmed, with Nilsson pointing a double-barreled coach gun at me. He made sure that he stood far enough away so I couldn't have a go at disarming him. I moved into a position so that if Mick had to shoot at him and possibly missed, there weren't any houses behind him as those projectiles could have been a threat to people residing in the immediate vicinity.

I couldn't see Mick anywhere at this point, so I just had to wing it.

Had I been armed, I think I would have given serious consideration to shooting Nilsson, but I wasn't, and this left only one option, and that was to persuade him to surrender. Several times earlier in my police service, I had needed a firearm to resolve a situation. This occasion was the first time I didn't have one. I started talking to this individual with the vain hope that he would surrender peacefully, but it soon became apparent that he wasn't going to. The only reason this lunatic hadn't fired at me, and he couldn't miss with a short, double-barrel shotgun from that range, was because he didn't know where Mick was. I could see him looking around frequently, trying to spot him, and decided to work on his insecurity. Trying to convey confidence in this deteriorating situation, I said,

'Shoot this bastard Mick.'

Nilsson instantly looked wildly about him but kept the shotgun pointed at me. I expected at any instant a gunshot, resulting in Nilsson going down, but that didn't happen. Instead, to my amazement, Mick suddenly appeared from the darkness emerging from the nearby shrubs. He rushed forward in a propulsive lunge and grabbed Nilsson's gun, forcing the barrel downwards. This development gave me enough opportunity to move in as well. With both of us tackling him, we managed to disarm Nilsson while pinning him to the ground. I only just managed to resist the temptation to give him the stomping of his life.

We arrested the man and took him over to the watch house, where we charged him and put him in the cells. We then returned to the caravan park and found the two wounded victims of the shooting. After organising transport to the hospital for them, we started making our inquiries as to what had transpired. It appeared that Nilsson had arrived at Gibbo's van to 'hoot' him. But his aim was wrong, and he missed shooting his intended victim. Instead, the pellets hit his thirteen-year-old daughter in the knee and his mother-in-law in the forearm. Both survived, but the old lady had to have about an inch or so of her forearm removed.

After we'd advised headquarters, two detectives arrived later that day by aircraft and charged Nilsson with several offences. The Department of Public Prosecutions amended the charges, and Nilsson eventually appeared in the circuit court. Here he faced two counts of grievous bodily harm and one of going armed in public so as to cause fear. As it turned out, this man had been in a similar situation in Longreach three years earlier. There he had shot a man over this same woman. The man survived, and astoundingly Nilsson escaped a conviction at the behest of a stupid jury. The "happy couple", Nilsson and his wandering girlfriend, reunited and went on their merry way until they became our problem in Burketown. It seems the jury in the Longreach trial thought that shooting a man under those circumstances, was quite acceptable, and the rule of law didn't necessarily apply.

At our trial, the defence barrister was an ex-politician. He had a policy of calling a voir dire where the evidence is heard in the absence of a jury. It gave him an idea of what the evidence was against his client. This development was truly fortunate for me as he wasn't expecting a bushwhacker uniform cop to know any rules of evidence. He said to me while in the box,

'Have you ever heard the accused going around, saying he was going to shoot someone?'

My answer was 'No, but he said he'd shot a man in Longreach three years ago and got away with it.'

Hearsay evidence was admissible in voir dire proceedings. The Barrister roared,

'I didn't ask you that.'

He had no further questions. The judge was looking intently at Nilsson over his glasses. I thought that this was a good thing, but unbelievably the Mount Isa jury returned with a verdict of "Not Guilty". Incredibly, on being given the good news, the accused started walking over towards us, the police. It was apparent that Nilsson intended to shake hands with us. And in an incident which I'd never witnessed before or since, the judge, scarlet faced, roared at him,

'Nilsson, Get out! Get out of my court!'

Mick and I returned to Burketown, amazed that a jury could be so stupid but questioning the court's decision is not our remit, so we just let it go. Back in Burketown, Nilsson turned up at the police station and demanded his firearms back. We had seized several of them after his arrest. I grabbed him and threw him down the steps, and told him to get lost. He got up off the ground and stalked off, muttering all sorts of threats, so we decided to play it safe and take things a bit further. I rang the district inspector, who took out a prohibition order on firearms on him. I handed in Nilsson's weapons, and I never saw him again.

Some months later, I was at the Gregory Downs

annual canoe races held in the Gregory River near the pub. I was in the bar when I was approached by a significantly overweight, loud individual who said to me,

'Sergeant Cahill, I'm Superfry, I was the foreman of the jury in the Nilsson trial, and I suppose you are wondering why we came in with a not guilty verdict.'

I replied, 'I'm not wondering, but I have a feeling that you are going to tell me anyway.'

He said, 'This is Mount Isa, and up here our interpretation, "his interpretation" of grievous bodily harm is for a man to be knocked down and kicked in the head with miners' boots and taken to Brisbane for treatment.'

I was astonished and didn't have an answer for an exercise in gross stupidity like that, so I just looked at him in disbelief, then turned around and just walked away. That incident forever dispelled any ideas of the notion "judged by your peers". I decided there and then that if I were ever in the position of being accused, I would, if guilty, opt for a jury or, if innocent, a judge sitting alone.

This whole saga, unfortunately, hadn't finished. In a conversation with Mick years later, he had found out that Nilsson had an open contract hit on me, Mick, and the District Inspector. The worse thing was that the police department knew, but no one had thought to let us know. So Nilsson and the other family members moved to the Northern Territory, including his reunited wife and shooting victims.

It had been an awfully close call. I've thought since that, given some of the other awards for bravery I've seen given, Mick and I should have received some recognition, but that didn't happen. Still, some years later, Mick did receive a bravery award for his actions during another incident.

TROPICAL CYCLONE ALERT

There was a severe tropical cyclone warning, and one of the areas on alert was the Gulf of Carpentaria. Cyclone Sandy was expected to cross the coast in the vicinity of Burketown in the early hours of the morning. Everyone had been tracking the cyclone, which had reached a windspeed of one-hundred and seventy kilometres per hour with gusts of two hundred and twenty kilometres per hour with reports coming in of twelve-metre swells.

The country around Burketown is very flat and the Gulf very shallow, thus making it ideal conditions for a storm surge. The Weather Bureau was expecting a five-metre surge, and back then, police were not permitted by the legislation in force to divulge the possibility of a tidal wave to the wider public. I couldn't see a rational explanation for why this was so, but that was the law. Regardless though, during the early afternoon, when the storm surge became a strong possibility, I took the opportunity to go around to the town's residents and without breaching the provisions of the relevant Act, I suggested they head down to Gregory Downs about sixty miles south.

There had been a severe storm surge many years ago at Burketown, which had resulted in several deaths, but the blokes from the local State Emergency Service offered resistance. They believed that going down to the Gregory wouldn't be any safer and said that the cyclone would veer off its current course before making landfall at Burketown. In my view, however, those extra sixty miles could just make the difference. Fortunately, the rain hadn't started to fall, leaving the dirt road south still open for traffic. A bit of rain would turn them into mud, making the dirt road completely impassable, entrapping the entire community. A couple of hundred people understood the seriousness of the looming danger and took my advice. The group made use of the small window of opportunity and headed off towards the Gregory Downs pub.

Happy to have accomplished their leaving, I went back to the station to wait it out. The preceding days had been full-on, and I was getting tired. I hadn't had a decent sleep for four days. Amazingly the phone lines, which were always first to go, were still intact, enabling me to speak to the Weather Bureau staff. The bloke on the other end of the line said,

'At eleven-thirty tonight, regretfully, the last thing you will see in your life is a five-metre storm surge. I'm sorry and good luck.'

And with that, the phone went dead. Great! All the drama and stress of recent times had caused me severe heartburn, and to ease the pain, I had been swigging an antacid. But now, with the end looming, I decided to have a few cold beers instead. I had no choice other than to sit around and wait for the inevitable.

The cyclone veered off at the last minute and moved westwards along the coast towards the Northern Territory border and Borroloola township. Like a lot of Northern Territory towns, residents found refuge in their local state school. They are all constructed to double as cyclone shelters. Along the entire coastline, up to this township and beyond, there wasn't a leaf left on the trees in the wake of the cyclone.

When I went into the State Emergency Service's office early in the morning, the blokes were quick to tell me they had been right. I had to agree with them as the cyclone indeed had veered off at the last minute.

'But,' I said, 'Have you looked out the window?'

The sight that greeted those blokes extracted a variety

of colourful exclamations as everything was underwater. The Gulf had come in around twenty kilometres covering the huge saltpan. Cyclone Sandy was the second near-miss cyclone during my time in Burketown.

CARDIO-PULMONARY RESUSCITATION

Police officers are required to learn how to use CPR, Cardio Pulmonary Resuscitation. At the time, it never occurred to me that I would ever find myself in a position where I would have to perform this chest compression, mouth-to-mouth, first-aid technique.

Late one night before hotel closing time, I was in the bar when the hospital's matron rang and said there'd been a vehicle rollover south of the township and a young, injured, and unconscious man was brought in by his friend, who had been following behind him in his car. The friend managed to get the man out of the car and bring him to the little hospital, where the matron performed CPR but needed assistance. I immediately drove up to the hospital with two constables to help the matron with the injured man.

The Royal Flying Doctor Service was organising a doctor and an aircraft, arriving in about an hour. We received the added instructions to keep performing CPR until the doctor arrived. To prevent exhaustion, we performed CPR in relays while the matron supervised and administered the oxygen. After a while, it became apparent to us that this man was dead. However, as only a doctor can pronounce life extinct, we were required to continue. I heard and felt ribs and sternum cracking due to the prolonged resuscitation efforts, but apparently, that happens and is regarded as normal under those circumstances. It was about an hour and a half later when the doctor arrived, which wasn't too bad considering the distance from Mount Isa.

There were no lights on the small remote airport, and with the runway shrouded in darkness, we needed to illuminate the strip. So a few blokes went out to mark the runway's perimeter by placing milk tins filled with diesel and sand and lit diesel-soaked rags along its length. These, together with the activated headlights of several vehicles, provided enough illumination for the flying doctor plane to land safely. It was standard practice in isolated places back then. Fortunately, most outback township airstrips today have automatic lighting activated by the pilot of any aircraft wanting to land.

With not being able to save the young man's life, it hadn't been a great night, and though I wasn't personally acquainted with the deceased, I had seen him around the place. It is a drawback of being in small communities, especially in vehicle collisions and farm accidents. One positive thing, I guess, that did come out of it was to have to carry out practical CPR under the supervision of the matron. It was by far more beneficial than the occasional practice on a first aid dummy.

POINTED WITH THE BONE

One Sunday morning, I received a message via the Royal Flying Doctor Service base in Mount Isa. A man was acting in a strange manner outside the Gregory pub about seventy-five miles south of Burketown. The owners of the hotel were away for the day and left the barmaid in charge. The governess was also there, minding a couple of children, and they were understandably very worried. The man tore around like a lunatic with wild flailing arms. His piercing screams were enough to scare even the bravest of the locals. Seemingly terrified himself, he climbed under an old disused bus across the road from the pub.

My blokes were away on another matter with the police truck, so I decided to go down in my old Dodge to see what I could do. As I was getting ready to leave, Berney, the grader driver who lived next door in the van park, came over. He thought I might like to head up to the local pub for a beer with him. I told him where I was going, so he said,

'I'll come along for the run and give you a hand.'

I was happy with his offer, having dealt with mentally ill people before. I knew how strong they could become. So Berney and I headed off in the truck for the Gregory Downs pub. Upon arrival, I spotted about half a dozen stockmen at the bar; this meant that at least the governess and the barmaid would be safe. The governess pointed at an old rusted-out bus lying abandoned across from the pub and told me that the man was hiding underneath. I walked over and crouched down to have a look. I could see his face and a pair of wild eyes looking back at me, and it was clear that whoever was hiding underneath wasn't in a hurry to come out.

Berney suggested, 'Let's have a beer first.'

It had been a hot, dusty drive down, so I agreed.

From the pub, I kept an eye on the man while having a few beers. Suddenly he slithered out from under the bus and took a full gallop straight towards me. Berney, a big bloke, said as he was getting off his barstool,

'I'll take him.'

I thanked him for the offer, but as the running figure approached, I could see an expression on the wild man's face that indicated some other emotion. It was of fear and panic, certainly not aggression. I was wearing my police uniform, and this wild-eyed man, once inside the bar, headed straight for me. He now had a look of terror on his countenance. The stockmen had all turned towards me and were openly looking on with interest. As soon as the man reached me, he went to stand right beside me so close that he ended up leaning up against me. He said nothing but absolute dread remained etched on his face, and he looked utterly exhausted.

The consensus was that the man was possibly suffering from delirium tremens or the horrors I had encountered before. The condition, causing uncontrollable tremors, intense feelings of impending doom and panic attacks, is a severe manifestation of alcohol withdrawal.

I finished my beer and quietly guided the man, who still hadn't spoken, out to the Dodge. He appeared more than happy to accompany Berney and me, and what I noticed was that my uniform seemed to give him some feeling of security. I decided to take him to the hospital in town and leave any diagnoses or treatment up to the matron. So I drove off back towards Burketown with the man sitting quietly in the back. But that didn't last long.

The Dodge had an aluminium canopy with two sliding glass windows. Unfortunately, there was no way of locking them, which hadn't presented a problem before as there were usually two attack German shepherd dogs in there. The man started screaming incoherently, and in one movement, I could see him in the rear vision mirror as he took a dive through the driving side canopy window. He was hanging by his knees outside at eighty kilometres per hour.

As quickly as I safely could, I brought the truck to a complete halt. Berney and I jumped out and ran over to the man, hanging suspended, from the canopy window. I found out that he could speak, and in a difficult to understand rant, he told me there were demons inside the canopy. They had jumped out the other window, and others were grouped around the rear doors waiting for an opportunity to drag him out onto the road and kill him. I was now sure he was in the horrors. As we still had a considerable distance to travel, I decided to try and keep him calm until the matron could see him. I kept a tyre lever under the truck's seat, so I retrieved it before walking around to the rear of the vehicle. I could see the terrified man, whom I had put back into the canopy, staring intently at these non-existent demons. I took a few wild swings with the lever in the air, delivered a couple of kicks and looked up at the man in the back.

The look of relief on his wretched face was unmistakable. I repeated this process twice more, dropped Berney off at the hotel in town and drove up to the hospital where the matron was waiting with a Largactil injection. After receiving the sedative injection, for want of a better place of safety, I took him back to the watchhouse. Here I could keep a close eye on him until the morning. I safely confined him in one of the cells and went back to the hotel to see what I could find out regarding this bloke. He had no identification on him, and no one at the other pub where I had found him knew anything about him either. He was an Indigenous man, so I figured that the best place to start inquiries would be with the local blokes. I went over to a group of men near the general store. I knew them well and had a decent level of rapport with the group. I explained to them what had happened during the past four hours, and I barely finished speaking when a look of fear crossed all of their faces.

Several panicked voices instantly said,

'That's Harry Nondo!'

Then they all bolted in every direction towards their respective homes. Shortly afterwards, I heard vehicles starting up, saw people on foot, heading off into the scrub that surrounded the township. This development was extremely unusual and perplexing, however, I now had a name to go on. I found a local who had chosen to remain behind and asked him about this man Harry Nondo. Could he explain why the mention of Harry sparked so much panic amongst the locals? He replied,

'He has had the bone pointed at him further south and has run on foot all the way from Mount Isa to where you found him. So no one will want to be around him much now.'

I thanked him for the information and advised the matron that I'd keep an eye on him until the morning. Harry seemed to have a reasonable night's sleep until the following morning when I let him go. I had no legal reason to keep him there. He wasn't as disturbed as the previous day; however, there was still a look of fear in his eyes. He again refused any food and walked out the back gate of the police reserve towards the town. I didn't see him again as he managed to get a ride out to a community about one hundred kilometres west. His appearance there again sparked a panicked mass exodus. From that place, he then boarded a flight to an island community to the north, and for a third time, people were going everywhere.

This unfortunate man died very shortly afterwards despite efforts to save him. I never did find out any information as to what sparked his ultimately fatal predicament.

THE VIDEO CAMERA

It had been a reasonably quiet afternoon, so I thought I'd make the most of it by catching up on a bit of bookwork. Once I had that thought, the phone rang. The local storekeeper told me that there was a decent sized fight going on outside his store. Not wasting any time, I got in the police vehicle and drove down to where the melee was taking place. Upon arrival, I observed the proceedings for a short while, deciding that if I locked up the leading contender in the bout and eliminated him from the struggle, the situation might fizzle out.

I walked over to the man and advised him that he would be spending some time down at the slammer. He sure took exception to the plan and decided to fight me instead of his previous opponents. He wasn't a local, as I had made arrests previously without even exiting the car. I would say to the arrestee, 'get in the back,' which they invariably did. But not so this stranger.

Anyway, I wasn't worried at all, even though he was considerably bigger than me, and after dodging a few wild drunken swings, I knew that he'd consumed more than just a few drinks. I put him in a restraint hold with his arm in a figure 4 lock, when at the same time, out of the corner of my eye, I noticed a movement. It was to my left at the front door of the hotel across the street.

A tourist was in the process of raising his video camera and was about to start filming me while I arrested this bloke. I didn't like that one bit and yelled out,

'Point that thing at me, and I will come over there, take it off you and shove it up your fucking arse.'

He immediately lowered the camera and bolted back inside the pub to the encouragement of a drunk yelling,

'I'll get the Vaseline Sarge! This is going to hurt!'

Loud, raucous laughter spilled from inside the bar. I put the prisoner in the truck and drove him back to the watchhouse for a bit of a rest. Later that evening, after work, I went back up to the pub for a beer. A sheepish looking bloke came over to me and said he wanted to apologise for coming out with the camera. Said he only wanted to film a bit of outback police action to show his mates in the force back in Sydney. He bought me a beer, and that was that.

CRASH-LANDING IN THE DARK

Late one night working back in the office, I was startled by my neighbour Jack. He had a bit of land around the area on which he ran a few head of cattle. Jack was a quiet bloke and slightly eccentric, but we got on well. I arrested him once on a warrant for non-payment of fines from the Australian Tax Office, for which he had to serve ten days imprisonment in the watch house.

Once Jack became aware that he had to spend time behind bars, he drove a bullock into the police yard and offered the beast as payment for the fine. However, predictably enough, this wasn't acceptable, and I arrested him without incident and placed him in a cell. As Officer in Charge, I was also responsible for the supervision and provision of meals for prisoners. However, Jack indicated that his wife was quite happy to feed him and, as she was only across the road from the lock-up, that wouldn't be an issue. In the end, we agreed that it was easier for him to go home at mealtimes and return immediately afterwards to the watch house. Jack quietly stuck to the routine and never gave me any trouble.

One night, some months later, he came in highly agitated and wanted to make an official complaint about someone trying to kill him. I managed to calm him down enough to elicit some information and listen as Jack explained that he had been standing on the back of his ute to look out over his property when some unknown person in an aircraft flew so low that he nearly hit him.

On the face of it, the story sounded preposterous, but something must have happened involving a plane, so I decided to go out and have a closer look at the situation. It turned out that there was an aircraft flying down so low that it crash-landed in the darkness and gloom not far from where Jack had been standing in the back of his ute. The small plane had run out of fuel, with the pilot needing to make an emergency landing in the dark in unknown terrain. It could very well have collided with Jack and his ute, but there certainly wasn't any intention of killing the complainant. It was just sheer luck that it passed over him instead.

I soon located the pilot and passengers who had been out prawn spotting when the pilot lost his bearings. As a result, the aircraft ran out of fuel requiring the pilot to put his plane down in the dark on an unknown surface. For all he knew, there could have been trees, cattle or, as reported, Jack in his ute, directly within his landing path. Amazingly no one travelling in the aircraft had been injured, which demonstrated that the pilot had a fair degree of skill to land the plane under those circumstances. However, any brownie points he accumulated with that creditable effort were more than cancelled out by the fact that he had committed a primary cardinal sin by running out of fuel. Landing in a cattle paddock isn't the smoothest ride and one in which the aircraft incurred a fair bit of damage, and a few days later, the plane was trucked out.

I furnished the relevant reports required easily as this was the sixth aircraft crash, I'd attended in the past thirteen years.

TV COMES TO BURKETOWN

For many years, radio reception was limited, with only ABC on AM coming through in early mornings and evenings. Television didn't exist anywhere where I worked in remote areas until 1984. ABC programs could be accessed in the Gulf town if the locals would raise enough funds for the installation of a three and half thousand-dollar satellite dish. The population of Burketown was not large, but everyone was keen and happy with the prospect of owning a satellite dish. A mate of mine took it upon himself to collect the money.

The collection met with enthusiasm where everyone donated that which they could afford. Within weeks the satellite was ordered and on its way to the small gulf town. Locals jumped in their utes and left for the more prominent centre of Mount Isa to buy their first-ever television. Everybody was happy to now have access to daily state and national news broadcasts. It might not seem like a big deal in today's fast-moving world, or even back then if you happened to reside in a large coastal city. However, it really was something in a remote area and certainly a vast improvement on a weekly newspaper and mail service.

THE WILD PIG HUNT

Constable Mick and I took a drive in the police Toyota to make an enquiry regarding an accident at Lawn Hill. On the way back, as we drove past the entrance to Gregory Downs cattle station, we saw two pigs trotting along the side of the road heading in the same direction as us. One was jet black, the other brown, and both appeared shiny and well-fed. I had serious doubts about them being feral pigs. However, they were out in the middle of nowhere, and wild pig numbers were increasing. It's estimated that Australia has up to twenty-four million feral pigs roaming free and they are considered a pest in Queensland.

My offsider grabbed his rifle, a .223 Ruger semi-automatic, and started blazing away. Now Mick had plenty of good points, but accurate shooting at two moving pigs from a moving vehicle wasn't one of them. He pretty much emptied a magazine before they finally went down. I thought it a strange thing that they didn't head into the scrub. Those pigs kept running along the road until finally succumbing to the gunfire or was it perhaps from the weight of the lead projectiles.

Following the successful pig hunt, we eventually arrived at the Gregory Downs Pub. It was good to sit down with a cold beer as it was still one hundred and twenty kilometres of dirt and bulldust before we got back to the police station. While we were in there yarning away with some locals, I noticed the manager of Gregory Downs station enter the bar. He walked over to us, and after exchanging a few pleasantries, he got around to asking about the shooting. Said he found the dead pigs along the road, and we had to admit that we had, in fact, been the ones involved. He added,

'Those were the house pigs you shot. They broke out of their pen and escaped.'

The manager, who wasn't a bad bloke, went on to say that he wouldn't hold it against us, as these pigs had been a bit of a nuisance anyway. So, after another beer with him, we left and headed home as soon as we could. We hadn't broken any laws, but in hindsight, perhaps we should have given the condition of the pigs a bit more thought. It might have saved us from a bit of embarrassment.

CHRISTMAS MORNINGS

Christmas Days in the Outback were always quiet days. Burketown, in that aspect, wasn't any different. I had a couple of constables with me, and as we were all single blokes, Christmas morning usually went by quietly without family gatherings and presents.

As there were several more people on their own, the thought of an informal gathering came to me. So, I invited locals over the age of eighteen to come out the back of the police station for a beer. As far as I was concerned, it made no difference if someone had been in the watchhouse the night before, every male was invited to come along. And they did. It felt good to sit around peacefully with our six-packs and talk about anything and everything. Then, when lunchtime came around, everyone went their separate way to wherever Christmas dinner was served for each bloke.

The wives and partners were happy with the idea, and we repeated this light-hearted informal gathering for the three Christmases I was there. I am pretty sure it went a little way towards improving police and residents' relations.

CAHILL'S LAW STATES

I'd been in the Gulf Country for well over a year, and everyone seemed to know me. One day I was with a mate of mine who had been a 'tunnel rat' during the Vietnam war when a man approached me with a query, to which I gave him an answer. After the bloke left, my mate said with a laugh,

'Cahill's Law States.'

I asked him what that was about. He then told me that the saying had sprung up due to my sometimes adapting the rules to suit any given situation. Unbeknownst to me, it was used many times by the local blokes who knew me well.

OUTBACK CHARACTERS

During the time I spent in the Gulf Country, I met a lot of interesting characters. They resided in these far-flung communities, not to hide from the law, but more from society, and were perfectly happy to remain on the fringes. One of them was a tough decent bloke, a contract fencer who never wore shoes who attended a function at the local pub in honour of something or other with several dignitaries in attendance. He was a bit of a tourist attraction with his preference for bare feet and didn't disappoint anyone that night, including the governor, as he went over to meet him dressed in suit and tie, but no shoes.

Another was a massive, big Slavic bloke named Barra, a professional fisherman on the Albert River. Barra operated by himself and made enough income to provide himself with food, a carton of beer and two packets of cigarettes daily. I never knew or asked him his correct name but understood that he had served in the French Foreign Legion at one stage. Before that, Barra had been a pilot in the Yugoslav air force. Then, having decided to flee Yugoslavia, he stole a Mosquito Bomber and flew to Austria, then joining the Legion to escape his communist pursuers. He eventually ended up in Australia, where he took up the occupation of crocodile shooter and fisherman.

There was a large encampment of army personnel at the local airport, and an army major and a warrant officer had opted to stay at the courthouse. They were from an intelligence unit and had many questions about the area concerning the old disused airstrips. We sat in the police residence talking while having a few beers when I heard a loud noise like a vehicle colliding with a fence. As a matter of fact, it was my fence, out the front of the police residence. I went out for a look and spotted Barra stumbling away from his old Toyota and the fence he had just collided with, carrying a carton of beer on his shoulder. Now drunk driving wasn't at the top of my list of priorities or of many other cops in remote areas in those times.

Nevertheless, Barra came inside, took a seat, and opened his carton of beer. The army blokes were fascinated with the ex-legionnaire, and it turned out to be an interesting night as they each told their stories. Eventually, the army blokes went to bed, and Barra left for his camp on the Albert River some twenty km away and returned in the early morning hours with a rope to repair the fence damage. I was saddened to hear of his death a year after I left the town on transfer.

There were community police members at a settlement about one hundred kilometres west of the township. The officer in charge was an Indigenous man named Richard Brookdale. He was a decent man who, in addition to being a first-class stockman and rider, was as good a tracker I had encountered. I had worked with a few and never ceased to be amazed by their ability. Richard performed a few tracking jobs while I was there, one from the back of a ute at forty kilometres per hour. On another occasion, not only did he successfully track a man's footprints, but he could also tell me whom the tracks belonged to, well before we caught up with the fugitive simply by the way he walked, with a limp.

We became close friends, and when I told him of my upcoming transfer from the Gulf, he immediately resigned from the community police job he had held for the past thirty-five years and went back to being a stockman.

BURKETOWN FAREWELL

By the time two and a half years had passed, I decided it was time to move on. Although I was still unaware of it, due to the continuous exposure of assaults and violence, my post-traumatic stress disorder was steadily increasing. I believe it to be the reason I felt like going somewhere else. I rang the district inspector, who gave me a choice of five police stations. I had done an excellent job for the police force, he said. I opted for a sugar cane growing town, Tully, on the coast south of Cairns, and made arrangements to get my gear shipped out and said my goodbyes to the people of Burketown. The night before I left, there was a large gathering of people, both Black and White, at the council administration area to see me off. They told me that it was the largest send-off they'd ever held for a departing police sergeant.

The following morning, I hooked up my boat and left for the coast with my brother-in-law Kemo Sabe, who had travelled up from Brisbane to accompany me on my way down. I arrived in Tully some days later and moved into the single men's barracks attached to the station.

TULLY

THE PHONE CALL

Upon arrival at my new police posting in Tully on the North Queensland coast, there was a phone call from Burketown. I was spoken to by a deputation of eight elders of the tribe led by the recently retired Community Police sergeant, Richard Brookdale. They let me know they had voted at a community meeting, where it had been decided that they wanted me to return to the Gulf. I was astounded that I was held in such esteemed regard but, for me to return to Burketown was simply not possible after having been assigned to a new district. During the time I had worked in the Gulf Country, I had been named in a national newspaper in an article by the then National Aboriginal Congress as being exactly the type of police officer required in Indigenous communities.

Richard Brookdale stayed in contact with me until he was well into his eighties, and then I heard no more. I have no doubt he has since gone to his reward, taking with him a set of skills that unfortunately has almost entirely disappeared from the younger generations of Indigenous people.

CYCLONE WINIFRED

Tully, as far as police work went, was unremarkable. It didn't have the excitement I was used to and had experienced in the outback. However, I met some great colleagues in Tully and got on well with one of the blokes, Graham Lohman. I worked with him on a regular basis attending to the general duties associated with small stations. Throughout the years, our paths crossed on several occasions, and our friendship remains strong today.

The year I spent at Tully was, as one could call it, peaceful, other than the category three tropical Cyclone Winifred, which crossed the coast north of Tully with wind gusts up to one-hundred and seventy-five kilometres an hour. Tully received over two hundred millimetres of rain in a twenty-four-hour period and was severely affected by floods from the flooded Tully River. During the time the cyclone raged, the strong winds caused a tree to fall onto the watchhouse at the rear of the station. Fortunately, I had released the two drunks who were inside before the arrival of the destructive cyclone. Looking at the damage that tree caused to the building, those two blokes had been very lucky.

Once it became quiet outside, I knew that we had entered what is known as the eye of the storm. One really shouldn't go out at that time, but I decided to take a chance and duck out in the police vehicle for a quick look around.

I came across a drunk stumbling around in the main street wearing nothing else but pair of shorts.

I said, 'What on earth are you doing?'

'I lost my thongs', he replied.

'Get back inside', I said and watched him stumble off in the direction of one of the pubs. The extensive damage caused by Winifred to the affected areas ran in the millions. In addition, there were three deaths reported and numerous accounts of property damage.

LIFESAVING ARREST

The only arrest I made in Tully was for a disqualified driving offence, with the driver wanted on a warrant for other offences elsewhere. It was fortunate for this bloke's girlfriend that I had pulled him up as I found her on the floor behind the vehicle's front seat, unconscious. I immediately organised an ambulance for transportation to the local hospital and was later informed that she had been in a life-threatening diabetic coma when I found her. Fortunately, she survived because of quick action, and the bloke himself spent nine months in Stuart Prison Townsville for his effort.

There was the army jungle training camp near Tully, and I spent my time there whenever I could. I socialised with the instructor staff, whom I found to be decent blokes. But, unfortunately, my back was deteriorating at a rate that it started to cause me enormous grief, so I got a transfer to Brisbane with easy access to a specialist and with a vague plan of perhaps leaving the police. I often thought about buying and living on a boat.

SANDGATE

SERGEANT FIRST CLASS

Once I settled into the Brisbane suburb Sandgate, I found that the city was not my type of environment anymore after having experienced the bush and other small places. So I put my intentions in motion to get a medical discharge from the police. It's when I encountered a local General Practitioner who, apart from having a lot of expertise in back injuries, also had personal experience with a severe back problem of his own. Through his manipulations, my fitness level rose to a point where I could ride my bicycle on a thirty-six-kilometre round trip to work every day

I read in the Police Gazette that a position for an Officer in Charge, Sergeant First Class, had become vacant. After giving it some serious thought, I withdrew my application for a medical discharge and applied for the Palm Island position. My application somehow went unanswered because it didn't take long for them to re-advertise the position. So, I decided to go to the Police Head Quarters and speak to the inspector in charge of personnel to find out why I didn't get the job.

The inspector told me that someone had made allegations that I was a racist, and therefore, my application was ignored. It was then that I started to realise I had one or two enemies somewhere. I produced the newspaper clipping from the Telegraph with the article in which the National Aboriginal Congress had named me the type of police officer they wanted in Indigenous communities.

The article was in addition to a reference from one of the Congress delegates. The inspector simply said,

'Best you get your stuff organised for transport, the job and promotion are yours.'

REMOVALISTS MEET WITH MY ATTACK DOG

Once again, I prepared for transfer. This move was a bit different than those I was used to during my outback postings. As in that, I needed to obtain the department's required quotes from three different furniture removalists.

On the day of quoting, I told the various removalist not to worry about my two elderly dogs, whom they could see locked away in the garage. They sat quietly and kept a watchful eye on the removalists through the shed's screen door. The blokes moved about freely, feeling safe enough, with the big dogs locked away.

Whoever it was of those three quoting companies that had decided to come back, and break-in had discounted the dogs as they were, after all, locked away. What they didn't know was that I had a third dog, one-year-old Conan. He had been away at a training facility run by ex RAAF personnel and had since returned home. Unbeknownst to them, this attack dog lived inside the house. And so, the fools decided to make a move.

I had gone out for the night, and upon my return, I found Conan sitting on the footpath, outside the yard, with the gates wide open. I quickly took score and found the wheelie bin knocked over, a set of side windows fully open and various items of furniture scattered about inside the house. There was blood splattered around inside the house, and it was evident that a tremendous struggle had taken place between the dog and the intruders. Further evidence in the form of claw marks and more blood splattered on the stucco exterior wall led me to believe that the dog had come out in front. Conan, uninjured, was a fully trained attack dog.

I didn't worry about reporting the incident. Then, about eight months later, I was talking to the Commissioner who had come out on an inspection visit to Palm Island, and I told him about the incident. Several days later, he rang me from his office and said that there had been scores of similar break-ins. All following furniture removalist quotations for police going on transfer in the Brisbane area, but there had been only one with an attack dog in the house at the time. Detectives investigated the incident, but no arrests were forthcoming though some people were strongly suspected of being involved.

PALM ISLAND

THE ISLAND

I covered the forty-eight sea miles from Townsville to Palm Island in a Police Boat. My immediate boss, a decent bloke I had known for many years, came with me for the trip over. He informed me that the job I was about to take on was, acknowledged to be, the worst job in the Queensland Police Force. During my time on the island, approximately two thousand four hundred Indigenous and around sixty Caucasian people lived there. Fifty per cent of those were under the age of seventeen. The island has made it into the *Guinness Book of Records for being the most dangerous place on earth to live outside of a war zone.

I was involved in investigating many horrific incidents, including the rape of an eighteen-month-old baby during the three years I was there. How some of the victims of these severe assaults survived their injuries is beyond my understanding. In the past, the community had been used as a type of penal settlement. And for several decades, the island was set up for the so-called "recalcitrant" amongst the Indigenous people of Queensland.

Members from over forty non-related tribes were relocated and sent to live on the island, creating a situation whereby possibly some traditional enemies suddenly found themselves, not by choice, lumped together on a small island.

*Great Palm Island-Wikipedia

https://en.m.wikipedia.org/wiki/Great_Palm_Island#cite_ref-Aust-131198_47-1

Having read historical newspaper clippings and being told anecdotal stories by local residents, I was not surprised that the current situation existed. I also formed the impression that the administration of the community in earlier years left a lot to be desired and, in my opinion, contributed to the current situation.

When alcohol restrictions were lifted for Aboriginal reserves and missions in the seventies, a canteen opened on Palm Island selling beer. With this ruling, drunkenness, disorder and inevitably, violence erupted which usually began during the day to continue well into the night. It was a daily and nightly challenge to keep the peace.

Apart from the obvious difficulties, the clerical work, including the clerk of court duties, had been untouched for two years. The police station was grubby, and the police house a "dive", with the description "dive" being a generous term. The three-bedroom house was filthy, and the house had been vacant for a while. Outside, the dense weeds had grown level with the windowsills, and it took me days of cleaning and shovelling dirt and debris from in, under and around the house to make it remotely livable.

Then there were the walls. Several holes in different locations suggested that probably heads had been bashed up against them well before the place became a police accommodation. The walls were so full of scuff marks and filth that even after a thorough scrub, they still looked like shit. There was only one option, and that was to cover them with cheap curtains and sheets. I bought seagrass matting to cover the torn pieces of very old lino that covered the floor. All the taps leaked, fencing was pretty much non-existent, and the rear door opened almost directly onto the street. And it was hot. It was sweltering hot!

I bought two refrigerated air conditioners and had them fitted by a Works Department carpenter. It made living in the house a lot more bearable during the humid, hot long summers. The bedroom faced the main road opposite a large, grassed area where the medivac helicopter landed, and, as I found out, it did so on a regular basis, ferrying the injured residents to the Townsville Hospital. The house windows were old-style glass louvres, which could be opened at any angle and adjusted to catch the breezes by simply moving a lever. Unfortunately, each time the aircraft landed, apart from the tremendous noise, the draft from the rotors invariably kicked up massive clouds of dust, leaves and small sticks. These were forced and blown through the louvre joins, inadvertently filling the bedroom and lounge area.

The people on Palm Island hailed from the Torres Straits and pretty much well from all over the state. This factor was very much to my advantage as I was well known to Indigenous people resulting from the many places I had worked and had, over time, earned their respect. These same people I had been around for years also had no problem advising their relatives on the island that I was okay. So consequently, they didn't resent me as much as they would a White police sergeant they didn't know.

One of the first requirements was for me to go to the hospital for my Hepatitis B injections. That's when I found out that these vaccinations are given with a large needle in the stomach. Not once but three times!

COMMISSIONER LEWIS

Several years earlier, in 1976, Terry Lewis had been appointed police commissioner and was the first commissioner to visit every police station in the state. I was at Coen in 1980 when he turned up there. The visit was only brief and lasted about ten minutes. My German shepherd dog Shiloh prevented the commissioner and his aides from entering my barracks during that short time as the dog regarded the quarters as his. The next time I encountered him was in a seafood restaurant in Fortitude Valley Brisbane a day or two before leaving for Thursday Island. I had taken my Mum out to lunch as I always did when in Brisbane, and coincidentally the Commissioner had the same choice of a lunch venue that day. The only interaction on that occasion was that I recognised him and nodded. He returned the gesture, identifying me as a young cop. He had since been knighted, Knight Bachelor, for his service to the Queensland police and was now Sir Terrence Lewis.

The third time was on Palm Island, where he, his wife and entourage arrived on a scheduled fifteen-minute visit. Time got away, so the Commissioner and his group decided to stay for lunch. Never failing to protect, Old Shiloh, who had been asleep under the stairs, awoke. Upon seeing a group of people enter his house, he lumbered out and prevented the last two, the secretary and pilot, from getting in. I told the old fellow that it was okay, and after satisfying himself that all was good, he went back to sleep under the steps.

After lunch, the Commissioner sent his aides and pilot back to Townsville and spent the next four hours with me on a tour of the island, station, barracks and watchhouse. Before leaving the island, he said,

'You can't work and live in a dump like this. This

place needs a new station, house and barracks.'

He was true to his word as within a few months, the builders arrived. Before he left that day, the Commissioner said,

'I wouldn't mind a photo', so we all lined up in front of the station, and sometime later, a copy arrived in the mail for me.

By now, though, some front runners and wannabees back at headquarters were enraged. How could the Commissioner choose to spend an afternoon with a bushwhacker uniform sergeant rather than their company? This fact, in itself, amused me rather than worried me, and it was to cause a great deal of stress down the track.

BREAK-IN AT THE BAKERY

One amusing incident occurred when one of the on-duty community police came into my office. The officer told me that Freddie had broken into the bakery, which was just a short distance from the police station, and had closed for the day. Freddie could be a bit nasty at times, which may have contributed to him, eventually, being stabbed to death. However, this time he wasn't aggressive, just a bit drunk and hungry.

I went in through the open side door of the bakery, where I saw the offender leaning up against a set of shelves. He had a loaf of bread in his hand, and a pack of Frankfurts shoved down the front of his underpants. Nothing unusual, if it weren't for a second offender in there as well, a horse, of which several wandered loose throughout the settlement at any time. One of them had on smelling the fresh bread, followed Freddie through the side door, which, considering the width of the doorway, was quite an achievement. The horse was quite happily munching on a loaf of bread and briefly looked up to see who else had arrived for afternoon smoko before going back to his meal.

After Freddie had been arrested, he was taken to the station, where no one was keen to handle the stolen pack of Frankfurts. The community police and I managed to coax the horse out of the bakery with a freshly baked loaf of bread. It was quite an achievement considering the size of the bakery internally. The horse went on its way, and Freddie went into the cells.

SUICIDE CARNAGE

I attended to a few suicides during my service, and despite my efforts to forget them, the following left an unforgettable and lasting impression on me. It was Saturday afternoon, and so far, it had been a reasonably quiet day at the police station. My colleague, Brian, and I were thinking about knocking off and going home for a beer when the phone rang. The caller was a well-known transgender person named Cleo, who worked as a bar attendant at the football grounds. In a near-hysterical voice, Cleo's screams came through the receiver.

'There's this bloke, and he has got a gun, and he is going to shoot someone.'

At that point, I heard a noise, and I realised it was a gunshot and the phone went dead. Brian and I grabbed our guns, jumped into the police car, and headed for the football fields. Halfway down, I saw another vehicle approaching which stopped, as it drew level with us. It was one of the locals, whom I knew well as he occasionally came round to the house on a social visit. He was a grey colour and had a thousand-yard stare. He was covered in what appeared to be brain matter. With a noticeable tremble in his voice, he said,

'A bloke down there shot himself.'

I replied, 'Head off home mate, I'll come and see you later on.'

It transpired that my mate had attempted to take the shotgun from this bloke, only to have had the weapon pointed at him. After his failed attempt to grab the gun, the bloke had turned the gun around and killed himself.

We continued on our way to the football oval. On our arrival, we were met with a situation I'd never encountered before, and one I have no desire ever to witness again. This is the only time I can recall dissociating.

The council had recently built a new chain wire fence surrounding the fields and clubhouse. However, the key to the vehicle access gate wasn't readily available. As a result, an enormous community policeman was attempting to remove the lock with a sledgehammer. I went through the pedestrian gate and over to where a crowd was gathered. Many of them were in varying states of shock and, upon seeing the situation, I fully understood why.

A man who had close ties with the ruling junta in Fiji thought he was going to be deported. It proved later that this wasn't the case, and it was therefore assumed that he either had been mistaken or had been misinformed.

Newspaper reporters from around the world rang from different time zones as there also had been a recent coup in Fiji, and links and connections were made. All of this made the average night's sleep on Palm Island even more fragmented than usual. Unfortunately, the area where this dreadful incident occurred was on the actual football oval, and up until I left the island, the players avoided it at all costs.

WINNING AND LOSING

Palm Island had thirteen community policemen, and their station was adjacent to the building of the Queensland Police. Over time, I replaced blokes who left with men of my choosing. I also experimented with hiring a female community police officer, however, her alleged efforts to supply prisoners in the local jail with hooch, despite the visible calming effects it had on the inmates, wasn't what I was looking for, and the exercise didn't last very long.

I managed to field a force of community officers comprised of decent blokes, at least three of whom weighed around one-hundred and fifty kilos. All were representative of the main tribal groups and regarded as respectable by the general community. They also regularly turned up for work.

One big bloke I hired was a huge man who walked into the station one morning and said,

'I'm here to pay a warrant.'

He told me that his name was Joe and that he had travelled over to Palm Island from one of the coastal Aboriginal communities. Computers hadn't moved into small police stations at that stage, so I telephoned the police from the Aboriginal community he had come from and advised them of the situation. Upon hearing the giant's name, he said:

'It took five of us to lock him up.'

Upon hearing that, I went back out to the counter and told the big fellow how much he had to pay, took the money, and issued him a receipt. As he was about to leave the office, I said,

'Do you want a job?'

He replied, 'What doing?'

I said, 'Community Police Sergeant.'

'When do I start?'

'How about now?' I suggested, 'I'll get you a shirt.'

I became good mates with this bloke who told me he no longer touched alcohol. He remained in his role as a community police sergeant for ten years, long after I had left. There were quite a few people on the island who originated from Joe's previous community, and as I didn't have any police from that area, it was a win-win all around.

Although slightly modified by not inviting the entire community, I had adopted my previous strategy in that all community police were welcome with their partners at the police residence on Christmas mornings for a beer, coffee or whatever.

One Christmas morning, towards lunchtime, Joe sat at the big table, drinking his coffee and just having a yarn, when we heard a commotion, shouting and screaming. I saw a man carrying an axe climb over the fence and rush towards us through the open roller door. I leaned over to the cabinet next to the table and grabbed my .357 Magnum revolver. I had no desire to shoot this bloke, still, if push came to shove, I would do whatever was necessary to preserve life. Joe's wife and toddler were there as well, and the big fella simply said,

'I'll take him.'

He walked up to the bloke and grabbed the axe off him, and held him in a vice-like grip. As it turned out, this bloke had whacked someone with the axe, and his victim's friends had taken up after him in hot pursuit. He was terrified of the retribution, which would come in the form of a couple of hits with that same axe, but this time, applied to him. So, he'd raced to the police residence for safety. He was fortunate Conan, the attack dog, was upstairs and not under the table near my feet as he usually was.

I did take on two blokes as community police officers who had served time for manslaughter. A bonus was that some of the younger blokes were frightened of them. However, these blokes had done their time, and on hiring them, I found them to be decent men. They had seen the error of their ways and were prepared to contribute to their community. There was one big quiet man, in particular, who originated from the Northern Territory. After he had left prison, he approached me and asked me to give him a chance.

He was a decent bloke, who I would often see gliding unasked into place, keeping an eye on my house each time I left on a night-time callout. I introduced a system of promotions for them whereby they were given one or two stripes for lengths of service or acts of good policing. The blokes liked the system and responded well to the incentive. The community police were shire employees but worked under the direction of the local state police sergeant.

There was also a community court system operating when I arrived. Although probably not strictly legal since 1984, it was both practical and accepted by the general community. It handled a lot of matters which would have otherwise necessitated numerous magistrates court hearings. It also meant that instead of spending time in the state-run jail in Townsville, the prisoners served their sentences on the island where their families could easily access them. The court hearings themselves were worth sitting in and observing.

There were two magistrates with the community senior sergeant as the prosecutor and one or two of his men as court orderlies. One thing about these court hearings was that they didn't waste any time or resources unless there was some point in the evidence that needed clarifying. The defendants were pretty much guilty as charged and rarely had any objections and, invariably, entered guilty pleas. I frequently sat in on the hearings out of interest and for entertainment. This is the scene:

Two magistrates are on the bench, and one of the community police officers brings in the defendant. Chief magistrate to the senior sergeant,

'What is the charge?'

Senior Sergeant, 'Drunk and fighting his uncle outside the canteen last night.'

Chief Magistrate 'How do you plead?'

Defendant, 'Not guilty!'

Chief Magistrate, 'You always were a fuckin liar! Fourteen days of imprisonment! Get him out of here.'

Another hearing:

Chief Magistrate, 'What's the charge?'

Senior Sergeant, 'Stealing food from his neighbour's table.'

Chief Magistrate, 'How do you plead?'

Defendant, 'Not guilty.'

Chief Magistrate, 'Got any witnesses?'

Defendant, 'One.'

Chief Magistrate, 'Well, the police have four! Fourteen days of imprisonment.'

Defendant, 'I can do that standing on my head.'

Chief Magistrate, 'Well, here's another fourteen, you can do them standing on your feet. Get him outta here.'

All these proceedings were conducted in earnest, and at times made me laugh, but I remained composed, as not to cause any disrespect. One real advantage of this system was that those blokes who were doing fourteen days were off the booze for that period and received three feeds a day. They also spent their time with other family members and friends and seemed to be laughing and joking for the duration of their sentence. It reminded me of a magistrate in Cairns who was in the habit of sentencing any bloke who appeared before him, three times in the one week for drunk and disorderly offences, to twenty days in the watchhouse. The watchhouse was always full, and at the end of the twenty days, the prisoners left detoxed to a certain extent. With three good meals per day, they had, in my opinion, consequently extended their lives, even if only by a few weeks.

There was a group of activists on the island, which included the former female community police officer I had employed. This group disagreed with the operation of the local court system, despite it having many distinct advantages, especially handling local issues that otherwise would have resulted in prisoners going to the Townsville prison. This hadn't seemed to worry the former officer while on the job, but it must've become a problem only after she had left. The result was that one morning, a community police officer came into my office on a scheduled court day and said,

'We might have a problem.'

'A big one?' I asked.

'There's a conservationist's boat anchored out a bit from the island. A reporter is on his way to do an expose on our court system.' he said worriedly.

I knew how vital the implemented court system was to the island, so I asked him,

'What do you reckon we do?'

He replied, 'It will finish up the courts forever. I will send the boys down to let the prisoners out of jail. It looks like this is it. I'll get it organised immediately.'

However sad it was, I knew that, unfortunately, he was right. And that was the end of the local court system on the island. A system that, up until then and to my knowledge, never had seen a suicide in the local jail. Unfortunately, that was about to change. It was an effective system widely accepted by the broad community, including the defendants who had appeared in it. However, a group with an axe to grind had brought it to a sudden end as they knew that it would never have passed the scrutiny of the global readers of the magazine.

Fortunately, their surprise attack failed because we had spotted them in time. It had allowed us to disperse the court and left nothing to see. We never discussed the incident or system again.

RAAF FA18 HORNET CRASH

Early one night around nine o'clock, I heard an FA18 RAAF fighter going over the police residence. I recognised it as such because at that time, the Royal Australia Air Force were conducting regular bombing runs with live ordnance on an island near the Palm Group named Rattlesnake Island. The media, both print and radio, advertised the events of the multiple bombing runs, and everyone knew about them. Also, you couldn't mistake the loud sound of the explosions. They continued this bombing practice with live bombs until the late nineties when they commenced using two-thousand five-hundred-kilo loads instead of the usual five-hundred kilo. It caused houses to shake violently and suffer structural damage resulting in the cessation of the activity. In recognising the sound of the aircraft, I noticed that this time the noise was slightly different. There was a howling as though it was climbing, and a second or two later, there was silence.

Feeling slightly uneasy, I went outside for a look. I didn't expect to see anything as those aircraft travel extremely fast. However, the thought of it colliding with the top section of Palm Island's Mount Bentley did cross my mind. I spotted a small group of community police heading my way who informed me,

'Sarge, a plane hit Mount Bentley, not once but twice. The first time we saw nothing, but when it hit a second time, we saw the flames.'

I rang the Townsville police and immediately advised them of the situation. Unfortunately, other than wait near the phone until daylight, there wasn't much I could do. The crash site was inaccessible in the daytime, let alone at night. Moreover, as the crash concerned a RAAF aircraft, I knew that they were infinitely better resourced in this type of situation. The following morning, a RAAF crash boat and two helicopters arrived with personnel and equipment.

I had arranged to meet up with a local who said he could easily find the spot. We assembled at the nearest point where access by foot was remotely possible. This bloke had previous military service, and I thought it would be a good idea to engage his services. As it turned out, it was a good plan but was fatally flawed when my "expert" turned up blind drunk! It was more than embarrassing, as I had informed the Commanding Officer of the recovery effort that this bloke could be of assistance. As I expected, the RAAF politely excluded everyone who wasn't defence force personnel from the operation and went ahead with their work.

In the meantime, a police inspector, whom I knew well, arrived from Townsville. He was aware that I had made it known that sending any further police over from Townsville, would be a waste of resources as the RAAF wouldn't let anyone else get involved. The recovery operation also included removing the hazardous material carbon fibre used in the construction of this aircraft, which becomes dangerous when handled pulverised.

The police inspector said that they had sent him over as a routine procedure. The bosses knew that I would never ask for assistance, as I was known to take on anything that came my way, including incidents such as this. The inspector was good company. He spent the day with us during our regular duties before leaving on the evening aircraft for Townsville.

The air force personnel were extremely busy over the next two weeks. First, there were helicopters winching people directly onto the crash site from where they would collect bags of debris. The bags were then taken to a central collection site for removal by the RAAF crash boat. They found the pilot's body and transported it to Townsville by helicopter. I had furnished reports for other civilian aircraft crashes but never for a defence force plane, so I contacted the Charters Towers police. I knew that some years previously, two Mirage fighters had crashed in their division. They were happy to help me out as those reports are a lot more involved.

The young pilot died on impact; he had just completed a bombing run and left the area. The findings were that through incorrect data in his navigational system, he had finished up too low and had crashed straight into Mount Bentley at four hundred and sixty knots, bounced, collided again and disintegrated. That explained the different sounds I had heard emanating from the aircraft on the night of the crash.

In a gesture of appreciation for the defence forces, but mainly for the young pilot involved in the crash, the locals took up a collection and erected a memorial to his memory.

ALWAYS ON CALL

The workload was unceasingly heavy, making a night's sleep impossible. There were constant callouts to fights, and there were the injured, the distressed and belligerent people turning up outside the police residence at any given time. Scenes such as people racing past being pursued by a man wielding an axe were not unusual. There was a man with a reaping hook embedded in his forehead. He almost scalped himself trying to negotiate his way through the after-hours door at the hospital. One man had a mattock lodged in his back and was still mobile, while another bloke jumped the police residence fence after being shot through the throat. These sorts of disturbances were nothing out of the ordinary. It wasn't long before I became accustomed to the nightly bursts of gunfire and the medivac chopper making regular appearances. It was only because of the people's basic physical toughness and resilience that there weren't many more deaths.

Though petty crimes were dealt with daily, for three days every fortnight, a magistrate, prosecutor, and legal aid flew over to Palm Island from Townsville to hold court, covering the more serious crimes. This was incredible for a community of two-thousand, four-hundred residents, including children. Suicides weren't uncommon, and rapes were a regular occurrence.

Constable Gavin and I were involved in one such rape investigation where the complaint was made three days after the offence. Someone had told the complainant that she'd been raped, but the girl herself had no knowledge of the incident whatsoever and had engaged in sexual intercourse since then. Unfortunately, DNA did not exist at that time, which brought the chances of an arrest down to zero. Gavin and I made several enquiries between us, but we had to drop the case because of a total lack of evidence. Further extensive investigations failed to locate even one creditable witness, and consequently, the matter was not proceeded with.

Since our time on Palm Island, Gavin and I have kept in touch, and occasionally, we still meet up for a beer.

There was one young woman with mental health issues who, during the cause of several weeks, reported to have been subjected to five rapes. I investigated each complaint only to find all those claims every time to be false. Finally, upon making the sixth complaint, I took details but regarded it as another false claim, and I simply did not believe her. However, I discovered later that this time she actually had been telling the truth. This incident happened near the end of my time in the community. I heard after I'd left the island that the perpetrators were caught. They were charged with the "sixth" rape of this young woman, as well as other criminal offences and were consequently jailed for several years. The main offender and his accomplice were one of the community police sergeants and his son.

One day I was having lunch with the Royal Society for the Prevention of Cruelty to Animals officer when a young woman ran up to the front fence, screaming hysterically. She shouted,

'Self-defence, self-defence.'

By her gestures, I gathered that she wanted me to follow her. So both the RSPCA officer and I followed her to a vicinity between two administration buildings. This area was obviously used as a public urinal as the overwhelming stench of urine that greeted us was nauseating and compromised our breathing.

I saw a man lying on the ground. His face was bloodied, and a pool of blood had formed around his head. Even though he first appeared dead, he wasn't because as we got closer, he lifted and turned his head towards us. Upon seeing this, the young woman immediately ran forward and delivered a terrific kick to his head, sending it back onto the ground. She then jumped over him and bolted. The bloke recovered pretty quickly and clambered back onto his feet and wasn't at all interested in making a complaint, nor did he wanted to be taken to the hospital. We watched him for a while as he walked off before we left the scene. There was nothing further that we could do.

I was having dinner when the phone rang. Answering its shrill tones, one of the doctors at the hospital told me that a woman had been killed. She was reported as lying in the street in the upper part of the settlement. He said that he hadn't been there himself and could I go and see what was going on.

I drove up to the scene and straight away saw the woman lying in the dirt not far from the edge of the gravel road. She had visible head injuries and suffered significant loss of blood. As I got closer, I detected the slightest movement in the woman's body. She was still alive. I organised transportation to the hospital via ambulance, operated by the community police. The woman then was post-haste transferred by helicopter to the Townsville hospital in a critical condition. A police investigation was launched, gathering witness statements and scene photographs. The object was to identify and locate the offender.

The guilty party had not been found when, thirty-six hours later, I was required to meet the morning plane to collect police correspondence. Standing at the entrance of the airstrip, I watched as the passengers disembarked. I was astonished when I saw the woman, who I had seen lying in the dusty road presumed dead, emerge from the door of the aircraft. She was a very grey pallor and required the handrails of the little passenger ramp to remain upright, but she made it out of the plane.

I found out that she had discharged herself from the hospital and had decided to return home. It was incredible. Obviously, a very resilient human being, to say the least. I can't recall the outcome of the court process, but the woman was still very much alive when I left the island at the end of my time there.

One bloke, in a blind rage, tried to shoot and kill several people at random. Fortunately for the intended victims, he had neglected to maintain his rifle, and it hopelessly misfired each time he pulled the trigger, which enraged him even more. We received information that the gun-wielding man had taken off to hide out in his house. Accompanied by constables Mick and Gavin, we entered the premises and found him hiding out in the lounge room, where we managed to overpower and disarm him. Just another day at the office.

Especially on paydays, there were countless domestic disturbances and fights fuelled by hundreds of drunken residents. Throughout my years on Palm Island, during confrontations that frequently erupted outside the police residence, I was never so grateful to have my courageous and powerful German shepherd dog Conan patrolling the yard. He took his job of keeping the house safe very seriously, and I never had any break-ins while he was there.

The only way of getting any peace was to leave the island altogether. Police in isolated stations were given "Leave Entitlement". This allocation allowed them to, once annually, take a run of five days off. During this time, we usually travelled to the nearest large centre to do the necessary shopping and tend to personal business. None of this could be done on the island and required more than just a day trip.

The usual way over to the mainland was via one of the ten-seater commercial aircraft. These planes flew every day, and all of them rattled badly and definitely had seen better days. Unfortunately, due to the dirt strip that served as an aerodrome, their condition worsened noticeably with every trip they made. The planes were also very hot and grubby. I sometimes had a beer before boarding the twenty-minute return flight, just to make it a bit more bearable.

One afternoon the aircraft had not long taken off when the adolescent male sitting across from me had evidently neglected to visit the toilet before departure. While looking at me, he raised his leg up onto the seat and dropped a solid lump of poop out of his shorts onto the seat. He then lifted up his foot and kicked the turd onto the aircraft floor, totally unconcerned for the rest of the flight. Talk about the stink.

Another early, very foggy morning flight, the aircraft was not far from the Townsville airport. I sat in the seat behind the pilot and saw that he was reading a map. Suddenly he threw the chart out of the way, grabbed the yoke, and put the aircraft in a very steep climb to the right. The engines screamed with the sudden acceleration, and looking behind me, I saw the grey-ashen faces of the other nine passengers. They had gripped their seats with white knuckle intensity, and fear had rendered them incapable of uttering a sound.

I didn't ask any questions. I was just ever so thankful that we avoided colliding with what I suspected to be Mount Cook. The pilot was on his last day with this company before commencing with one of the major airlines the following Monday. Now there was a worry!

I, however, had reservations about flying from there on in and preferred using the barge service. I knew the skippers and crew, and we had become great mates over the time I was there. Travel time was longer but infinitely safer, with an added bonus that I now could take my dogs with me.

KARMA

While stationed on Palm Island, in addition to my attack dog Conan, I acquired a female German shepherd. She was a homeless dog and given to me on one of my visits to the mainland. The dog had no known name, so I decided on Karma, meaning action, and that she had plenty. She turned out to be an excellent guard dog to the extent that a RAAF dog trainer said he'd wished he'd seen her first. The dog did an excellent job of protecting the police residence and, after entering her breeding season, produced a litter of pups with Conan. The mating process went smoothly even though neither dog had been involved in breeding previously. Sixty-two days later, the puppies started to arrive.

The event was much anticipated by police staff, and two constables, my mates Mick H and Gavin, put in an order for a pup. The birthing process, which took place in the kennel underneath the police residence, was running smoothly. Karma proved to be an excellent mother who knew instinctively what to do. Big Conan fussed around, trying to help in his way. Later that afternoon, just after the fifth pup had arrived, there was a commotion outside the fence. Karma pricked up her ears, and mid-labour was off like a shot. We ran out to see what was happening and were astonished to see the dog clear the high fence that surrounded the yard. Here she nipped a bloke outside the fence in the backside and jumped back over the fence, and ran back under the house. I don't know what this bloke did. The last I saw of this man was him racing drunkenly down the footpath.

Back under the house, Karma got on with her job and gave birth to three more pups, after which both parent dogs settled down to raise their litter. However, I noticed that one pup seemed to be struggling during feeding, and on having a closer look at the little fellow, I discovered he had a cleft pallet. The milk he was trying to swallow was going straight into his tiny lungs, effectively drowning him. Concerned, I contacted a vet on the mainland who confirmed what I had suspected. Living on an island without a vet, sadly, my only option was to euthanise the puppy.

Getting this bunch of excitable puppies immunised was a logistical nightmare. I chartered an aircraft for the occasion and flew Conan, Karma and the seven pups to Townsville. As usual, the dog squad blokes were great and collected the entire crew at the airport and, after the visit to the vet surgery, took them all back to the airport. On the way over, the pilot was unconcerned with all the dogs running loose throughout the aircraft objecting only to Conan's usual request to ride in the front seat next to the pilot. He loved riding in planes. However, another pilot was to fly us back, and he was of a totally different mindset. When we pulled up in the dog squad van and let all nine dogs out onto the tarmac, he became very nervous and yelled,

'Get those fucking dogs in the plane. Quick before the tower spots them.' The dog handler and I rapidly rounded up the dogs. We milled them around Conan, who was waiting near the entrance door to the aircraft with eager anticipation for the upcoming flight. He had flown to Townsville with me on other occasions and always selected his own seat upon boarding. He then spent the flight looking out the window, oblivious to the ashen faces of the other passengers who were terrified of this big dog acting like a human being.

After eight weeks, the puppies went to good homes except for one, which I decided to keep. I named the pup Barrabas. It soon became evident that he indeed had inherited both his parents' great traits. Karma continued to be an excellent guard dog. She was also very intelligent, as not only could she undo gate latches, but was also capable of unwinding wire tied to secure gates. Unfortunately, it was just a matter of time before she got into strife, and when I eventually moved to the city, she escaped from the house yard taking Barrabas with her. Unfortunately, one night they were bumped by a car. For her safety, I rehomed her with a security company, where she performed her duties admirably until her death, caused by those who think it's hilarious, throwing poisonous baits into a dog's house yard.

PERILOUS LEAVE

My turn for isolation leave came around, so I arranged for a ride on the police boat with my dogs. My mate Nick decided to come over with me. But as usual, the promises made of a regular service and ready access to a police boat disappeared with the inspector who had made them. His replacement wasn't all that well disposed towards me, and consequently, the boat arrived three days late. That left only two days out of the five, one of which was Anzac Day. The trip over to the mainland, forty-eight sea miles, was slow and rough with nonstop rain and strong winds whipping up three-metre swells. Initially, the boat had been designed to be three and a half metres longer than it was, but budgetary constraints shortened it, and consequently, the boat rolled badly. The dog squad was waiting in the

Townsville harbour to give us a lift to a house in West End. A friend, who worked as a civilian clerk at the police station, was away on holiday, and she was kind enough to let us have the use of the place in her absence.

As it now was Anzac Day, there was nothing open in the way of supermarkets and the like, but I managed to score a carton of beer. Nick's friend Lyn called in for a few beers, and we settled down for a bit of relaxation, and it felt great to be away, if only for a couple of days, from the constant violence and full-on police lifestyle of Palm Island. My two German shepherd dogs also seemed to enjoy the peace and tranquillity and soon fell asleep at my feet.

It wasn't to last. Glancing at the clock, it was just after eight in the evening when both dogs became restless and started to growl. Their behaviour unmistakably indicated that someone was near the house in the backyard. After hearing the sounds again, I told the dogs to stay, grabbed my torch and walked out the back door. On the back steps of the house was a large wild-eyed male. He was much bigger than me, had long dreadlocks and wore a grubby T-shirt, jeans, and joggers. He also appeared to be affected by a substance that I knew wasn't alcohol. A drunk is uncoordinated in his movements and slurs his words. This bloke did neither. I guessed that he was under the influence of drugs. I asked this bloke,

'What are you doing here?'

He replied that he was looking for a supply of drugs. My friend, the owner, had informed me that a drug-producing motorcycle gang had occupied the house before she'd purchased the home. It was apparent that this bloke, standing in the backyard, was several years out of date insofar as his suppliers went. I grabbed him by the arm and walked him around the side of the house out into the street. I told him to leave and that he was wasting his time as there were no drugs on the premises. I watched him walk away in the rain until he was out of sight.

You wouldn't believe it, but about twenty minutes later, there were noises out the back of the house again. I went outside, and there's that boofhead again looking for drugs. I repeated the same process, and once more, I walked him out onto the road and watched him walk away. I hadn't been back inside ten minutes when there were sounds again, but this time he had chosen the front door and was attempting to force it open. I opened the front door, and yes, here's the same fool again. He started to get agitated because of my non-compliance in regards to supplying him with drugs. Being both off duty, neither my mate nor I were interested in arresting him. So we went outside, as well as the old dog Sabre, who managed to slip through the door. I decided to let him come with us and left the young attack dog inside.

It was becoming a bit repetitive and tedious. However, once again, I explained that he had the wrong place and added that he was about seven years too late, and both Nick and I walked him out onto the road. Old Sabre was also starting to display an interest in the intruder. Although the old dog had only a few teeth left and had his big head permanently tilted to one side because of a prior ear infection, he still had plenty of fire in him. Sabre had one problem though, the dog seemed to be unaware that he wasn't three years old anymore. Therefore Sabre made an executive decision of his own and started moving towards the drug-crazed man to give him a good bite.

All we wanted was for that fool to go away, so I grabbed the old dog's collar, preventing him from attacking the man. In hindsight, I should've let the old dog have a go because the moment I turned with

Sabre, the fool king hit me. He hit me in the right eye with a massive punch causing me to lose sight in that eye instantly. For the next half hour, I could only see a grey coloured mist and nothing else. I didn't go down but let go of the dog.

I rushed forward and grabbed this idiot by his dreadlocks and threw him out onto the road. In the rain and darkness, Nick and I tried to restrain this lunatic, who seemed utterly impervious to pain. Understandably, neither of us had a set of handcuffs, which is the last thing you would take on leave. Nick put a leg lock on the man while I placed a solid arm lock on him. We held him down, but his extremely violent struggling, screaming and wildly thrashing made it exceedingly difficult to hold him. The man managed to sink his filthy teeth in during the struggle and bit almost through Nick's forearm. Within a few minutes into the fight, I felt the bloke's shoulder dislocate, but that didn't deter him. He just seemed to get worse, displaying maniacal strength and rage.

To keep the dog out of the way, Lyn locked Old Sabre back in the house and rang the Townsville police station. The request was for urgent assistance as Sergeant Cahill and Nick were in a massive fight trying to bring a big lunatic under control. Now, this is again where things started going awry. The police officer on the other end of the line simply put the message over the radio as,

'Fight in the street.'

The result was that the three cars on night shift didn't place the call at the top of their priorities. By now, the rain was getting heavier, Nick had a severe bite wound to his forearm, and my back problem was starting to cause me problems. I had no other choice than to escalate the restraint plan, so I struck him hard with a bottom fist to his kidney. His response to that was that he immediately urinated and defecated himself. He stank something awful and continued to fight. The last thing I now needed was for this bloke to break loose and to get back onto his feet. He seemed impervious to pain, and I decided to slow him up with a bottom fist to the side of his head. It gave us a minute of reprieve while we remained in our positions. With the time that had passed, I thought a patrol car wouldn't be far away.

Wrong. Within no time, this individual regained consciousness, and he immediately resumed his violent rage. I had no choice but to hit him again. By now, we had been on the ground with this man for probably twenty minutes. Still, there was no sign of a police vehicle, nor of this man's violence abating.

Then there was a crash of glass breaking from the house. Big Conan, the RAAF trained attack dog, had become enraged with the commotion outside. The man's unintelligible roars had Conan charging at the set of glass louvres and crash his way through them. He raced out and immediately attacked the man with the only available biting space left for him and set to this bloke's backside with the incredible enthusiasm he always employed. The lunatic's enraged bellows added to the tremendous cacophony in the already disturbed night.

Lyn managed to coax Conan back inside the house and rang the police station again. This time the phone was answered by someone who put the call over the radio that,

'Sergeant Cahill was on the ground with a violent man and needed urgent assistance.'

Thirty-five minutes had passed since we first engaged in fighting when finally, three police vehicles arrived, with one being a paddy wagon. Mortified, the six police officers that arrived on the scene explained that they had no idea that the incorrect message that had come through in the first instance concerned their old boss. They took the bloke to the rear of the paddy wagon and placed him inside. The police officers locked the door behind him, and the arrested prisoner was conveyed to the watchhouse. After he was charged, they took the man to the hospital as he needed treatment for injuries received during the desperate struggle.

The following day, Nick and I got to spend the day at the hospital. Nick received treatment for his bite and me for my damaged hands as well as my eye. The doctor advised me that it would be seventeen years before I'd know of any permanent damage to my eye. That type of injury takes that long to manifest symptoms. The day after our time at the hospital saw us on our way back to Palm Island. The bloke appeared in court later, and his solicitor entered a plea of guilty. In addition to a fine, the magistrate ordered him to pay us both compensation for the injuries he had caused us. He said that he had no recollection of the events which occurred on that night. His injuries were described as having been dragged along the bitumen for some considerable distance.

A few years later, after leaving the force and working for Armaguard, I was in the driver's seat of the armoured truck when I saw the drug user walk by along the footpath. I could see him staring at me. I guess he was trying to remember where he had seen me before, gave up and continued his way. Seventeen years passed, and fortunately, I have had no further problems with that eye, and it was a tremendous relief to know that no permanent blindness would develop.

GROUND ZERO

Life returned pretty much to normal after that wasted trip to Townsville, or at least, what was considered "normal" for Palm Island. The usual violence continued. I was also on the alert for problems caused by interferences from our various politicians and newspapers. Several people from different clans had direct lines to some of these politicians, all of whom had their own agenda. By now, the constant stress and lack of sleep were starting to bite, causing weekly flare-ups and recurrences of my malaria. I was gradually getting more and more fatigued as the months went by. The symptoms of PTSD added to the difficulties that went with doing "the worst job in the Queensland Police Force".

The local government elections came around, and as it happens in small communities, the tensions started to run higher than usual. Still, I had never experienced anything like the one in Palm Island. There were two main clans in addition to the thirty-eight smaller groups. Some of these groups didn't have many people at all. As the counting of votes progressed, a lot of dissatisfied voters started to voice their anger. There were ute loads of people racing around the streets, accompanied by the sounds of occasional gunfire.

Then the alcohol-fuelled hand to hand fighting started, and although there wasn't much, I could do with four constables, I still had to make an effort to try and quell the disturbances. There were too many conflicts in progress, all at the same time, and I was reluctant to involve the community police. They had their clan allegiances as well. I could, as well as my constables, wander around in uniform amongst the battling groups without being attacked. Their focus was on each other and not us, and if any of us did get injured, it would almost certainly be caused by a missile or rock meant for someone else. I hadn't bothered advising headquarters of the riot in progress as there was nothing much they could provide in the way of backup.

I came across a fight where I recognised one of my community police, a large and decent bloke. Unfortunately, in the heat of the results, he had gotten himself into a blue. He had a bloke on the ground and was winning decisively by choking him. I had to intervene as the bloke gasping for air wouldn't have lasted much longer. A murder in itself would be bad enough, but I could imagine the tremendous incendiary consequences which would follow. I immediately grabbed my bloke in a stranglehold to try and distract him from his current intent. Lots of people have long memories of wrongs done to their family or group. So they will take retribution whenever an opportunity presents itself, and here the locals were no different.

Trying to wrestle the giant to get him off the bloke he was strangling was starting to work. What happened next was incredible and unbelievably funny. I felt a hand tapping me on my right shoulder, and out of the corner of my eye, I could see Bernie, an old bloke in a community police uniform. I always got on well with Bernie, who had started to lose the plot a little. Every day he turned up for work, rostered on duty or not. While still maintaining my hold on the big bloke, I managed to turn my head slightly to see what Bernie wanted. The noise in the immediate vicinity was deafening, causing him to raise his voice well above his usual tone. He yelled while still tapping me on the shoulder,

'Sarge, can you do my tax for me in the morning?'

I couldn't believe what he'd just said, and as it turned out, nor could the giant I was wrestling. I released him, and he released his victim as we all burst out laughing.

Even the bloke on the ground laughed as much as he could, relative to his ability to breathe. I couldn't answer for a minute or two before replying,

'Yes Bernie, no problem.'

After that, the big bloke lumbered off in one direction and the bloke he had been strangling, in another, leaving me to continue wandering through the melee. The fighting, screaming, utes full of combatants tearing around continued and intensified. Then, on an impulse, I jumped into the police car and went around to the residence of a leader of one of the main clans to see what he had to offer.

I found him half full of booze. I had maintained a good rapport with this massive bloke, and after a short conversation, we left his house. I returned with him to ground zero of the riot, the level the disturbance had now reached. The leader morphed into a one-man riot squad. He stumbled around, shouting admonishments and obscenities at the numerous participants accompanied with plenty of judicious slaps around their heads. Now whether he was the sole contributor to the cessation of the disturbance, or maybe they were all just getting tired, I don't know. But, from there on in, it wasn't long before things started to become relatively quiet. Well, for there anyway.

The phone started to ring almost nonstop, with newspapers wanting the details of the riot. They had been alerted by someone, but I always made it a point to suppress news of incidents like this as much as possible. The place already had a bad reputation, and I didn't see the point in making it any worse. The only paper I provided information to, was the local Townsville Bulletin. On being asked about the riot the following morning, my reply was,

'A few people were running around yelling and waving their arms around, but nothing too serious; "I've seen more fights on a pay night".'

To my surprise, that one-liner made "Quote of the Week" in the paper.

Once again, I made it into the paper when a reporter asked me about the sly grog trafficking on the island and the inference that I was turning a blind eye to the nefarious activity. I responded with,

'There's no doubt it goes on here, as Palm Island is no different from any other town on the mainland. If anyone has any information which could help us get this activity stopped, I urge them to come forward, and we will act on it.'

Nobody came forward for several reasons, amongst them being the need for alcohol and fear of retribution. The system was such that someone could access cheap flagons of wine any day they wanted them. They then could depend on a visit on pension day for payment of those already downed flagons, which generally had a mark-up of at least five hundred per cent. To stamp out this behaviour would require constant surveillance day and night by police. I didn't have the numbers to make that happen as there were numerous other problems we had to deal with daily. In some of the places I had served, I could recall flagons containing half cheap wine, topped up with methylated spirits and water, creating devasting results immediately and long term.

I was generally perceived to be doing an okay job in difficult circumstances by the bosses. However, that was soon to change with the arrival of a new inspector who became my immediate superior. I'd had a run-in with him a few years earlier in the Gulf. He had started mouthing off at me half-drunk one night at a cattle property. Another inspector who was there at the time prevented me from giving this bloke the hiding he so richly deserved. I remember thinking later; this is the last bastard I'd want as my boss. Now that time had come.

Another senior officer decided to team up with this bastard, who incidentally was universally disliked by a lot of police. Between them, they started to make my life even more stressful. So now I had an extremely difficult job with failing health and was hounded by a couple of individuals hell-bent on getting at me. I was in the habit of keeping a diary, particularly of conversations I had with various people, and I knew that I had not applied for a transfer. Neither would I have done so for an unspecified destination, which was the allegation.

I immediately telephoned the police union. The president said he'd follow it up and get back to me. Half an hour later, he returned the call and told me to forget about the transfer but that I had a serious enemy. I realised that the writing was on the wall.

The endless round of violence continued with one incident occurring, which gave me the opportunity for some impromptu negotiating with a man who had barricaded himself inside the local butchery and threatened to kill himself. I knew the bloke reasonably well as he had the local butcher shop. He had locked himself inside his shop and threatened to kill himself with a large sharp knife you would find in any butchery. He had already inflicted a few decent cuts to his arms and chest, and I wasn't sure he wouldn't follow through with his threat.

So, acting on a hunch, I rang this bloke and asked him could I put in an order for some mince and sausages, and as I guessed, he said yes and that he'd get to it straight away. I then walked over to the shop and stood out from the side door, making sure he saw me walk past the big front window. I had taken a constable with me who remained in the background, out of sight, but close enough to grab the bloke when he came out, hopefully with the meat. The butcher appeared holding a long-bladed knife in one hand and the mince and sausages in the other.

I walked towards him with a ten-dollar note in my hand, thanked him and managed to distract him long enough for the constable to tackle and simultaneously disarm him. The butcher had an astonished look on his face as he went down and dropped the knife and meat.

After being subdued, he said that I didn't fight fair by lying to him.

When he returned from the hospital a month later, the butcher came over and thanked me, and that was pretty much the last dealings I had with him. So the matter had a satisfactory conclusion.

WHEN THE GOING GETS TOUGH

Late one afternoon, once again, the phone rang. The caller informed me that a crowd had formed and were attacking a man on the beach not far from the canteen. It didn't take long for two of my constables and me to reach the scene of the reported incident. On my arrival, I saw a man aged about twenty cowering behind a community police officer, shielding him from a hostile, screaming crowd. Several large rocks lay strewn around which they had thrown at the frightened man. Between us four police officers, we managed to get the hunted man away from the mob and back to the police station.

The man was intellectually disadvantaged and slow in his speech. The community policeman who had kept him alive told us that the man had gone into the canteen carrying in his arms an eighteen-month-old girl. It had been obvious, even to the casual observer, that she had been sexually assaulted. The mob drinking in the canteen immediately reached the same conclusion that any group of drinkers in any bar across Australia would. They decided that the bloke carrying the child was the perpetrator, so they opted to take the matter into their own hands and chased him down to the water's edge. They could very well have killed him if it were not for the intervention of the community policeman.

One of the constables there at the time said to me,

'I know this bloke, and this isn't his go at all. I'll talk to him.'

As it turned out, this poor devil had gone home and had found this poor baby girl there, who was a relative of his. Trying to help, he had carried the baby down to the canteen, where he thought people might be able to help the little girl. Unfortunately, he almost got murdered for his efforts. Further investigations quickly located the real offender, who was arrested not long after that. Upon sentencing, he received a lengthy period of imprisonment in Townsville Prison. I can't even begin to imagine how these blokes can do such things.

LEPROSY

Not long after taking over the police station, I was outside my office one morning when one of the locals walked up to me and introduced himself to me by name. After the usual handshake greeting, we started a casual conversation. When he walked off, I noticed the looks of horror on the faces of the community policemen and my constables. I said to the group collectively,

'What's wrong? Has he got leprosy?'

I was astonished when they all answered almost in unison,

'Yes, he has.'

I blurted out, 'What?'

Regaining my composure, I added matter-of-factly, 'Oh, is that all. In that case, no worries.'

Quickly I made my way inside, thinking that surely it would take more than a brief handshake to contract this dreadful disease. But just in case and just to make sure, I scrubbed my hands thoroughly, and when I left the island three years later, this bloke was still alive and doing well, and so was I. Of course, the disease itself these days doesn't carry the stigma it did back then.

PALM ISLAND POLICE TRUCK.

The police Toyota Landcruiser ute on Palm Island had seen better days though mechanically sound enough, the unescapable, close proximity to the ocean made rust inevitable. One night Mick and I were in the ute in pursuit of a few blokes who had been in the act of breaking into the canteen. We'd received a phone call alerting us of the goings-on, but upon our arrival, the thieves spotted us and ran off. Mick pushed down the accelerator and, at speed, drove across the uneven ground with the result that the Landcruiser bucked and jumped all over the place. The rough ride caused the car key to fall out of the ignition and onto the floor. The problem was, there was a rusted-out hole in the floor, and of course, the key unerringly went straight through it and onto the ground outside as we raced along.

Eventually, we caught up with the three offenders and took them into custody, and after taking them back to the station, we retraced our path, and incredibly, we found the missing key. Mick and I remained friends throughout the years and have recalled this story a few times while sharing a beer, and several years later, he honoured me by being my 'Best Man' at my wedding.

ALMOST A DEEP SIX

One morning, after I had spent the very early morning hours in the office, I emerged at dawn with the intent of trying to take a day off. And after a bike ride and breakfast, I looked out over the ocean from my veranda and spotted several uniformed naval officers standing around on the wharf. I had a great view from where I stood, and I saw the sleek outlines of a grey warship in the distance. I made the executive decision that I'd done enough office work, and out of curiosity, I went down to the wharf.

As I wasn't in uniform, I introduced myself to the group of officers. It appeared that someone somewhere, not known to the ship's officers, had arranged for the ship to pull up and moor off the island. Groups of sailors were sent ashore to give them a chance to play a few games of football or cricket. Whoever this towering intellect was, who had told them to moor up, was unknown. It was evident that the level of planning didn't extend to advising either the captain of the warship or the island council. However, not in my wildest dreams could I have imagined what this day had in store for me.

I assisted in letting the locals know that the officers were on the island and arranged for them to organise a few games. The island itself had four football teams, so the sailors gave them a reason to have a few extra games. I used the police truck, a large paddy wagon with a rear cage, to provide the officers with a tour of the island. They were extremely interested in the wrecks of two WWII United States Navy Catalina flying boats. There had been a base on the island during the war hosting

United States Navy personnel. Aircraft operated out of Palm Island on anti-submarine warfare patrols.

Back at the police house, we had a few of my home-brewed beers and judging by the quantity consumed, the beer was more than acceptable. I dropped my newfound friends back at the wharf and didn't expect to see them again, and as it happened, I almost wished I hadn't.

Later in the afternoon, I was surprised to see a uniformed sailor at my front door. He saluted and said,

'Captain's invitation, he would like you to attend dinner in the wardroom on the ship tonight. The workboat will be at the wharf at 1800 hours.'

I said I'd be there, and away he went. I rang a mate of mine who had trained Conan and who had been a warrant officer in the Royal Australian Air Force to check on any procedures or protocol I should follow. I had been a junior naval officer in the Royal Australian Naval College at Jervis Bay before entering the police, but that was twenty years ago.

My mate said no to special procedures but did say to bring a couple of young blokes along as that is expected. When I put it to my constables, I found that I didn't have any shortage of volunteers for the job. So we trooped down to the wharf at 1800 hours sharp and jumped aboard the forty-foot cutter.

The HMAS Brisbane was anchored about three miles offshore towards the mainland. Heading out towards the ship, I saw its sleek lines and armaments, a beauty along with its menacing appearance. There were several sailors on board the workboat. They were in good spirits, having availed themselves of the hospitality of the canteen and other ways. It was with this happy crowd of temporary shipmates we all boarded the warship. The vessel was a modified Charles F Adams class destroyer displacing 4850 tons, 133.2 metres in length, with a complement of 311 officers and men. The distance from the main deck to the waterline was approximately 8 metres, and the draught was 6.2 metres. Both measurements have relevance to the story as it unfolds.

The hospitality the officers and stewards in the wardroom extended couldn't be faulted. They regarded me as the "Skipper" of the police station as in the police service, my ranking as a first-class sergeant was probably equivalent to that of a chief petty officer at the time. I thoroughly enjoyed the evening with great conversation and a three-course meal served by a never-ending supply of stubbies of beer.

I had tasked my two other constables, who had remained on the island, to give the duty lieutenant a hand rounding up the ship's crew. The sailors had dispersed celebrating around the settlement, and the report back was that those sailors had a great time onshore with the locals. However, the ship's doctor was thoroughly alarmed when the discussion came around to infectious diseases. I advised him of the eighty-five per cent rate of Hepatitis B in the community, and several had HIV, human immunodeficiency virus.

After some hours had elapsed, the time to leave arrived. I walked out to the steel ladder attached to the ship's side to descend and board the waiting cutter. Two commanders, with whom I had struck an affinity, accompanied me. After shaking hands, I put my feet on the top rung, and as it had been raining, the rungs were wet. Although I am not looking for excuses, I was in full uniform, including boots, not designed for descending slippery ladders. And even though I wasn't drunk, I did feel the after-effects caused by the never-ending arrival of stubbies at our table. I'll admit that I did have enough beer to impair my concentration slightly.

The deck was about eight metres from the waterline

and the waiting cutter, and this was the distance I fell after my boots slipped off the top rung of the ladder. Fortunately, I fell feet first, and it was my bum that collided with the gunwale of the cutter, slightly slowing up my unintended and unexpected descent into the water between the ship and the cutter. I never swore, yelled, or said anything on my trip down. After my collision with the smaller boat, I continued my trajectory into the dark waters of one of the world's largest tiger shark breeding areas. If it was dark before I hit the water, it was nothing compared to the blackness I was in now as I continued to descend into the ocean. The keel was 6.2 metres below the destroyer's waterline, and I estimated I must have at least been close to that when I pulled up. I started to make some immediate changes to my environment.

I was a strong swimmer with a lifesaving qualification. I had been putting in a decent swim in the lagoon on the leeward side of the island on an almost daily basis. One morning a small delegation of locals waited outside the gate of the police house to tell me

'Don't go swimming Sarge. There's a large tiger shark in the lagoon.'

After the arrival of the shark, I stopped going there. Apart from missing the exercise, I also missed telling any of the constables, who sometimes swam with me, that I liked their company because it decreased my chances of getting eaten by a shark by fifty per cent. The looks on those blokes' faces were always priceless.

Meanwhile, I am now about six metres underwater with numerous sharks I couldn't see but, which I knew, were lurking in the darkness. In a powerful swim, I immediately struck out for the surface. I was thinking clearly now but obviously not clear enough to give the cutter a thought. I hit the underside of it, with the impact nearly knocking me unconscious, but I managed to combat the inviting pull into the darkness of unconsciousness and remained alert.

I used the boat I'd just collided with to feel my way across until I surfaced. I broke the surface on the lee side, away from the ship's side and saw the yellow light flashing up on the deck and heard the message transmitted over the Tannoy,

'Man overboard, man overboard.'

One of the commanders became visible, leaning over the rail. Incredibly, I was still wearing my glasses. Two young sailors in the cutter looked at me, with eyes like saucers, as I pulled myself up onto the gunwale. I said to them,

'I thought I'd go for a swim before I went home, but I am a bit fucked at the moment. So give me a hand in, will you.'

I heard the commander yell out the order,

'Get him in the boat.'

With that, the two matelots grabbed me, each by an arm, and hauled me over the side. It didn't take long for me to recover, and after a quick wave of the hand, the cutter moved off in the island's direction. I disembarked at the wharf and went home, starting to feel a lot of pain from my shoulders down to my feet, and I was more than thankful to have survived. If my head had hit first on the way down and not my bum, it could've been a fatal incident.

The pain over the next week or so was severe, and I could barely walk at times. However, I didn't complain, not one word, as you don't get chances like that every day. Eventually, the bruising faded away, leaving a solid lump where the point of impact had been, which after seven years disappeared as well.

VIOLENCE, DISILLUSIONS AND NEW BEGINNINGS

The violence continued among the residents of the island. One afternoon, I was to experience a series of events that I had never encountered before. Palm Island was a training station in that there were always four young constables there on a six-monthly rotational basis. I liked to think I got on well with all of them. There were a few who really liked the work and with whom I had an affinity. These constables stayed on for up to three rotations. Most of the blokes on leaving the island applied for detective, POS Public Order Squad, Special Emergency Response Team SERT or prosecuting positions, having acquired a fair bit of experience. Other blokes were happy with returning to general duty policing on their return from Palm Island. All in all, the constables were pretty much as good a group of young blokes you'd be likely to meet.

One constable arrived who possessed exceptional physical strength, which was not immediately apparent. He was a decent bloke, but this particular afternoon he inadvertently got involved in an altercation that had the potential to flare up into a significant anti-police incident. What happened was, he had arrested an aggressive man, and as he placed him in the holding cell adjacent to the station, the man started threatening and abusing the constable. The cell was only a holding cell, and the barred door opened to the area used for parking the police vehicle. Members of the public could wander through this area at any time of the day or night as it was completely open. There were several people in the immediate vicinity of the cell, including family members of the arrested man. Allegations were that the constable had hit the man, however, I wasn't able to confirm that or otherwise. There weren't any obvious injuries to the man in the cell

During my time there, the actual violence directed towards the state police was far less than that in other places I'd been. I felt this was primarily because of the absence of violence from us. There was always the possibility of this changing in an instant, and this was turning out to be one of those times. In a noticeably short time, a crowd of very angry people had congregated around the police station. I was expecting the local field officer from legal services to turn up any minute. For many years, I had an excellent rapport with this organisation, but the people I had known and worked with, had since left, and strangers had replaced them.

I could see the unrest rapidly escalating to riot status if I didn't do something. It was then I remembered that the local barge was about to leave after it had made a freight delivery from Townsville. I was on good terms with the skippers and crew, who usually came to the police house for lunch. I immediately told the constable to change his shirt, head out the back door, and get on the barge. He did as he was asked and duly headed off for Townsville. I then telephoned the boss and said what I had done. He was more than happy with the result. I said that I would keep him posted and would attempt to calm the situation.

The field officer arrived a short time later. I advised her that the officer involved had not only been transferred but, in fact, had left the island. This information seemed to mollify the field officer a lot. I then set to work interviewing the witnesses and taking statements. However, the family weren't really interested in pursuing the matter and withdrew their complaint, effectively bringing the incident to a conclusion. The crowd slowly dispersed even though they weren't too happy about it. I was confident that this was the end of the matter; however, I was to find out otherwise.

In the months before this incident, disturbing revelations had begun to appear in the media about corruption on a grand scale within the Queensland Police Force and Government. Allegations of protected non-existent brothels and casinos and massive bribes to police over decades led to a royal commission that was to change the police culture and operations forever. The corruption was pretty much confined to a relatively small percentage of cops, mainly in the vice and licensing branches. The rest of the people were doing the jobs they were supposed to do. Commissioner Lewis was accused of being the ringleader of "The Joke", as its participants had named the system of corruption. He was stood down as the process rolled inexorably on.

In return for immunity, crooked police were turning on their colleagues, and the stories surfacing were reprehensible. While this inquiry was going on, all transfers and promotions ceased, effectively punishing honest cops. For me, this meant that, even though I had qualified externally in the Senior Sergeant examinations, I was forced to remain where I was. It was well past the required two years expected of a sergeant in an isolated, stressful position like Palm Island. But there was nowhere to go that would suit me. I also realised that, because of the forged attempt to get me transferred several months earlier, I had enemies and wouldn't receive a fair go. So then, almost overnight, the seniority promotion system was axed, and it's then that I knew for sure that I would never reach a job such as OIC, Officer in Charge, of a larger country station such as Longreach or the like.

Already it seemed that there was a purge going on

with operational police of my rank. It appeared that they deemed my rank to have the most impact on new police. Not only were we involved in running training stations, but we also instructed the young constables during operational work. They didn't like the influence we had, and they wanted it changed. I knew of other sergeants, who hadn't made an enemy as I had, but who also had been treated abominably. The end result for those sergeants was a, more or less a forced departure from the force. The rank soon was abolished, and Force became Service.

I have already outlined the only dealings I had with the now-disgraced Commissioner Lewis in a previous chapter. For some reason, which I presume to be "payback" by those shunned during Lewis's visit to the island, my nemesis, the inspector and the frontrunners had me consequently tagged as a "Mate of Lewis". A source informed me that I was on a list of twenty-six cops in the same boat. Subsequent investigations revealed that I was simply an honest policeman, uninvolved in any criminal activity, which probably was also the case for the rest of those listed. I could see even more writing on the wall.

After I had submitted my complete file on the incident involving the immediate transfer of that young bloke, I was surprised to receive a visit from a relatively new inspector. I had a few dealings with him in the previous months, and he was a decent sort of bloke without any animosity towards me at all. Nevertheless, he was required to come over and issue me with a formal caution over the incident. He told me that the way I handled the near-riot situation was the best he had ever seen in effectively smoothing things over. However, at some stage before or after the "near riot" occurred, there was an empty Coca Cola can on the floor of the cell, which according to, whoever was driving my harassment, amounted to a total lack of supervision of the constables and watchhouse. I didn't know about the existence of the empty can or how it had become known in Townsville. As a result, I was officially cautioned. Of course, it was incredibly petty to caution a sergeant over an empty soft drink can, but that is how far things were deteriorating.

The writing on the wall was increasing in size and became huge and threatening. The time had arrived for me to decide what I wanted to do with the rest of my life. I could continue my work with failing health, constant harassment and white-anting, character assassination, no prospects whatsoever of promotion or even a decent transfer. That plus the enormous stress of running the worst station in Queensland for three years and being regarded with suspicion. All this on the say-so of some cowardly individuals who declared me an associate of the disgraced commissioner. I could also leave the Force altogether. The decision was straightforward in that I didn't have a choice.

So, one day I rang an inspector I had worked with previously. He was a decent bloke who always had a lot of time for his men. I told him I would retire on medical grounds and could he please come over to conduct a complete station inspection. Following this, I would cease duty and start the process of retiring. He agreed to this and duly arrived the following day to conduct his inspection. I wanted there to be nothing that could be deliberately misconstrued or fabricated in further efforts to damage my standing. That same afternoon he wished me luck as I went on sick leave until I received my notice to retire. However, during that waiting time, another inspector tried extremely hard to make my life as difficult as possible. He still saw a need to badger me.

By now, I was suffering badly from PTSD, which had

a firm grip on me. So I saw a doctor, John, in Townsville who got the ball rolling for a medical discharge from the police and then referred me to another doctor who told me that an increasing number of police were diagnosed with war neurosis, as PTSD was called back then. John has remained my doctor, and I still see him at his surgery, thirty-two years later.

I decided to avail myself of an offer to manage a small RSL motel to gain a bit of knowledge in the private sector. That went well as it was a bit like running a watchhouse. Only the inmates could come and go as they pleased. A few months went by before I received my retirement notice, and somewhat relieved, I headed off towards Townsville and a new life.

I was glad I had been able to follow in my family tradition of being a policeman. I was confident that the job I had joined in 1967 had changed, not only in name and rank structure but also in how policing was carried out. The effective methods of the past were now deemed criminal behaviour, and it would have ended badly for me. I was looking forward to a new career somewhere in the private sector. As it turned out, I acquired work in a very satisfying position, but that's another story.

Always on Call

OFFICE OF COMMISSIONER OF POLICE

Brisbane, 6 OCT 1987

Sergeant 1/c P.A. CAHILL
Police Station
PALM ISLAND

At the SEP 1987 examination of Candidates to qualify for the rank of SENIOR SERGEANT you passed the examination, and your official file will be noted accordingly. Issued subject to the provisions of Police Rule No. 27.

MARKS OBTAINED:

Law 83 %

Police Duties 69½ %

Acting Commissioner of Police

PASS

GLOSSARY

A
A CARTON - A cardboard box containing twenty-four bottles or cans of beer.
A COUPLE OF ROADIES - Usually a beer to consume in the car on the way home.
AFL - Australian Football League.
AMBOS - Ambulance medical staff.

B
BARK - To abrade one's skin.
BARRA BLOKE - A barramundi fisherman.
BEAT-COP - Inoffensive slang for patrolling police officers.
BIG SMOKE - The city.
BIKIES - Motorcycle gang.
BOGGY - Wet and muddy, marshy.
BOOFHEAD - A fool.
BOOZE - Alcoholic drinks.
BOOZER - A pub or bar.
BROADSIDE - The widest dimension in front.
BUGGER IT - Implying dissatisfaction.
BUGGERED - Tired.
BULLSHIT - Untrue talk, talking nonsense in an attempt to deceive.
BUSHIE - A person who lives in the bush away from town.

C

CAMP - Having a snooze.
CB RADIO - Citizen band communication system.
CHOOK - A chicken or fowl.
COCKY - A cattle or sheep farmer.
COLT - A young man learning the trade.
CRIMS - Criminals, thieves.
CROOK - Dishonest person - Feeling unwell - Unpleasant situation.
CROSSED A FEW DRY GULLIES IN HIS TIME - Had a lot of life experience.
CSIRO - Commonwealth Scientific and Industrial Research Organisation.

D

DAIA - Department of Aboriginal and Islanders Affairs.
DARK AS BUGGERY - Absolute absence of light.
DC3/C47 - 1930s/1940s twin-engine aircraft used for cargo and passengers.
DEEP SIX - Burial or discarded at sea.
DERELICT - Person without a home or job.
DOCO - A documentary.
DOJOS - Rooms for judo and martial arts practice.

E

ESKY - Portable cooler or icebox.
EYEBALLING - Looking at something.

F

F100 - Ford truck.
FEELING BUGGERED - Extremely tired.
FIRIES - Firefighters.
FLAGON - A large bottle in which wine or cider is sold.

GLOSSARY

FLOPHOUSE - A cheap dirty hotel or apartment.
FOUR EYES - A person who wears glasses.
FOUREX STUBBY - 375ml bottle of the brand XXXX beer.

G
GSDS - German Shepherd Dogs.
GARBOS - Slang for rubbish collectors.
GONADS - Testicles or balls.
GOBSMACKED - Astonished, astounded.
GRAVEYARD SHIFT - Work shift from midnight to morning.
GURNEY - A stretcher with wheeled legs.

H
HANDY IN A DISTURBANCE - Skillful in battle.
HE HAD NO BALLS - An absolute coward.
HIDING - a physical beating.
   HITTING THE GROG - Getting drunk.
HMAS - His (or Her) Majesty's Australian Ship
HOLDEN UTE - Early model Holden utility model.
HOONS - People who drive recklessly.

J
JACKY HOWE SINGLET - Navy blue singlet.

K
KIDDY COP - Fresh-faced police officer.
KNOCKABOUT BLOKES - Great mates.

L
LEPROSARIUM - A place to isolate lepers.
LEPROSY - A chronic bacterial infection of the skin and superficial nerves.
LOSING BARK - To graze one's skin.

M
MALARIA - A life-threatening disease caused by parasites transmitted to humans by way of bites of infected female mosquitoes.
MARQUIS OF QUEENSBURY - A code of fair play presumed to apply in any fight.
METHO - Methylated spirit.
MGB - Morris Garage Model B-series.
MIDGES - Biting flies about the size of a pinhead.
MORON - A foolish or stupid person.
MOZZIES - Mosquitoes.
MUCKING AROUND - spend time doing things that are not useful or serious.

N
NASHOS - National Servicemen Association of Australia.
NOT THE SHARPEST TOOL IN THE SHED - Not very bright.

P
PADDY WAGON - An enclosed vehicle used to transport prisoners. Police van.
PANNIER - Bag in pairs attached to the sides of a motorcycle.
PLAINS TURKEY - Large inland open country dwelling bird.
PONG - Unpleasant smell, reek.
POS - Public order squad.
POSTIE - The postman.
PRETTY HANDY BLOKE - Useful man, skilful.
PTSD - Post-traumatic stress disorder.

Q
QLD - Queensland

R

RAAF - Royal Australian Air Force
RACKET - A loud, unpleasant noise.
RDO - Rostered day off.
RECKON - Be of the opinion. Believe.
REEFER - Cannabis cigarette.
REGO NUMBER - Vehicle's registration number.
RING BARKER - One who barks tree trunks circularly to destroy them.
ROO SHOOTER - Kangaroo hunter.
ROOS - Kangaroos.
RSL - Returned Service League.
RSPCA - Royal Society for the Prevention of Cruelty to Animals.
RUN LIKE THE CLAPPERS - Running off fast, bolted.

S

SAUSAGE DOG - Dachshund.
SCUM BAG - A despicable person.
SCRAWNY - Skinny and boney.
SERT - Special Emergency Response Team.
SERVO - Fuel service station.
SHOVEL - A tool resembling a spade.
SHOWIES - Travelling sideshow operators.
SIX-PACK - Six 375ml bottles of beer held together with cardboard or plastic.
SLAMMER - Prison.
SLIM DUSTY - Late Australian country music icon.
SLIPPER TREATMENT - Delivering a kick or two.
SMOKO - A rest from work for a coffee break.
STAR PICKET - Three-sided, steel fencing post.
STIRRER - A person who deliberately causes trouble.
STOCK SQUAD - Police who investigate stock and other agricultural thefts.

STOCKHOLM SYNDROME - A situation where victims bond with their captors or abusers.
STUBBIES - 375 ml bottles of beer. Men's shorts.
SWIG - A large swallow or drink.

T
TALLY – Tall-ee. Long neck, 750ml *bottle* of *beer*.
THONGS - Cheap casual rubber open footwear like flip flops.
TURD - Obnoxious person or poop
TURDS - People regarded as obnoxious or a collection of poops.

U
USSP - United States Shore Patrol.
UTE - Utility vehicle.

V
VB - Brand of beer, Victoria Bitter.

W
WHACK – Striking someone or something with a sharp blow.
WADDIES/NULLA NULLA - An Australian Aboriginal hardwood club or hunting stick.
WALLABY - Australian marsupial.
WASN'T THE SHARPEST TOOL IN THE SHED - Not very bright and slow to perceive or understand something

Y
YARNING - Chat, talking, communicating.

www.ingramcontent.com/pod-product-compliance
Lightning Source LLC
Chambersburg PA
CBHW051417290426
44109CB00016B/1335